THE WORD'S GOTTEN OUT

ALSO BY WILLARD R. ESPY

The Game of Words

An Almanac of Words at Play

Oysterville: Roads to Grandpa's Village

Another Almanac of Words at Play

O Thou Improper, Thou Uncommon Noun

A Children's Almanac of Words at Play

Espygrams

☞ Being a Gallimaufry of Reactions to Thoughts from Books, Magazines, ual Array of Espy Knittelverse (Called Doggerel by the Unin- Words Are Generally More Interesting Than the Things

Newspapers, Speeches, Conversations, and Letters; formed); and a Great Deal of Excellent Ad- They Represent, and Always More

ing Memories; a Word Puzzle or Two; the Us- flecting a Long-standing Impression That

THE WORD'S GOTTEN OUT

Certain Remain- Whole Re-

Including Also vice — the Amusing.

WILLARD R. ESPY

CLARKSON N. POTTER, PUBLISHERS ☞ NEW YORK

Acknowledgments to reprint previously published material
are to be found on pages 353–354.

Published by Clarkson N. Potter, Inc.,
distributed by Crown Publishers, Inc.,
201 East 50th Street, New York, New York 10022

CLARKSON N. POTTER, POTTER and colophon are trademarks
of Clarkson N. Potter, Inc.

Manufactured in the United States of America

LIBRARY OF CONGRESS CATALOGING-IN-PUBLICATION DATA
Espy, Willard R.
    The word's gotten out / Willard R. Espy.
        p.   cm.
    1. English language—Miscellanea.   2. Commonplace books.
    I. Title.
    PE1095.E87   1989
    818'.5403—dc20   89-3991
                                                        CIP

ISBN 0-517-57061-0

Designed by Beth Tondreau Design/Jane Treuhaft
10 9 8 7 6 5 4 3 2 1

FIRST EDITION

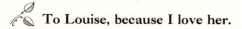 To Louise, because I love her.

To Charles F. Dery, for arguing gently
that the title should be *The Word's Got Out—*
got being preferable to *gotten* as the
past participle of *to get*.

And to Bob Williams, for comforting me.
"After all," says Bob, "don't the Germans
say *'Gotten Himmel'?*"

PREFACE

On Geography . . .

SOME OF THE RECOLLECTIONS that bob up in the pages ahead were written in New York, some in Oysterville, and a few in England or Scotland. You can generally tell where I was from the context, but it doesn't matter much.

Bud Goulter, who runs cattle on the Ocean Beach Road back of Oysterville (which is located on the southwestern coast of the state of Washington), says it had to be some other hermit, not Jimmy Anderson, whose dead body was found standing and wrapped in blackberry vines (page 53), because Jimmy died considerably after the time indicated. I told the story exactly as my mind holds it, but circumstantial evidence says Bud is right. If you draw any moral from this book, it may be that memory—even mine, which I consider to be among the best—is fallible.

PERHAPS YOU ARE AMONG the lucky ones with a mind like pure running water, forever attending to business—the kind of mind that is good for whoever sails on it, or swims in it, or kneels to sip cool drafts from it as it hurries past on its way to the sea.

Unfortunately, mine is no such mind. If I were to compare it to water, it would be to that at the bottom of a country well, waiting to be pumped up. When the pump is dry from disuse, you have to find priming water, and bring it in a bucket, and pour it down the rusty iron throat with one hand, while you work the handle with the other. The pump squeals and gasps and tries to catch its breath. Sometimes it fails, and all you have to show for your effort is the wet bottom of the bucket.

If you are hard to discourage, however, and lucky, the rubber valves inside the pump soak up the priming and swell until they are watertight. Then the gasping turns to a sucking and the sucking to a gurgling; water begins to leap out with every stroke of the pump handle. At first it is reddish from the rust in the pipe, but it is clear and safe to drink once that has been flushed away; you need only deflect the occasional skeleton of a leaf or the cadaver of a drowned field mouse.

That is the way of my mind. It had to be pumped and primed to start every entry in this book. Consider, before you criticize the rust and leaves and field mice too harshly: a letter from someone very much like you may have started the whole thing.

✍ ACKNOWLEDGMENTS

. . . .

MANY OF THE ENTRIES IN THIS BOOK arrived by way of the transom, and I thank all who sent them, as well as those whose offerings cannot yet be used. Wayne Moseley mailed a rebus in immigrant dialect (*Word Ways* was the source of several others); John Furneval relayed an invertogram by Silvester Houédard; Dr. Wombat (a pen name) explained when "pure" was not pure; Dudley F. Church supplied unfamiliar locutions for animal droppings; Paul Bonner quoted little-known anagrams (and Will Shortz sent one in Polish); Scot Morris showed treasures of wordplay from his column in *Omni;* Professor John Niven discovered that Michelangelo signed only one of his works (and Professor Frederick Hartt said not to take that too seriously); Ned Naumburg let me peep at notorious poems, so bad they are good; Avery Fisher gave me the English translation of a speech Mark Twain delivered in German; Dr. Goodwin Breinin provided material ranging from the muting of birds to his pen drawing of a homunculus; Professors J. Lyndon Shanley and Elizabeth Witheral explained how Thoreau taught geese to honk; Derek Pell provided an endless farrago of vile puns; Paul Grabbe's remarkable discovery about his Russian great-grandfather led to still more remarkable discoveries about the Library of Congress; Clement Wood invented the funniest palindrome I know; E. J. K. Read, James Benenson, Jr., Kate Delano Condax, and Frank Johnson revealed themselves as closet poets; Oma ("Amy") Woodcock Singer provided the missing link of minimalism, a one-hundred-year-old letter written by her grandmother; Buddy Basch posted nymbles and James H. Rhodes an impossible rhyme on *orange;* Edgar Tafel yarned about Frank Lloyd Wright; Edgar Watkins forwarded *bouts rimés;* Charles R. Eisenhart, Jr., passed along some unconventional views on the problems of our lower schools; Jessica I. Gretch frightened me with a sonnet, and Colin Smith delighted me with a limerick; Charles F. Dery gave me a word puzzle involving reduplications (he also explained the difference between paparazzi and mamarazzi); Peter Heckes reported a bond between sea gulls and oysters (and revealed why Liney Seaman never married); Barbara Williams (now Barbara Geisler) exposed a spectacular misconception (or was it the opposite?) on the part of her late father-in-law, Rees Williams; R. P. Boas composed a love song to a computer; Dr. S. A. Rosenthal defined a doohickey; George Johnson discovered why My True Love no longer sends a partridge in a pear tree on the first day of Christmas; and Tony Kischner threw disconcerting light on the complexities of one dissolving marriage.

At least a half dozen entries first caught my eye in Alison Henning's inimitable, unforgettable *Christmas Commonplace Book*. She distributes a new edition annually to a few fortunate friends—and to me, because I begged for it. If it were not for Alison Henning's book, I might never have completed mine, and I am grateful.

Generally, when I think I might like to include a contributed tidbit in some vaguely planned collection, I drop it into a cardboard box or spring binder containing several hundred others. This file is labeled (though only in my mind) "Once and Future Things." Unfortunately, it has neither head nor belly nor tail, though it does have rhyme and reason. I either forget what is there, or can't locate it or the name of the contributor, or (in the case of clippings) the printed source has vanished by the time I need it. Some contribution of yours may be mouldering there at this instant. If it is, or if somehow I used a whimsy of yours and failed to credit you, I am bitterly sorry, and will try to do better next time. I thank you now, anyway.

THE WORD'S GOTTEN

O U T

1

You asked me once. To quiet you,
I told you everything I knew.

A lifetime of happiness! No man alive could bear it;
it would be hell on earth.
—GEORGE BERNARD SHAW

THE SEATTLE *POST INTELLIGENCER* says that a couple in Leigh, England, was denied the right to adopt a child because of too happy a marriage; they would not be able to expose a youngster to enough "negative experiences." Explained the authorities: "It would seem from the interviews and reports that both of you have had few, if any, negative experiences when children yourselves, and also seem to enjoy a marital relationship where rows and arguments have no place."

Those two should apply again; they have now had at least one negative experience.

His Honor Denies a Petition

False-hearted pair, stand facing me,
And undergo the third degree.
Your love is tranquil? That's immoral;
True love is proved in lover's quarrel.
How can you claim you really care
If you don't pull each other's hair?
You must, ere either one forgives,
Spell out the other's negatives,
And fan, through prefatory fight,
The fiery passions of the night.
You mock this honored court; I grieve
To learn that, since you can't conceive,
You seek some guileless babe, to raise
In these same unrepentant ways—
With "love" and "law"—which you define
(Good God!) as *discipline benign!*
Your application we refuse:
We cannot sanction child abuse.

—W.R.E.

Ted Bernstein,* damner
Of bad grammar,
Takes up considerable room
In Whom's Whom.
—W.R.E.

THAT SHOULD HAVE SETTLED the petty quarrel over "who" and "whom" once and for all; but no, only this morning a letter came from a woman who claims still to be confused, "though," she says rather peevishly, "I must have read every word you have written on the subject."

What you need, my friend, is an authority you can understand. Like James Thurber:

> The number of people who use "whom" and "who" wrongly is appalling. Take the common expression, "Whom are you, anyways?" That is, of course, strictly speaking, correct—and yet how formal, how stilted! The usage to be preferred in ordinary speech and writing is "Who are you, anyways?" "Whom" should be used in the nominative case only when a note of dignity or austerity is desired. For example, if a writer is dealing with a meeting of, say, the British cabinet, it would be better to have the Premier greet a new arrival, such as an under-secretary, with a "Whom are you, anyways?" rather than a "Who are you, anyways?"—always granted that the Premier is sincerely unaware of the man's identity. To address a person one knows as "Whom are you?" is a mark either of incredible lapse of memory or inexcusable arrogance.†
>
> —JAMES THURBER

. . . .

The First Double-Entry System

"In the first minute of class," says Michael A. Haughney in a letter to *The Wall Street Journal*, "students in Accounting 101 at the University

---

* Mr. Bernstein was for many years arbiter of language usage at *The New York Times*.
† Humorist George Ade had an equally good time with "who" and "whom." The ages will remember his eloquent one-line tribute to the American way of learning:
  "Whom are you?" said he; for he had been to night school.

of Edinburgh are taught that Noah is the patron saint of all accountants, since he 'floated a limited company when the rest of the world was in liquidation.'

"He also employed a system of 'double-entry.' "

It is impossible, in our condition of society, not to be sometimes a snob.
—WILLIAM MAKEPEACE THACKERAY

DURING THE BATTLE OF BRITAIN, troops were sometimes billeted within the property of landed aristocrats. A private might walk out of an evening with a downstairs maid, or a commanding officer sit as an honored guest at the great house. A socially ambitious military man might well dream of developing a lasting friendship with his host. Evelyn Waugh tells here of such a man; but in view of the events described, it seems unlikely that Colonel Durnford-Slater, D.S.O., and the unlucky Lord Glasgow ever became chums.

THE TREE THAT DID NOT FALL ON A SIXPENCE

So [the officers] were very anxious to be chums with Lord Glasgow so they offered to blow up an old tree stump for him and he was very grateful and he said don't spoil the plantation of young trees near it because that is the apple of my eye they said no of course not we can blow a tree down so that it falls on a sixpence and Lord Glasgow said goodness you are clever and he asked them all to luncheon for the great explosion. Col. Durnford-Slater D.S.O. said to his subaltern, have you put enough explosive in the tree. Yes, sir, 75 lbs. Is that enough? Yes sir I worked it out by mathematics it is exactly right. Well better put in a bit more. Very good sir.

And when Col. D. Slater D.S.O. had had his port he sent for the subaltern and said subaltern better put a bit more explosive in that tree. I dont want to disappoint Lord Glasgow. Very good sir.

Then they all went out to see the explosion and Col. D. S. D.S.O. said you will see that tree fall flat at just that angle where it will hurt no young trees and Lord Glasgow said goodness you are clever.

So soon they lit the fuse and waited for the explosion and presently the tree, instead of falling quietly sideways, rose 50 feet into the air taking with it ½ acre of soil and the whole of the young plantation.

And the subaltern said sir I made a mistake, it should have been 7½ lbs not 75.

Lord Glasgow was so upset he walked in dead silence back to the castle and when they came to the turn of the drive in sight of his castle what should they find but that every pane of glass in the building was broken.

So Lord Glasgow gave a little cry & ran to hide his emotion in the lavatory and there when he pulled the plug the entire ceiling, loosened by the explosion, fell on his head.

This is quite true.

Latin . . . was a cultural tongue of the highest order, second only, if at all, to Greek.
—MARIO PEI

READERS OF *THE NEW YORK TIMES* argue occasionally about the propriety of mixing Greek and Latin roots in an English word. Norman Fine says the inviolable rule is not to. Dankwart Rostow asks, Does Mr. Fine plan to turn in his automobile (Greek *auto*, "self," + Latin *movere*, "to move") for an all-Latin *ipsomobile* or an all-Greek *autokinete?* Emmanuel Mesthene estimates that Mr. Fine is at least a millimeter (Latin *mille*, "thousand," + Greek *metron*, "meter") off the mark. Harry Weber recalls a similar tempest in a teapot forty years ago when we began talking about television (Greek *tele*, "far off," + Latin *videre*, "to see").

When Latin Cleaves to Greek

Whenas, impelled thereto by primal urges,
Greek quitteth Greek and cleaveth unto Latin,
Wherefrom a hybrid progeny emerges,
Pray tell me, is it *Leek?* Or is it *Gratin?*

Ah, "millimeter" turns my senses hot,
And "television" makes my members tinglish,
For they have simmered in the Melting Pot,
And come out English.

—W.R.E.

Slow sail'd the weary mariners and saw,
Betwixt the green brink and the running foam,
Sweet faces, rounded arms, and bosoms prest
To little harps of gold.
—ALFRED, LORD TENNYSON

DRIVING PAST STACKPOLE SLOUGH this morning, I was reminded of an event long ago that started me on a lifelong quest for a mermaid.

As everyone knows, Stackpole Slough debouches into Willapa Harbor (more aptly called Shoalwater Bay before various Chambers of Commerce began prettying things up) about two miles north of Oysterville. At high tide the water of the harbor, or bay, presses against the eastern shore of the North Beach Peninsula, then gives up and retreats until next time.

At the period I speak of, I was a Tenderfoot in the local Boy Scout troop. We were proceeding at low tide—"marching" would be a euphemism—over the wooden bridge that crossed the mouth of the slough. Below, in the pool left when the tide departed, we espied, forlornly paddling about, a hair seal pup that could not have been more than a few days old. Of the mother there was no sign; presumably she had followed the tide out and was now separated from her offspring by a half mile of sand flats.

As I look back, it is clear that we should have left the pup there; its mother would have returned with the tide. But have you ever seen an infant hair seal? It is irresistible. The hair is glistening white, with black spots the size of a silver dollar. It has white mustachios and great brown eyes that shine with instant love and demand instant reciprocity.

At that instant a mermaid rose from the water. . . .

Moreover, it is so small and light that a twelve-year-old boy can easily carry it in his arms.

So I took the poor wet thing home.

But there was a problem. In those days, the 1920s, no hot line existed over which one might learn the technique of feeding a newborn seal. It was not old enough for the fresh smelt we offered; it would not take warm milk from a bottle. We had no idea then that unweaned seals suckle only under water. After six hours of fruitless efforts, we realized, or at least my father did, that the infant* was doomed to starve. He ordered us to return it to the bay in the faint hope that its mother would find it.

So we carried it down the lane—that is, *I* carried it; my older brother Ed carried the oars—to the bay, the tide by then being full; rowed (Ed did) east a quarter of a mile toward the channel; tossed the seal into the water; returned to shore at top rowing speed; and ran home (our home was perhaps four hundred feet inland). I am afraid we were both crying.

Moments later there was a sound on the porch. It was not vocal, but a rubbing or scratching. I went to the door, and there, looking up through those eyes to drown in, was the baby seal. It had swum back in our wake and hauled itself across four hundred feet of land to come home.

Again and again we tried to return that seal to the bay, and again and again it followed us back. Its skin grew looser, its eyes dimmer. In a week it died, and we buried it in a hole left behind the previous winter where a storm had uprooted a cypress tree in our yard.

Soon afterward I dreamed that Ed was rowing the dinghy up a broad silver path stretched across the bay by a rising moon; I sat in the stern, petting the seal. When we were a long way out, he rested his oars: I hugged the small thing one last time and tossed it into the moonlight. At that instant a mermaid rose from the water and caught it to her breast; for a long moment she poised there, head and upper body upright above the surface, studying us, the seal in her arms; then she dived, her scaly tail flashing for an instant in the moonlight.

Doubtless the dream involved pubescence somehow; no matter.

---

* "Infant" is from a Latin word meaning "(still) unable to speak." It could therefore be argued that any dumb animal—not just my seal pup—is infantile.

Two times more, perhaps three, it returned. To this day that mermaid swims somewhere just beyond the bounds of my vision. Before I die—or perhaps after; it makes no difference—I shall see her rise from the water again, and this time she will smile at me and hold out the great-eyed seal for me to stroke.

Les mots font l'amour.
—ANDRÉ BRETON

OR WAS M. BRETON SIMPLY QUOTING from Arthur Rimbaud—who in any event hypothesized that words metamorphose by "their friction with each other, their copulation"? Anyone who has watched words when they think no one is around knows that they are as ridiculous as you and I about falling in love, exchanging first kisses, having spats, pledging eternal devotion, changing (in the case of female words) their names, procreating, sulking, separating, reuniting, divorcing, holding grudges, and failing to pay alimony.

Words do, though, possess a singular advantage over humans in the area of the affections: they have solved the problem of Narcissus. He could only moon over his reflected image in the water and waste away. He was inaccessible to himself. But by a process that a worm might call parthenogenesis, words can not only caress themselves, but create new words, and new meanings for old words, in the process.

What ardor must have been involved in such metamorphoses as these!

- *Glad* once meant "smooth, bright, shining" (L *glaber*, OHG *glat*).
- *Plant* meant "sole of the foot" (L *planta*), used for tamping seeds in the soil.
- *Beldam* meant "beautiful girl" (F *belle dame*).
- *Chum* and *crony* mutated from *chronos*, Greek for "time"—you spend time with people you like.

- *Dapper* meant "heavy, powerful" (OHG *tapfar*).
- *Gentle* is from Latin *gentilis*—"of the same clan or race." But so is *gentile*, "of another clan or race"—to the Jews a non-Jew, to the Pakistanis a non-Moslem, to the Mormons a non-Mormon.
- *Weird* was once man's fate, destiny—the weird sister was one of the Fates. Then Macbeth's witches showed up, and weird became . . . weird.

There are also eerily connected words, perhaps the result of some ages-old liaison—*widow* and *void*, for instance, both with the overtones of "emptiness, being emptied." And mind you, I say nothing about what happens when two words are in love with each other instead of one with itself. Far be it from me to mention how *hand in cap* united in *handicap* ("contesting parties and the umpire depositing forfeit money in a cap or hat") or how handicap went on to mean a disadvantage or, the other way around, an advantage given to the weaker side. If I were not confining myself to the results of verbal narcissism, I might even remind you how the French *m'aider*, "help me," hobson-jobsoned itself into May Day, while retaining the original meaning.

Me, I stick to one subject at a time.

. . . .

Tails, Heads? Both Win

Julian Barnes points out that if you cut a flatworm in half, the head will grow a new tail. Even more surprising, the tail will grow a new head.

. . . .

We have unmistakable proof that throughout all past time, there has been a ceaseless devouring of the weak by the strong.
—HERBERT SPENCER

MR. SPENCER MAY HAVE THE RIGHT of it as far as living creatures are concerned, but when it comes to grammar, the weak devour the strong. Strong verbs are dying out, and weak verbs are inheriting the language. Strong verbs are those in which the body of the word itself changes to show a change of tense—go, went, gone; begin, began, begun. Weak verbs change only by adding -ed: walk, walked, walked; chuckle, chuckled, chuckled. (Perhaps words like "hit" belong to a separate class of ultraweak verbs—hit neither changes its root spelling nor adds -ed: I hit you now, I hit you yesterday, I have hit you every day since I have known you.)

No new strong verbs are coming along to make up for the loss of the old ones. Every new verb that enters the language is weak.

Maggie Sullivan, writing in *The New York Times*, proposes to change all that. She would require that every new verb pass a test for strength, and that some existing words be turned into strong verbs even if they are not now verbs at all. Here are some of her suggestions, with examples:

> *Summit, summote, summut.* "Would that they had summut on cultural exchange as they summote on trade!"
>
> *Gentrify, gentrifo, gentrifum.* "The newcomers gentrifo one block, and now the whole neighborhood is gentrifum."
>
> *Furlough, furlent, furlon.* "All soldiers were furlon except those the captain furlent last week."
>
> *Subdue, subdid, subdone.* "Nothing could have subdone him the way her violet eyes subdid him."
>
> *Frisbee, friswas, frisbeen.* "Although he had never frisbeen before, after watching the tournament he friswas every day, trying to frisbee as the champions friswere."
>
> *Pay, pew, pain.* "He had pain for not choosing a wife more carefully."

Commemoreat, commemorate, commemoreaten. "At the banquet to commemoreat Herbert Hoover, spirits were high, and by the end of the evening many other Republicans had been commemoreaten."

Ms. Sullivan concludes: "It's hard to imagine anything that could undermine a language as strong as that."

The Italian dish made of pasta strings smaller than those of spaghetti (the word spaghetti, *from* spage, *literally means "strings") is called* vermicelli, *a diminutive form of Latin* vermis *("worm").*
—Morton S. Freeman, The Story Behind the Word

PASTAS MAY BE RANKED by thickness, thus:

Mamma Mía, How We've Grown!

Pasta starts in teeny-weeny
With the thread-like *capellini;*
Spaghettini, slightly coarser,
May be taken for a horsehair.
Vermicelli, thickening,
Has the look and taste of string,
While *spaghetti* widens toward
The diameter of cord.
Thicker yet is *bucetini;*
Next in line is *maccheroncini;*
Maccheroni has the scope
And the chewiness of rope.
Lacking *ziti* on the table,
Simply substitute a cable.

—W.R.E.

As headlong as an allegory on the banks of the Nile.
—MRS. MALAPROP, IN RICHARD SHERIDAN'S THE RIVALS

LAST NIGHT AT DINNER I SAT next to a young woman who could make an excellent living from her looks but has done famously by using her brains instead. Her name is Hannah Demaray; she is a professor of English at Marymount College, and her specialty, I gather, is seventeenth-century literature, with particular attention to Milton.

Last night, however, she was instructing me in malapropisms, which she had been acquiring from student essays. One young man cited an unlikely source of support for a prophylactic device currently in the news:

• St. Paul condoms sex

A second advised:

• One should not expose oneself pubically

A young woman anthropomorphized a particular concern of the New Testament:

• The St. James Virgin of the Bible

The twisting of Biblical messages into malapropisms must be a student specialty. Thayer S. Warshaw, who at last word was teaching high school English at Newton, Massachusetts, presented his class with a quiz based on the Holy Scriptures and received the answers I paraphrase in the knittelverse below:

Let There Be Light—But Not Too Much

Hark to the Bible as portrayed
By students of the eleventh grade
At Newton, Massachusetts, where
The Scriptures seem in poor repair.

- "This lesson I brought home from chapel:
  Eve was created from an apple."
- "For we see darkly now, alas!—
  God furnished us an eye of glass."

- "Of all Commandments Ten, the root
  Is 'eye for eye, and toot for toot.' "
- "Jesus instructs by stories. These
  Are known to us as Parodies."

- "He maketh me, his faithful daughter,
  To lie down safely in green water."
- "Unto each day that passes by,
  Sufficient is the evil eye."

- "When asked to dance, Salome said,
  'That seems the way to get a head.' "
- "Said David, lolling on his throne,
  'Man does not live by sweat alone.' "

- "Love great as Petrarch's love for Laura
  Was that of Sodom for Gomorrah."
- "And for her sins, it came to pass
  That Jezebel was Balaam's ass."

One of Mr. Warshaw's students provided a particularly ominous warning for longtime lovers of the musical stage:

Thy God's a jealous God, thou vermin;
Thou canst not serve both God and Merman.

—W.R.E.

· · · · · · ·

> *Sir, I admit your general rule,*
> *That every poet is a fool,*
> *But you yourself may serve to show it,*
> *That every fool is not a poet.*
> —SAMUEL TAYLOR COLERIDGE

A SHORT TIME BACK, having committed a series of particularly graceless verses, I groped for a name that would encompass them all and came up with the word *knittelverse*. (I sound the *k*.) (Knittelverse is German for the Latin term *rhopalic*, "club-shaped"—a justifiably forgotten verse form in which each metric foot was a syllable longer than the one before.)

I disagree, as my dog does, with the general assumption that these verses are *doggerel*. *Amphigory*—verse that seems to have meaning at first glance but turns out to be nonsense—applies no better. I considered *nominy*, but that fits any rigmarole—wordy tales as well as verse. Another possibility was *crambo clink*, a parlor game in which players match rhyming lines. There was also *crambe repetita*, taken from the Latin for "sodden cabbage, twice served"; the reference is to warmed-over stories.

But knittelverse sounds classier than the others, except perhaps crambe repetita; and I object to that for reasons having less to do with aesthetics than with my taste buds. Henceforth knittelverse will be my name for all Espy rhymes.

Such as this one:

Darius Green Wasn't Such a
Hot Pegasus, Either

Now bounds from crag to crag my Word,
Equipped to vault the sky.
That mist, about its shoulders blurred—
Is't wings, revved up to fly?

It soars!—no, plummets!—to the heather's
Flung down!—and there it lies.
What *was* that shoulder mist? Horsefeathers?
Or (likelier) *horseflies?*

—W.R.E.

You will note that in the first line my Word appears to be a mountain goat, while in the last two it is clearly a horse, or the remains of one. Such little inconsistencies are the charm, even the glory, of knittelverse.

Here is the first of several knittelverses of a particularly pointless sort; they feature words beginning with some arbitrarily chosen letter of the alphabet. In this case the letter is *b*.

B. Song for a Biotic[1] Dance

Swing and sway with me, my dear,
In our band of biosphere.
As we circle we shall pass
Other clumps of biomass,
All biota,[2] each with home
In some suitable biome,[3]
Heeling, toeing, to the fiddle
Of a biologic riddle.

—W.R.E.

[1] Biological. [2] Flora and fauna, collectively. [3] Formation.

A word square is made up of words of equal length that read both horizontally and vertically. In most word squares the words are the same in both directions, but in some (sometimes called "double word squares") the horizontal words differ from the vertical ones.

—TONY AUGARDE

SAMUEL JOHNSON SAID a woman's preaching is like a dog's walking on his hind legs—it is not done well, but you are surprised to find it done at all. He is wrong; women have been preaching, and well, since the day that Eve preached Adam into eating the apple. But I would have agreed with Dr. Johnson if he had applied his analogy to word squares. They are remarkable accomplishments, though of no use except to wonder at. Only a word square could fall in love with another word square.

If I were a word square, I would fall in love with this one by Allen Tice:

*And Now the News**

```
Wherenowhowhat
Herenowhowhath
Erenowhowhathe
Renowhowhather
Enowhowhathere
Nowhowhatheren
Owhowhathereno
Whowhatherenow
Howhatherenowh
Owhatherenowho
Whatherenowhow
Hatherenowhowh
Atherenowhowha
Therenowhowhat
```

* Copyright © 1987 Allen Tice

You will see below what happens when a verse is incorporated into a square. To get the drift of this you need only break up the succession of letters into words—"hasgone," for instance, becomes "has gone." (Incidentally, if you follow the letters of the two lines forming the X, reading first from top left down and then from bottom left up, you will discover an entropic law that has distressed many lovers.)

Bear two points in mind as you decode the square. First, when Zeus the Swan lay a-chatting with Leda on long winter nights, he called her "hon," short for "honey." (The Greek word is *miel.*) Second, he customarily borrowed for his amorous expeditions a phenomenal asset of the god whose name takes up the first line.

Farewell Note on Leda's Pillow

P	r	i	a	p	u	s
H	a	s	g	o	n	e
N	o	s	h	e	e	p
N	o	r	s	w	a	n
T	o	s	p	i	l	l
S	e	d	n	o	w
L	e	d	a	h	o	n

—W.R.E.

> *Far from all resort of mirth,*
> *Save the cricket on the hearth.*
> —JOHN MILTON

EACH TIME WE RETURNED from the country I would unlock the apartment door, reach inside to turn on the light, and push our suitcases across the threshold with my foot. This time something in the apartment chirped. Louise asked, "What was that?"

"I have no idea."

We went around opening windows.

"Chirp!"

"Could it be a cricket?"

"In midtown Manhattan? On the tenth floor? Don't be silly."

"Chirp!"

Louise said, "It *is* a cricket."

But where? We tried the study. We tried the bedroom. For a while, silence. Then it chirped loudly, certainly within four feet of my ear.

"I think it's following me."

"We bought some African daisies a few days before we left. Maybe it came with them. The *Times* said that a department store once filled a display window with flowers, and all of a sudden the store was infested with crickets."

The remains of the daisies were still in their vase; there was no cricket.

But it went on chirping. Louise worried about it.

"What does the poor thing have to eat?" she asked.

I told her the *World Book* said crickets thrive on such odd diets as book lint. We had a lot of that.

We felt guilty whenever we left town. The cricket would be lonely. It might even die of loneliness.

But it always welcomed us back.

"Chirp!"

A cricket is nice to come home to.

I began chirping back. "Good night, cricket," I said each evening as I crawled into bed.

We sold our apartment and bought another. The time came to depart.

"Louise," I said, "we can't leave the cricket."

"Why not?"

"Maybe the new owners don't *like* crickets. Maybe they'll call in an exterminator."

We decided to write a note, asking them to watch out for the cricket and let us know if they caught it; we would pick it up.

The night before we started packing, Occy Romaine came by to drink a stirrup cup with us. I said, "We hate to leave the cricket."

"Cricket?" said Occy.

"You haven't heard the cricket? Listen."

He listened.

"Chirp!"

"That's no cricket," said Occy. "That's your smoke detector."

"Our what?"

"Smoke detector. When the battery's low, it chirps."

He was wrong. The cricket must have been smart enough to smuggle itself into our luggage, for we had no sooner unpacked in our new apartment than it began chirping. And it is chirping as I type these words.

I once told a Slavicist I know that I particularly liked a Russian poem I had read in translation. "It loses a lot in the original," he responded.
—*MARTIN PERETZ*

ENGLISH HAS CAPTURED THE RUSSIAN words *glasnost* and *perestroika* recently, as it did *sputnik* earlier. On balance, though, I suspect that the Russians are getting the best of the war of words. They have turned our "hooligan" to *gooligan;* our "budget" to *byudzht;* our "telephone" to *telefon;* our "champion" to *chempion;* our "hot dog" to *khot dog;* our "coffee" to *kofe;* our "jazz" to *dzhaz.* (There is, to be sure, a certain moral equivalence here. We had appropriated most of these words from other languages ourselves.)

Russian is forbidding to the eye (my eye, at least); nor is it particularly seductive to the ear. It is a useful language to know, though, and you can learn it easily. You need only memorize the newspaper clipping, somewhat yellowed now, that surfaced from my files the other day.

It reveals that *Tartar,* for instance, is a sauce used on halibut, swordfish, sole, and scallops, while *Siberia* means "Russian suburbia." It also provides the translations cited below. Fix them in your mind, and you will know all the Russian you are ever likely to need.

Everyman's Guide to Russian

A *Petrolgrad's* a station
For autos low on gas;
A *Cossack* is a garment
For altar boys at mass.

Black See? Sunglasses . . . maybe.
And *Minsk?* A lisping mink.
And *Ogpu's* "talk for babies"
(Like "icky-poo," I think.)

What's *nyet?* "Not yet," contracted
(What Russian maidens say
When, though perhaps attracted,
They won't go all the way).

Still, if you ask permission,
And certain *Steppes* are taken,
You may achieve fruition—
In Russian, "burn the bacon."*

---

* I have never heard that "burn the bacon" is a Russian expression, but it sounds as if it might be.

2

You asked me twice, and I again
Politely made the matter plain.

THE FOLLOWING ADVICE FOR THOSE attending a royal tea in Dallas appears in Alison Henning's *Christmas Commonplace Book:*

YOU HAVE RECEIVED

AN INVITATION TO TEA WITH

HER MAJESTY

THE QUEEN OF THAILAND

AT THE HOME OF

MRS. RICHARD MARCUS

ON THURSDAY, OCTOBER 29.

THE EMBASSY OF THAILAND

WOULD LIKE TO SUGGEST

SEVERAL ITEMS

OF PROTOCOL AND TRADITION:

THE QUEEN

IS ADDRESSED AS

"YOUR MAJESTY."

ONE MAY BOW OR CURTSY,

BUT THIS IS NOT NECESSARY.

IT IS SUGGESTED

THAT ONE NEVER MENTION

THE KING AND I.

IT IS SUGGESTED

THAT ONE NEVER SHOW

THE BOTTOMS OF THE SHOES.

KEEPING THE FEET

FIRMLY ON THE FLOOR

WHILE SEATED

WILL BEST ASSURE

THAT THE SOLES

NOT BE REVEALED.

BASICALLY,

HER MAJESTY

IS VERY GRACIOUS, NOT FORMAL,

COMMANDING THE RESPECT

ONE WOULD NATURALLY GRANT

SUCH AN HONORED PERSONAGE.

Look closely at the letter C, and you will know why it should never be trusted. It will offer you a trip around the world, but leave you marooned before you reach home.

—W.R.E.

C. Dirge in C

When my craft first set to sea,
Never chopa[1] swam by me,
Showing me the way to go;
No,
I was frequently adrift,
Squiffed,
Or at tropic isle ashore;
For
Capripede[2] I made my role—
Chose to dance the carmignole[3];

---

[1] The rudderfish, said to accompany ships. [2] Satyr. [3] A lively song and dance of the French Revolution.

With the great-eyed maidens croodled,[4]
Sighed and trembled and canoodled.[5]
Now, where once sang gay conquedle,[6]
Digs the sexton, prays the beadle;
Now, where hair sprang fair and flaxen,
Sits askew the stringy caxon[7];
Cheek, once redder than an apple,
Now capple[8];
Eyes, once eager, twinkly-sparky,
Now carky[9];
Voice, once honey in its talk,
Now cawk.[10]
Grudgingly I face my culp,[11]
And gulp.

—W.R.E.

That which we call a rose
By any other name would smell as sweet.
—*WILLIAM SHAKESPEARE*

GOODWIN BREININ SAID A SEA GULL had muted on him. *Muted.* When I looked the word up, it turned out to derive not from the familiar Latin *mutare*, "to change," or *mutus*, "mute," but from the quite unrelated Teutonic *émeutir*, "to digest, melt." This kind of mute seldom ventures outside of unabridged dictionaries, but the meaning is forthright: "to void excrement." As a noun, it means "dung."

I cast about for other elegant terms related to animal excretion. Gretchen Salisbury, my editor, remembered hearing her father call horse manure "road apples." Several friends suggested "scat" (reserved in some areas for wolf droppings); but scat does not sound at all

---

[4] Nestled together. [5] Caressed. [6] Bobolink. [7] A much worn wig. [8] Pale and sickly looking. [9] Troubled, anxious. [10] Croaking, as a crow. [11] Sin, guilt.

elegant to me, though it had exactly the same meaning in Greek. (Hence our "scatology," for filthy literature, or, in medicine, "diagnosis by means of the feces.") Guano, the accumulated excreta of sea fowl, is a common and respected usage. More colloquial are buffalo chips and cow pies, for the droppings of these two beasts. *Bois de vache*, borrowed from the French, substitutes for either. When dried and used for fuel, these droppings are also referred to as "cowshard" or "cowsharn," from the Anglo-Saxon; "argol," from the Mongolian; or "upla," from the Hindi.

A member of the National Puzzlers' League who writes under the pseudonym "Dr. Wombat" (the wombat is a kind of burrowing marsupial) suggested I turn to the Eleventh Edition of the *Encyclopaedia Britannica*, volume 7, page 9, and note there the word *pure*. I did. The passage lists exports from Constantinople during the opening years of the twentieth century, among which were included the following:

> . . . refuse and waste materials, sheep's wool . . . and skins from the slaughter-houses . . . horns, hoofs, goat and horse hair, guts, bones, rags, bran, old iron &c, and finally *dogs' excrement, called in trade "pure," a Constantinople specialty, which is used in preparing leather for ladies' gloves* [my italics —W.R.E.].

I discovered later that the usage was common in western Europe in the last century. By comparison with pure for dog dung, mute for dung in general is but a minor oddity.

Then Dudley F. Church forwarded the following lines from *The Rebel Angels* by Robertson Davies:

> And in the Middle Ages, how concerned people who lived close to the world of nature were with the faeces of animals. And what a variety of names they had for them: the Crotels of a Hare, the Friants of a Boar, the Spraints of an Otter, the Werderobe of a Badger, the Waggying of a Fox, the Fumets of a deer.

There are those who, hitting their thumb with a hammer, cry, "Oh, ——!" If they cried, say, "Oh, friants!" one time, and "Oh, fumets!" the next, would they not relieve their feelings and broaden their vocabulary at the same time?

Rhopalic. A snowballing line or passage in which each successive word has one more syllable (or letter) than the last, as in Dmitri Borgmann's "I do not know where family doctors acquired illegibly perplexing handwriting."

—W.R.E.

AN ESPYRAMID UP IS A rhopalic built around missing words. The first consists of a single letter, and each of the others contains all the letters of the preceding word plus one, in any appropriate order. Thus:

> * man named Seth, when ** the point
> Of death from fasting, *** a joint
> Of beef. "I **** all meat," said Seth,
> "But not as much as I hate *****."

The missing words are a, at, ate, hate, death.

See how long it takes you to determine the missing words here:†

> *Faith Rewarded*
>
> * sailor, ** he set to ***
> To bring back **** from Barbary,
> Prayed, "Father, ***** me and I swear
> I'll ****** Thy glory everywhere!"
> He ******* the Lord, nor felt surprise
> To wake next morn in ********.

> *And They're Smooth Going Down*
>
> * man ** dinner would not ***.
> He said, "Of **** I like food sweet.
> Please ***** what you serve to me;
> I best ****** to sugared tea
> And *******. They are cloying, but
> They do not ******** the gut."

† You will find them in Answers and Solutions, at the back of the book.

At Least He Knows What He Wants

* critic ** an *** display
Could scarcely **** himself away;
He said, "I'll ***** my Paul Gauguin
With ****** joy for your Derain.
To excellence my eye is *******;
I know what's fine, and what is ********.
Your canvas is *********, I see,
But that does not ********** me."

—W.R.E.

> *If all else fails, immortality can always*
> *be assured by spectacular error.*
> —JOHN KENNETH GALBRAITH

THERE IS MUCH TO BE SAID in favor of error (and consequent failure), not least being the pleasure of one's friends. The difficulty is to fail in so dramatic a way that they will notice, since in the usual course of things even your best friends do not reflect about you very often. For help in choosing the most embarrassing way to fail, I recommend to you *The Book of Heroic Failures,* by Stephen Pile. It contains scores, if not hundreds, of humiliations; there must be one that is right for you.

THE MOST UNSUCCESSFUL TV COMMERCIAL

In 1973, while making a breakfast cereal advertisement, the comedienne Pat Coombs forgot her lines twenty-eight times. On each occasion she forgot the same thing—the name of the product.

THE VET WHO SURPRISED A COW

In the course of his duties in August 1977, a Dutch veterinary surgeon was required to treat an ailing cow. To investigate its internal gases he inserted a tube into that end of the animal not capable of facial ex-

The jet of flame set fire first to some bales of hay. . . .

pression and struck a match. The jet of flame set fire first to some bales of hay and then to the whole farm, causing damage estimated at £45,000.

The cow escaped with shock.

THE LEAST SUCCESSFUL WEATHER REPORT

After severe flooding in Jeddah in January 1979, the Arab news issued the following bulletin:

"We regret we are unable to give you the weather. We rely on weather reports from the airport, which is closed because of the weather. Whether we are able to give you the weather tomorrow depends on the weather."

THE LEAST PROFITABLE ROBBERY

Intending to steal cash from a supermarket in 1977, a Southampton thief employed a unique tactic to divert the till girl's attention. His method was to collect a cart full of goods, arrive at the till, and put down £10 by way of payment. She would then take the money and open the till, upon which he would snatch the contents.

He arrived at the cash desk and put down the £10. She took it and opened the till; but there was only £4.37 in it. Undeterred, the thief snatched it and made his getaway, having lost £5.63 on the raid.

 Shakespeare is in the singularly fortunate position of being, to all intents and purposes, anonymous.
—W. H. AUDEN

I RECEIVED THE OTHER DAY a list of fifty familiar expressions, all cited as having originated with Shakespeare. But several had not.*

Take the expression, "fool's paradise"[1] (*Romeo and Juliet*, 1593). Juliet's nurse certainly said it, but it goes back at least to the *Paston*

---

* See Answers and Solutions for more on the footnoted phrases.

Letters (1462), written more than a hundred years before Shakespeare was born. Similarly, "without rhyme or reason" appears in *The Merry Wives of Windsor* (1599); but Edmund Spenser, who *died* that year, had written—complaining about a promised pension that failed to arrive— "I was promised on a time/To have reason for my rhyme;/From that time unto this season,/I received nor rhyme nor reason."

The list includes "I'll not budge an inch,"[2] "to be in a pickle," "to give the devil his due," and "I have not slept a wink." But all these appear as well in Cervantes's *Don Quixote*, the two parts of which came out in 1605 and 1615. It is hardly likely that either the Englishman or the Spaniard deliberately stole the lines, even assuming one could read the other's language.

"Dead as a doornail" is indeed unrecorded before its appearance in *Henry VI*, but the chances are that it was common currency long before that. (Most readers today associate it with Charles Dickens's remark in *The Christmas Carol*, 1843, that "Old Marley was as dead as a doornail.")

Then came the attribution "But me no buts." It certainly *sounded* like Shakespeare but did not show up in my concordance (I thank you for that concordance, John Niven!). Robert Kasanof read somewhere that Rabelais used it; I cannot for the life of me imagine how it would come out in French. The first reference I can be sure of appears in Susanna Centlivre's *The Busy Body* (1709), when someone says, "Sir, I obey; but—" And Sir Francis replies, "But me no buts." (Robert Ehrenberg, who called the Centlivre citation to my attention, says also that Henry Fielding used the same expression in *Rape upon Rape*, c. 1740.)

William Shakespeare

"Who said it first?" What difference who said it?
That Willy Shakespeare always steals the credit:
"Cold comfort"[3]; "tongue-tied"[4]; "be that as it may"[5];
" 'Twas Greek to me"[6]; "a matter of fair play"[7];
"More sinned against than sinning"[8]; "without rhyme
Or reason"[9]; "in a pickle"[10]; "it's high time"[11];
"An eyesore"[12]; "make short shrift"[13]; "the more fool you"[14];
"The game is up"[15]; "to give the devil his due"[16];

"Dead as a doornail"[17]; "if the truth were known"[18];
"A laughing-stock"[19]; "the crack of doom"[20]; "a ston-
y-hearted villain"[21]; "it's all one to me"[22];
"To make a virtue of necessity"[23];
"Slept not one wink"[24]; "to dance attendance"[25]; "your
Own flesh and blood"[26]; "or not to be"[27]; "done more
In sorrow than in anger"[28]; "a foregone
Conclusion"[29]; "we've seen better days"[30]; "stand on
No ceremony"[31]; "foul play"[32]; "truth will out"[33];
"Lie low"[34]; "the wish is father to the thought"[35];
"Now what the dickens?"[36]; "vanished into thin
Air"[37]; "playing fast and loose"[38]; "the devil in-
carnate"[39]; "green-eyed jealousy"[40]; "the long
And short o't"[41]; "keep a civil tongue
Inside your head."[42]

                  All these the high Bard versed;
Whoever said it first, *he* said it first.

                               —W.R.E.

Shakespeare's Word Coinages

Though Shakespeare is credited with inventing 1,700 words, we really
know only that there is no record of their earlier use. Among these
Shakespearean "firsts" are

    assassinate • suspicious • barefaced
    castigate • countless • critical • dwindle
    gnarled • hurry • impartial • lapse
    laughable • leapfrog • lonely • misplaced
    monumental

*The pangram, an ancient form of wordplay,
is an attempt to get the maximum number of different letters
into a sentence of minimum length.*

—SCIENTIFIC AMERICAN

ANYONE WHO HAS STUDIED touch typing has tapped out "The quick brown fox jumps over the lazy dog," which, containing as it does all 26 letters of the alphabet, gives practice to every finger. The sentence is a 35-letter pangram and makes sense of a sort. As pangrams shrink toward the irreducible 26, the sense oozes out. "Why jab, vex quartz-damping flocks?" asks David J. Porter in a pangram of just 28 letters. One can but murmur, "Why indeed?"

Slightly more intelligible are "Bawds jog, flick quartz, vex nymphs" (27) and "Quick wafting zephyrs vex bold Jim" (29), both from *Word Ways*, the magazine of recreational linguistics. I have no doubt of the meaning of "Victors flank gyp who mixed job quiz" (30). And "Jackdaws love my big sphinx of quartz" (31), credited to Marvin Moore, will certainly mean something to Egyptologists, among others.

Paul Bonner sent me, from Edward Ronthaler's book *Life with Letters*, a page of pangrammatic headlines written by an unidentified journalist. Between 36 and 45 letters each, they are as lucid as some headlines that actually appear in newspapers:

- Doxy with charming buzz quaffs vodka julep (36).
- Raving zibet chewed calyx of pipsqueak major (38).
- Wolves exit quickly as fanged zoo chimp jabbers (40).
- Oozy quivering jellyfish expectorated by mad haw (42).
- Six big devils from Japan quickly forget how to waltz (44).
- Lazy jackal raiding from Xebec prowls the quiet cove (44).
- Guzzling of jaunty exile wreaks havoc at damp banquet (45).

Word Ways carried this Polish pangram, using each of the 32 letters in their alphabet once only:

Pójdź, kińże tę chmurność wgląb flaszy.

The sentence, explains contributor Will Shortz, is supposed to cheer up someone who is morose from drinking. It means "Come, throw the gloom in the bottle."

Is it true that schools do not teach grammar any more?
—*JULIA HURTT*

N O, IT IS NOT TRUE. It just seems that way to you and me, because we are growing old. There may be some truth, though, to the rumor that children are no longer willing to *learn* grammar, which shows they are sensible; if they spoke grammatically, who could understand them?

Just in case you have some odd young friend who would like to know, say, the nine parts of speech, but cannot get the teacher to tell because the teacher does not know either, here is an old rhyme by an unknown author that can slide them all into any young head. It dropped out of teaching a long time ago—clearly it is not in the public interest to have people walking around with their heads cluttered up by the parts of speech.

The Nine Parts of Speech

Three little words you often see
Are ARTICLES, *a, an,* and *the.*
A NOUN's the name of anything;
As *school* or *garden, hoop* or *swing.*
ADJECTIVES tell the kind of noun;
As *great, small, pretty, white,* or *brown.*
Instead of nouns the PRONOUNS stand;
Her head, *his* face, *our* arms, *your* hand.
VERBS tell of something being done;
To *read, count, sing, laugh, jump,* or *run.*
How things are done, the ADVERBS tell;
As *slowly, quickly, ill,* or *well.*

CONJUNCTIONS join the words together;
As men *and* women, wind *or* weather.
The PREPOSITION stands before
A noun, as *in* or *through* a door.
The INTERJECTION shows surprise;
As, *oh!* how pretty! *ah!* how wise!
The whole are called nine parts of speech,
Which reading, writing, speaking teach.

 The word around the world is English, more or less.
—TIME

WRITES OTTO FRIEDRICH IN *TIME:*

The ads in Italy's *Corrière della Sera* for just one day included the words *personnel, administrator, quality audit, contract manager,* and *know-how.* Germans routinely refer to their employer as *der Boss,* who is expected to be a good *Manager.* . . . Japanese ads, posters, and shopping bags are full of a special kind of American English, often starting with an enthusiastic "Let's," as in "Let's hiking" or "Let's sex.". . .

The French still cling to *ordinateur* instead of computer, but in Italy even the schoolchildren call it by its American name. Also floppy disks, lasers, compact disks, software. Germans buy *Tapes,* not *Magnetbänder.* In fact, they call the whole field *HITEC.*

And the athletic life. A French magazine called *Vital* (pronounced Veet-al') is full of terms such as *le rafting* and *le trekking.* The Germans go in for *das Joggen,* while Italians turn to *il body-building.* . . .

This combination of money and technology, show biz and sex appeal, strikes many foreigners as the epitome of the American success story, and so they adopt English words that imply success itself: super, blue chip, boom, status symbol, summit. . . .

Foreign languages do not simply acquire American terms, of course, but adapt and rework them in a sort of hybridization variously known as Franglais, Spanglish, or Japlish. The Germans . . . now add English to

German as though creating a polyglot strudel. *Powerstimmung,* for example, means a great mood, which can make a German *ganz high* or even *ausgeflippt.*

The Japanese, though, are the past masters at making such words pay their way. It was inevitable that the Japanese would import "word processor" and just as inevitable that they would shorten it to *wa-pro.* Then the younger generation seized it and made it stand for "worst proportions," meaning an unattractive woman. . . .

Lillian Chao, professor of English Emeritus at National Taiwan University, fears that the spread of English is doing subtle damage. "China has always been a civilization of great politeness and courtesy," she says. "But now our young people, through the English they're studying, are learning to be offhanded. They say 'Hi' to everyone they greet, and everything is 'O.K.' " Well, exactly.

Don't Kiss Me

Slip: In France and Italy, not a woman's underskirt but a man's underpants.

Bronzing: In France, sunbathing.

Twenties: In Germany this is abbreviated to "twens," a clothing store category that follows teens.

Salvage: In the Philippines, to execute someone.

Kiss: In Nigeria, to collide—and not gently—with the rear of another automobile, as warned of by a Lagos bumper sticker that says DON'T KISS ME.

—*TIME*

> *Phoenicia first, if fame be truly heard,*
> *Fixed in rude characters the fleeting word.*
> —*LUCAN*

BUT THE EGYPTIANS, CHINESE, AND Tuaregs, whose firsts we shall examine later on page 109, were not far behind; nor were the Cretans, Semites, early Greeks, and others.

1. The Cretans and the Semites

When first on sheets papyral
Lads moaned of love bereft,
The Cretans' moan was spiral,
The Semites', right to left.

2. The Early Greeks

To placate spirits chthonic*
Did those first Greeks indite
In lines boustrophedonic†
Left-right, right-left, left-right.

—W.R.E.

Boustrophedon

The oxen plow from gee to haw for Jill—
　　.eeg ot wah morf ,kcaJ roF
And so between the two of them, they till
　　.ylhguoroht dleif-naeb ehT

　　　　　　　　　—W.R.E.

* A word for gods sojourning
Behind hell's triple locks.
† A word defined as "turning,
As turns the plowing ox."

I can't make a damn thing out of this tax problem.
I listen to one side and they seem right—and then
I talk to the other side and they seem just as right,
and here I am where I started. God, what a job!
—PRESIDENT WARREN GAMALIEL HARDING

WHEN CONGRESS DECIDED THAT WITH only ten days between Lincoln's and Washington's birthdays it would save time to take care of both of them at one go, they picked the third Monday in February as a convenient middle point and called it Presidents' Day. The third Monday, by inference, then, honors all forty-one presidents. For your reference, here is the full list, with two lines devoted to each. Some presidents deserve several pages; but on average, two lines seems about right.

A Potpourri of Presidents

1. *George Washington*   *Today*, George, what would you advise?
   1789–1797   We *are* entangled with Allies.*

2. *John Adams*   Adams? Not the man that backed
   1797–1801   The Alien and Sedition Act?

3. *Thomas Jefferson*   As prez, he bought one claim to glory:
   1801–1809   The Louisiana Territory.

4. *James Madison*   The White House burned down undeterred;
   1809–1817   Let's hope Jim had it well insured.

5. *James Monroe*   His doctrine's dead—for which, "Hosanna!"
   1817–1825   Cries Señor Castro of Havana.

---

* Washington warned against "permanent alliances." It was Jefferson, however, who called (in his 1801 inaugural address) for "honest friendship with all nations, entangling alliances with none."

6. *John Quincy Adams*
   1825–1829

He was a good man. (Sadly, gents,
They don't all make good presidents.)

7. *Andrew Jackson*
   1829–1837

"The winner gets the spoils," said Andy.
Immoral—but it comes in handy.

8. *Martin Van Buren*
   1837–1841

Just plain hard luck that his accession
Began a five-year-long depression.

9. *William Henry*
   Harrison, 1841

A month in office, and he's dead.
Too long, the opposition said.

10. *John Tyler*
    1841–1845

Paste one gold star on that blank slate:
He brought in Texas as a state.

11. *James Knox Polk*
    1845–1849

He made a bow to "Manifest
Destiny," and grabbed the West.

12. *Zachary Taylor*
    1849–1850

It took Zach barely half a term
To trade the White House for the Worm.

13. *Millard Fillmore*
    1850–1853

The North and South were waxing wroth.
Who blamed it all on Millard? Both—

14. *Franklin Pierce*
    1853–1857

Then, still more furious and fierce,
They blamed it all again on Pierce.

—W.R.E.

The rest of the presidents will jog past on page 124.

Hypallage, pronounced hi·pal′a·jē, *when a sentence is said with a contrary order of words, as, He took his ear from his fist; Open the day, and see if it be the window; I would make no more ado, but take a door and break open the Axe.*
—HENRY PEACHAM, 1577

THERE ARE GRAVE ARGUMENTS against drinking to excess, but none can deny that the practice leads to rhetorical tropes of stunning power, unavailable to most of us when we are sober. Hypallage is not the least of these, as may be seen from the knittelverse below:

Oh-h-h-h, My Head!

Oh-h-h-h, my head!
    A drink or two, and scarcely more . . .
    At maximum say three or four . . .
    Or even at the most prolix
    It might have come to five or six . . .
    They villainously overstate
    Who talk of seven or of eight . . .

Oh-h-h-h, my head!
    I mooned on the gaze, and I songed pretty sangs;
    I heeled up my kicks and I starred at the looks;
    I girled all the kisses, and belled all the rangs;
    I bluffed every call, and I diced all the shooks.

    I ruled all the brokes, and I homed to my went;
    I tanked at my pause, and I fished all my fed;
    I showered a took, and I kneed to one bent,
    And prayered my utters, and bell into fed.
    Oh-h-h-h, my head!
—W.R.E.

Throw a cat over a house and it will land on its feet.

—ENGLISH PROVERB

PERHAPS A QUARTER OF A CENTURY AGO I read in the Topics column (since deceased) of *The New York Times* a report that has permanently changed my view about cats. The clipping has long since crumbled to dust, and I must paraphrase, memory being porous; but the essence of it is branded into my mind, this way:

> Some people like cats, and some people hate them. Me, I am neutral. I can take cats or I can leave them alone. But I must tell you one thing: not all the superstitions about cats are true.
>
> One of these superstitions is that a cat, tossed into the air, will always land on its feet. I happen to live in the suburbs, and my last chore before going to bed each night is to toss our cat down the cellar steps. I have learned to give it a certain twist that will make it land on its head every time.

Instruction for getting rid of an unwanted cat in a city apartment: Put cat in elevator, press 1.

—SALLY FLY

Michelangelo faciebat

—SIGNATURE ON THE PIETÀ IN
SAINT PETER'S CATHEDRAL, ROME

MICHELANGELO'S SCULPTURE OF THE Virgin Mary mourning over the dead Christ is perhaps the most famous of all Pietàs. John Niven, back from Rome, mentioned noticing that the statue bore the carved legend *Michelangelo faciebat*. I found this astonishing. *Facere* is Latin for "to make"; *fecit* is the simple past, "made";

faciebat, if my Latin teacher in high school knew what she was talking about, means "was making"—was still in the process; the work was not yet finished. Was Michelangelo actually saying his masterpiece was incomplete?

I wrote for an opinion to Frederick Hartt, a Michelangelo scholar. He did not share my excitement. He replied that the only signature he knew of on any of Michelangelo's works was that on the Pietà, but he added, "I am sure there are many other examples in which Trecento and Renaissance artists employed the imperfect tense. I should be inclined to attribute this lapse to their imperfect acquaintance with the rules of Latin grammar, rather than to any profound teleological speculation."

But *Michelangelo?* He was no illiterate. His skill in Latin was scarcely less than in the covering of canvas and the chopping of stone. He wrote, says the *Encyclopaedia Britannica*, as he painted and carved—"with labor and much self-correction." Would he be so cavalier as to err, the one time he left his name on a work of art?

I contend that Michelangelo deliberately carved "was in the process of making" into the stone of the Pietà. Perhaps he had to quit before he was through. Perhaps he was signaling that there could be no such thing as a completed painting or sculpture.

Says the *Britannica* sketch: "The only work which in all his life he was able to complete as he had conceived it was . . . the decoration of the Sistine ceiling."

So he would have signed the Sistine ceiling Michelangelo *fecit*, not *faciebat*. All his other works, the Pietà included, were, to his mind, unfinished.

Faciebat. Not a bad legend for a tombstone, it seems to me. "John Jones faciebat." "Willard Espy faciebat." Here we are, painting away at our personal Sistine ceilings . . . nowhere near to accomplishing what is in our hearts . . . and Someone calls us down from the scaffolding.

. . . .

*For four wicked centuries the world has dreamed this foolish
dream of efficiency; and the end is not yet.*
—GEORGE BERNARD SHAW

IT IS A PLEASURE TO FIND A VIEW on which Mr. Shaw
and I hold common ground. I am almost as opposed to efficiency as
I am to logic.* Whoever sent me the following unattributed clipping
obviously hates efficiency, too.

A MANAGEMENT SURVEY TEAM REPORTS ON A PHILHARMONIC ORCHESTRA

For considerable periods the four oboe players have nothing to do. Their
number should be reduced and the work spread more evenly over the
whole of the concert, thus eliminating peaks of activity.

All the 12 first violins were playing identical notes. This is unnecessary
duplication. The staff of this section should be drastically cut. If a large
volume of sound is required, it can be obtained by means of electronic
amplifier apparatus.

Much effort was absorbed in the playing of semi-quavers. This seems
an excessive refinement. It is recommended that all notes be rounded up
to the nearest quaver. If this were done, it would be possible to use
trainees and lower grade operatives more extensively. There seems to be
too much repetition of some musical passages. Scores should be drastically pruned. No useful purpose is served by repeating on the horns a
passage which has already been played on the strings. It is estimated that
if all redundant passages were eliminated, the whole concert time of two
hours could be reduced to twenty minutes and there would be no need
for an intermission.

The conductor agrees generally with these recommendations, but fore-
sees that there might be some falling off in attendance. In this unlikely
event it should be possible to close sections of the auditorium entirely,
with a consequent saving of overhead expense, lighting, salaries for ush-
ers, etc.

* See pages 131 and 153.

Eye-rhymes, sight-rhymes. Words that have the same
spelling but different sounds where the identical-sounding
conclusion of a rhyme would be, and therefore are not
rhymes at all: herein, rein; baked, naked.
—W.R.E.

Duck, Poet! Here Comes Another Sight-Rhyme!

How nicely *panache—ache—Apache*—would rhyme
Were eyes the sole judges! But *ears* need a chime.
Ears rhyme *ache* with *steak* and *opaque;* rhyme *panache*
With *ash* and *rehash* and *bedash* and *abash.*
Ears know that a rhyme for trochaic *Apache**
Has endings like *scratchy, hibachi, seecatchie.*

Ears know, too, that *passage* won't rhyme with *massage,*
Which has a last-syllable stress, like *barrage.*
(As far as I know there's just one rhyme for *passage*—
"A charge for expenses of coinage" called *brassage.*)

The eye sees accord between *science* and *prescience;*
The ear knows that *prescience*† rhymes only with *nescience,*
While *science* has *giants, alliance, defiance,*
And ten or so others in rhyming compliance.

Take *naked* and *baked;* it is wise to recall
That *naked*'s a word that has no rhyme at all.
And *shallow*'s unable to rhyme with *allow,*
But matches with *hallow; allow* rhymes with *cow.*

---

* Member of a certain Indian tribe. But *apache,* meaning "a Paris hoodlum," does rhyme with *panache.*
†*Pre-science,* though, hyphenated, rhymes with any word that *science* does.

And finally, *eat* does not rhyme with *hereat*.
No; *eat* rhymes with *feet*, and *hereat* rhymes with *cat*.

The moral? *Appearance is often deceiving.*
Best not take for granted that seeing's believing.

—W.R.E.

> *Recently I noticed that the word* dollop *reads the same way*
> *upside down. Would you call it an "invertogram"?*
> —JOHN M. CULKIN

"INVERTOGRAM" SOUNDS FINE TO ME, JOHN. By the way, what would you call a word that becomes a *different* one when turned upside down? Take, for example, *deus*, Latin for "god," which opens and closes the lines below. (A monk named Silvester Houédard drew the word, and John Furneval relayed it to me.)

Too Late

deus, till I lay here dying,
I forgot You frown on lying.
Till no time was left to live,
I was sure You would forgive.
I ignored, in days of lust,
That the ways of God are just.
Till my time to take the rap,
I thought heaven was a **snap**.

—W.R.E.

The names of three populated places in Guatemala—
Xecchavox, Xetonox, and Xix—begin and end with X.
—PHILIP COHEN

X Marks the Spot

Down below our neighbor Mex,
In the land of Guatemala,
You will find no wild ibex,
No koala, no impala—
But, instead, the letter X.

X's running, X's walking,
X's thundering in herds;
X's sunning, X's stalking,
X's crowding into words;
X's reading—writing—talking.

X no x's out to fix
Names of towns, should you stay in them;
In the cities or the sticks,
X's end them and begin them.
You may ride a mule in Xix . . .

Eat a pig in Xecchavox . . .
Swat a fly in Xetonox . . .

—W.R.E.

3

The third time I replied once more,
But not so kindly as before.

But I must not go on singling out names, as our dear queen
was telling me at lunch only yesterday.

—NORMAN ST. JOHN-STEVAS

THE ONLY TIME LOUISE ACCUSES ME of dropping names is when I tell about our dinner with Lillian Gish. She interrupts me before company to announce that the story is only an excuse to brag that Lillian Gish once spoke to me.

What I cannot make Louise understand is that this is a special case. I was just nine years old when I saw Miss Gish in *Orphans of the Storm*, and I have been in love with her ever since. Besides, the story she told me is well worth repeating.

It was one of those affairs where you know only a few of the guests, and Louise and I went to the table and found our name tags and sat down, and there she was between us. After a while she told this:

Once, she said, she was one of several guests aboard a Trump-size yacht idling among the Aegean Islands. For several days a sloop of modest dimensions kept pace with them, and Miss Gish, with one or two other passengers, fell into the habit of coming across by tender and socializing with the husband and wife who were the only humans aboard.

There was, however, one nonhuman—a sea gull that the couple had nursed back to vigor after it broke a wing. The sea gull considered them its family and the sloop its nest. Its favorite pastime, apart from eating fish, was sitting on laps; and once it discovered Lillian Gish's lap, that was the lap it preferred. You would have felt the same way.

Though a tender-hearted sort, she found the bird a bit of a fardel— a word I use in Hamlet's heavy sense.

"You cannot imagine," she told us, "the dead weight of a sea gull. That bird must have weighed at least fifteen pounds when it first settled down, and it kept getting heavier.*

"Fifteen pounds dead weight," she repeated. "And I am told that a sea gull eats more than its weight every day. And sea gulls are

---

* She was hyperbolizing. Two or three pounds would be more like it.

everywhere. Say there are a billion of them. They would need fifteen billion pounds of food a day. In tons, that comes to—"

"Seven and a half million," I said, dividing by two thousand on my napkin.

"All right. Say there are four billion people in the world. If you divided those seven and a half million tons among four billion people you would have—"

"Three and a third pounds of fish per person per day," I said.

"You might grow tired of so much fish," said Miss Gish. "But just think—there would be no more hunger. Why—" (I could see she was throwing the challenge directly into my teeth) "—if someone could just persuade those sea gulls to diet . . ."

That is the whole story, and I admit that it would be less interesting if Lillian Gish were not part of it. But honestly—am I name dropping? Don't answer; Louise has not been able to persuade me, and you can't, either.

. . . .

Waiter, Freeze

At Ciro's last night, D. seemed to have caught a chill and she complained that the hot room was very cold. "It's very draughty," said she. "I don't feel any draught at all," said I. She said, "It's when the waiters pass."

—ARNOLD BENNETT

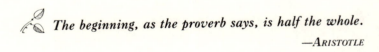

The beginning, as the proverb says, is half the whole.
—ARISTOTLE

ETYMOLOGY—THE STUDY OF WORD origins—makes clear that Aristotle was right, at least about words. They may change their meanings dramatically over the centuries—nobody knows how to stop that—but whiffs of the earlier definitions still emanate from them, as here:

Broker (Latin, broccare)

Broccare meant "to tap a cask,"
And then, "to deal in wine":
And then, "to take on any task
As middleman"; and fin-
ally meant "broker": "one who scouts
For stocks and bonds and such."
It once meant "pimp," too. Some have doubts
The meaning's altered much.

—W.R.E.

Chattel, Cattle, Capital (Latin, capitalis)

"Chattel" 's to "cattle" as brother to brother—
Words that took suck from the same Latin mother.
"Capital," too, from that word *capitalis*
("Head-man's possessions") debouches and sallies.
Chattel and *cattle* are part of the *capital*
Owned by the "head-man"—the one who can tap it all.

—W.R.E.

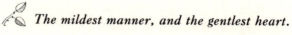 *The mildest manner, and the gentlest heart.*
—*HOMER*

I ONCE WROTE OF BEING, as a boy, part of a group that
found the body of Jimmy Anderson, my favorite of the Oysterville
hermits, slumped over the sink in his kitchen. Blackberry vines had
crawled in through the doorway and climbed up his legs, and other
blackberry vines coming in through the raised kitchen window had
twined down his midriff to meet them.

We called him and others of his sort—old widowers or bachelors—
"hermits" because they lived in leaky shacks in the deep woods, tramp-
ing in to the post office–grocery store perhaps once a week to pick up

*. . . Blackberry vines coming in through the raised
kitchen window had twined down his midriff. . . .*

such staples as coffee, tobacco, and occasionally bread. Jimmy considered himself a cut above the others, for he owned a fiddle, given him in boyhood. This he played at hoedowns, shrilly. He was convinced beyond argument that it was a Stradivarius; his mother, he said, had told him so.

He was also the village weather prophet. Whenever he and I met—he, I suppose, in his sixties, I not yet in my teens—on the graveled road that was our main street, he would pause and greet me with courtesy as elaborate and genuine as if I had been the schoolmistress, instead of a tousle-headed boy in brown coveralls. Then he would cock his head toward the sky, pause one calculating moment, and, if it happened not to be raining, say, "Yup, it is going to rain." He was always right.

Winter after winter Helen Heckes watched him trudging past her house in sluicing downpours, always wearing the same clothes: a broad-brimmed felt hat with large holes in the crown; neatly patched overalls; and a wool shirt. Never, though, a raincoat to fend off the storms.

Finally Helen could stand the sight no longer. She ran out in the rain one day and insisted on giving him a worn but still serviceable slicker, which after many demurrers he accepted with as many thanks. But never did she see him wear it.

Barbara Kemmer lived on the same street, and she worried about Jimmy, too. His abode, she knew, was more holes than roof or walls, and the winter sou'easters found it easy passage. She demanded of him once whether he had a quilt for his bed; he hesitated; and she forced him to accept one. Jimmy could not have been more grateful. Indeed, several months later Barbara, unlike Helen, did receive an accounting.

"I want you to know I am taking real good care of that quilt of yours, Barbara," he said. "I keep it wrapped in Helen's raincoat."

· · · · · · ·

Perhaps there never was a publication more implicitly to be relied on for the authenticity of its statements and the exactness with which every fact is detailed.

—*LORD BRAYBROOKS*
(ON PEPYS' DIARY, WHICH HE EDITED)

EXCEPT THAT PEPYS NEVER SAID how his name should be pronounced. Oh, admittedly there is a consensus; but every new reader of the *Diaries* must start out by abandoning one mispronunciation after another, finally to settle on the one that, from the appearance of the name to the eye, is the unlikeliest of the lot.

On The Pronunciation of Mr. Pepys' Name

Oh Samuel, who on some folks' lips
Are designated Samuel Pips,
While others follow in the steps
Of those who call you Samuel Peps—
At Cottenham the proper step is
To sound the y and call you Pepp-is—
To such ignorance all Magdalen* weeps
Well knowing you are Samuel Peeps.

—THE JONSONIAN NEWSLETTER

But I still say Peps, as this ESPYramid shows:

It Was John Buchan

* is a vowel, like A, I, and O;
**, though now rare, is the plural of "you."
*** has the opposite meaning of "no."
These further facts may be useful to you:
**** did not write *The Thirty-nine Steps*—
Though, come to think of it, neither did *****.

—W.R.E.

*Magdalen (the college Pepys attended at Cambridge) is pronounced "maudlin."

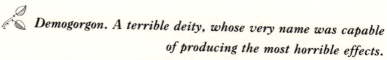

Demogorgon. A terrible deity, whose very name was capable of producing the most horrible effects.

—BREWER'S DICTIONARY OF PHRASE AND FABLE

DAMNATION. DEVIL. DEMOGORGON. There is a dreadful dimension to data dominated by D, as you may deduce from the doleful drama delineated in the D words below.

D. No Ranks of Inalienable Law for Demogorgon
(With the Barest of Nods to George Meredith)

Great Demogorgon, on a daggly[1] day,
Uprose diversivolent[2] to the light.
Daspygal[3] and disomous[4] too he lay
Until a tender virgin hove in sight—
A dryad, toothsome and devorative,[5]
Who, puzzled, paused and gave the fiend the eye.
"No roots . . . no leaves," she murmured. "As I live,
Here is an object hard to classify."

She was dendrophilous[6]—a lass who weened
All strangers to be variants of trees.
Some dotty dotterel,[7] she thought the fiend;
She figured she could chop him down with ease.
But he proceeded to dilaniate[8] her,
And ate her.

—W.R.E.

---

[1] Drizzly. [2] Looking for trouble. [3] Hairy-assed. [4] (pronounced di.sō′mus) Having two joined bodies. [5] He could swallow her in one bite. [6] Living in trees and loving it. [7] A decaying tree, or an old fool ("dotty dotterel" is redundant). [8] Rend to bits.

Every day in every way I'm getting better and better.
—ÉMILE COUÉ

OR IF *I* AM NOT, AT LEAST the nation's schoolchildren are. A recent *Northwest Magazine* report indicates, indeed, that by comparison with those of the 1940s they are nearly angelic. To illustrate the point, the publication draws this comparison between present-day discipline problems and those of a generation ago:

1940s	*1980s*
Chewing gum	Assault
Dressing inappropriately	Drug abuse
Not putting paper in wastebaskets	Possessing alcohol
Passing notes	Possessing weapons
Skipping classes	Skipping classes
Running in the halls	Theft
Talking	Vandalism

No longer do our wee ones chew gum, drop paper on the floor, pass notes, or whisper in class. At least nobody bothers to make a note of it. The improvement deserves a tribute, and I am not one to fall silent when my voice is needed.

I Think the Earth Nears Heaven

I think the earth nears heaven—so
Devoutly disciplined
Schoolchildren are, who years ago
In these dread fashions sinned:

One: Some unblushingly *chewed gum!*
Two: Sloppy clothes some wore!
Three: Some *passed notes!*—and also some
Four: Dropped stuff on the floor!

Five: In the halls, some kids would *run!*
Six: Other kids *skipped class!*
Or, *Seven: whispered,* just for fun!
(And some kids *didn't pass!*)

But nearly fifty years have gone,
And good have schoolkids grown:
The sins that they once doted on
Today are quite unknown.

Now sins are trifling: *One: assault;*
Two: dope (to ward off stress);
Three (who would count this as a fault?):
Persistent *drunkenness;*

Four: weapons (just for self-defense);
Five: skipping class (a shame
To count this trifle; common sense
Says parents are to blame);

Six: when the time's propitious, *theft;*
(But prudence here applies—
A few possessions must be left
To, *Seven: vandalize*).

Thus true-blue heart and snow-white soul
Pervade each flawless class;
All muggers make the honor roll,
And every kid will pass.

                                        —W.R.E.

If it were not for the capacity for ambiguity, for the sensing
of strangeness, that words in all languages provide, we would
have no way of recognizing the layers of counterpoint in meaning,
and we might be spending all our time
sitting on stone fences, staring into the sun.
—LEWIS THOMAS

THE WEEKLY NEWSPAPER THAT COVERS Oysterville, a village in Washington State where I spend part of each year, reported a search for "a dog belonging to a doctor that had gotten loose." Edith Olson sent a letter asking for clarification. The story said the dog had been found, she noted, but what about the doctor? "Is he still loose? How did he get out? Did someone smuggle in a key or hacksaw blade? Did the people panic when they heard there was a doctor loose? Anyway, I hope he doesn't get caught. He was ingenious enough to break loose; let him go."

A young woman confided to Georgia Penfield that she and her poossl-q* were "thinking of telling our friends we are married." Georgia is still wondering whether that meant the lovers were already married and now planned to admit it, or were unmarried but going to say the opposite.

Even majestic financial institutions are not immune to ambiguous language. The Chase Manhattan Bank ran a series of advertisements headlined WHEN MY FUTURE BECAME CLEAR, I PUT THE CHASE BEHIND ME. Not quite what Jesus meant when He said, "Get thee behind me, Satan!" (Matthew 16:18).

I am told that a tutor at an Oxford College, asked to give a reference for a notoriously indolent graduate, wrote: "You will be lucky to get Mr. Bloggs to work for you."

Then there are the verbal ambiguities that are also double enten-

---

* Not *possl-q*. To me, *poossl-q* means "persons of opposite sex sharing living quarters"; *possl-q* (which I spell *posssl-q*) means "persons of *same* sex sharing living quarters." Besides, *poossl-q* sounds smoochier.

dres. I have a deplorable weakness for them, as you may already have noticed. I treasure this newspaper headline:

SLIPPING AND FALLING IN
BATHTUBS IS OFTEN DUE TO
CURVED BOTTOMS, IT IS SAID

And this letter to a columnist for the troubled:

"You can't imagine how out of things I feel, never to be able to discuss how my husband hasn't touched me in months, the way all my girl friends do."

A young woman, asked to review a book titled *Have You Had It in the Kitchen?*, could not resist writing, "No—in the back of a car, on the seashore, in a cave, on a table, but never in the kitchen." I am told the review did not appear.

A little uncertainty in such matters is all to the good, it seems to me. "To be uncertain," said Goethe, "may be uncomfortable, but to be certain is to be ridiculous."

Lewis Thomas would subscribe to that.

• • • • • • •

Writes Robert Michael Pyle in *Wintergreen:* "My grandfather used to have a saying that he repeated at every Sunday dinner: 'This is a mighty fine dinner, what there is of it; and there's plenty of it, such as it is.'" Sounds like a classical ambiguity, but not so; it is a ringing tribute to the cooking of Mr. Pyle's grandmother.

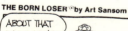

THE BORN LOSER ®by Art Sansom

Reprinted by permission of NEA, Inc.

> *Therefore is the name of it called Babel; because the Lord
> did there confound the language of all the earth.*
>
> —GENESIS 11:9

EVER SINCE GOD SABOTAGED the Tower of Babel, well-meaning souls have been dreaming up such artificial languages as Esperanto, Volapük, Occidental, and Arul for international use. They have won few converts. On a more practical level, though, international traders freely use various forms of lingua franca—a term originally applied to a mixture of Italian, French, Spanish, Greek, and Arabic spoken in Mediterranean ports and now to such jargons as

- Pidgin English,* frequently shortened to pidgin, a sound-approximation of "business." It combines corrupted English words with Chinese or Melanesian syntax.
- Bêche-de-mer. The Portuguese called the sea slug or sea cucumber (formally the trepang) *bicho do mar,* "sea worm," later Frenched to *bêche-de-mer,* "sea caterpillar." Much in demand for Chinese soup, it was fished so generally in the southwestern Pacific that its name was applied to a trade tongue combining English and Malayan.
- Chinook, after the Chinook tribe of Indians, includes words from several Indian languages, mixed with English and French. It was used for trade between whites and Indians of the northwestern United States and western Canada, particularly in the eighteenth and early nineteenth centuries.

Perhaps the most universal form of lingua franca, curiously, has never made its way into the reference books. It is called *hanka panka* and is often used in situations like the one described here:

* See page 81.

Hanka Panka

Use of wordless *hanka panka*
(Lovers' silent lingua franca)
Leaves observers unaware
You've begun a love affair.

One brief speculative look
Beats a question in Chinook;
Fingers barely brushing hair
More convey than bêche-de-mer.

Lowering your eyes a smidgin
Speaks more secretly than pidgin.
Hanka panka's still as able
As before God rubbished Babel.

—W.R.E.

*Among these writers a centripetal isolation prevails;
the world never extends illusionistically beyond
the cast assembled on the stage.*

—SVEN BIRKETS

MR. BIRKETS SAYS THE WRITERS to whom he refers—
a term sometimes used to describe them is "minimalist"—are
frequently the finds and protégés of a distinguished editor, educator,
and short-story writer named Gordon Lish, whose own sentences may
"capture the reader with their erratic and colloquial beat." He quotes
a Lish paragraph by way of illustration, and he is right; I am still a
captive to these sentences, though not exactly a willing one:

Alan Silver moved in. He moved in when there were seven houses and
four still going up. He was twelve. Maybe I was nine by then. So that's
the boys from two houses. The other five had boys in them too.

We are presented here with a problem in arithmetic, and it is a shame that the Lish story is no longer on my desk; it would be nice to see if he gives the answer at the end. Mathematics has always been hard for me. I suspect this particular problem involves algebra; the reader is supposed to turn the paragraph into an equation in which Alan = x. It is what comes between the Alan and the x that confuses me. The knittelverse that follows is an effort to sort these matters out.

Real Estate Development

When ONE Alan Silver moved in, moved in,
    With SEVEN new houses about
(Not counting his own, where once country had been,
And FOUR going up, or about to begin—
    FOUR added to SEVEN comes out

ELEVEN; the ONE makes it TWELVE) (that's the same,
    It happens, as Alan's own age)
(I know I was NINE, but confess to my shame
The house that I lived in, or even my name
    I cannot recall at this stage)

(The FIVE other houses had boys ONE and all,
    And Alan's and mine made TWO more)
(That's SEVEN, while Alan was TWELVE, you recall,
And I was just NINE) (I was born in the fall)—
    Now let's try to tote up the score:

ONE, SEVEN, and FOUR: FOUR and SEVEN again;
    ELEVEN, and TWELVE after ONE;
NINE, FIVE, ONE, TWO (but no six, and no ten)
Plus SEVEN, TWELVE, NINE: and the total is then
    A clear NINETY-TWO, and we're done

(Unless my addition has led me astray)
    But how many houses—and ages—
And boys? I'm afraid I can't possibly say;
    I haven't a clue—so let's leave it that way
      (Although I could go on for pages).

—W.R.E.

You will meet the great-grandmother of minimalism on page 146.

*Give me six lines written by the most honorable of men,
   and I will find an excuse in them to hang him.*

—CARDINAL RICHELIEU

I HAVE KNOWN FOR A LONG TIME that Ned Naumburg collects rare books, but until visiting him the other day I had no idea that he is also a collector of Impossible Poets. Richelieu would have hanged them all.

J. Gorden Coogler, a nineteenth-century southerner, would not have lasted beyond these two lines:

> Alas for the South, her books have grown fewer;
> She never was much given to literature.

Richelieu was not around, though, and Mr. Coogler survived to pen this:

> On her beautiful face there are smiles of grace
> That linger in beauty serene,
> And there are no pimples encircling her dimples
> As ever, as yet, I have seen.

And this:

> Thou immortal Byron!
>> Thy inspired genius
>> Let no man attempt to smother—
> May all that was good within thee
> Be attributed to Heaven,
>> And all that was evil—to thy mother.

Richelieu would also have hanged, higher than the ancient Israelis hanged Haman, one William McGonneggal, who in the nineteenth century retired the trophy for Worst Poet in the English Language. These lines would have been excuse enough:

> Beautiful railway bridge of the silv'ry Tay!
> Alas I am very sorry to say
> That 90 lives have been taken away on the last
>> Sabbath day of 1879.
> Which will be remember'd for a very long time.

At McGonneggal's side would dangle Julia A. Moore, "the sweet singer of Michigan." She too was moved by railway disasters:

> Swift passed the engine's call,
>> Hastening souls on to death,
> Warning not one of them all;
>> It brought despair right and left.

I hope Ned never reads one of my knittelverses. Better Ned Naumburg, though, than Cardinal Richelieu.

Authentic symbolism is present when something specific represents something more universal, not as a dream or a shadow, but as a living momentary revelation of what is inscrutable.

—JOHANN WOLFGANG VON GOETHE

PERHAPS GOETHE WAS HINTING that he was devoted to rebuses. (This would not necessarily be in his favor.) A rebus (from Latin *res*, "thing") is a riddle depicting words or syllables in terms of symbols, either verbal or pictorial, and often involving puns. The hidden message may be contained in words, parts of words, or letter combinations. *Child slept*, for instance, = *kid napped*, = *kidnapped*. *A chance n = an outside chance. Keet keet = pair o' keets*, = *parakeets*.

The rebuses below, all of the verbal sort, appeared in *Word Ways*. Helen Gunn, George Grieshaber, and Maxey Brooks were the suppliers. The answers are at the back of the book.*

1. Aallll
2. Dice misplaced
3. Off off on on
4. Stun
5. Always caution-light
6. Lev
       el
7. esroh
8. R / e / a / d / i / n / g
9. Cycle cycle cycle
10. Ecnalg
11. Knee
    lights
12. T
    o
    u
    c
    h
13. Death life
14. You just me
15. Man
    board

The following rebus, forwarded by Wayne Moseley, is self-explanatory if the elements are pronounced after the manner of an Italian immigrant who has not yet perfected his English:

U , ⌂ Rosie Mr. .

* See pages 168 and 230 for more letter rebuses.

The contribution made to the English language by the
sailing ship sailor is enormous. . . . The words and phrases
are among the most apt, the most colorful,
and the most popular in the language.

—BILL BEAVIS IN ENGLISH TODAY

THE KNITTELVERSE BELOW ENUMERATES several of the nautical expressions cited by Mr. Beavis. His account of their origins—listed here as footnotes— appears in Answers and Solutions.

The Lady and the Tar

The loveliest lady since Adam's lost rib
Admired a bold tar[1] for the cut of his jib.[2]
His muscular pectorals took her aback[3];
They brought her up short,[4] and her breathing went slack.
His smile took the wind from her sails[5]; when he grinned
She felt herself stagger, three sheets to the wind.[6]
She told him, "I'm listless[7] when we're not together;
I'm lost in the doldrums[8] and under the weather[9]!"
Said he, "Shake it up[10]; if you've something to say,
You'd better get cracking[11]; I haven't all day!"
She couldn't bear up[12] when she looked at his frown,
So, scant[13] though her breath, yet she boldly bore down.[14]
She feared she was sailing too close to the wind,[15]
But cried, "Dear, I love you; we've got to get pinned!"
It seemed touch and go,[16] but he answered, "I share
Your slant[17] on the matter; we two are all square."[18]
He's footloose[19] no longer, but home from the main;
Now Adam's one flesh with his lost rib again.

—W.R.E.

For rhetoric, he could not ope
His mouth, but out there flew a trope.

—SAMUEL BUTLER

ANYONE WITHOUT RHETORIC IS HANDICAPPED as a speaker, a writer, and, particularly, a thinker. I believe we should take a fresh look at the art, and to start off I am going to show here the simple meanings of three jaw-breaking rhetorical terms: enallage,* asyndeton,† and polysyndeton.‡

Pat Little Rhetoric—He Won't Bite

If you already can define *enallage,*
Or other bits of rhetoric here listed,
Just skip the ones you know, with my apology
And get along to any you have misseded.

Enallage is error by intention—
To show that *you're* the boss, when you insist,
And grammar isn't. (I need only mention
My use of "misseded" when the word is "missed.")

Omission of conjunctions is *asyndeton:*
"I came, I saw, I conquered," and its ilk.
Though Caesar is by chance the one I pinned it on,
It's used by Shakespeare, Keats, and Leonard Silk.§

But *polysyndeton's* in opposition;
It has conjunctions coming out its ears;
"I came *and* saw *and* conquered"—that's its mission;
Those *ands* and *buts* and *ors* go on for years.

—W.R.E.

* en.*al'*a.jē
† a.*sin'*de.ton
‡ *pol'*i.*sin'*de.ton
§ Mr. Silk writes on economic matters for *The New York Times.*

It is now quite lawful for a Catholic woman to avoid pregnancy by a resort to mathematics, though she is still forbidden to resort to physics and chemistry.
—*H. L. MENCKEN*

MY COUSIN BARBARA, UNCLE CECIL'S daughter, married Bronk (short for Brongwyn) Williams, one of the Williams clan that has proliferated so mightily a few miles south of Oysterville. This was the first link between us Espys and any other local tribe.

Barbara quickly became more Williams than the Williamses. She claims that they are livelier than the Espys, which is likely; louder, which is doubtful; and more numerous, which is certain. She was particularly fond of Bronk's uncle Rees, a bull-voiced man with a sociable disposition and a flair for telling stories—some stories of medium height, but most of them very tall. The Rees Williams story I like best, though, is not of his own telling; it is one that Barbara tells about him.

Rees had two sons—Tom, a high school senior, and Rees Jr., a student at the University of Washington. Young Rees frequently came home for weekends. During one of these visits he complained about the dinner gravy, which he said tasted like library paste.

In the ordinary course of things, Mrs. Williams, who was of Irish extraction, would have shriveled her firstborn with a blaze of words. Instead, though, she broke into sobs and fled the table. After an instant of confounded silence (an instant is a lot of silence for Williamses), Rees Sr. said, "Boys, I want to see you upstairs right after dinner."

They finished their meal and filed up to the spare bedroom. Rees Sr. seated himself on a straight-backed armchair. His two sons perched, edgily, on the bed. He huffed once, puffed once, and said:

"Boys, at a certain age women go through something called the Men-o-Pause, which means they can't have any more babies. It is a hard time for them, and they may become touchy for a bit; nervous, sensitive—what a man might call unreasonable. Well, boys, your mother is going through the Men-o-Pause right now; and until she is over it you must tread gently, very gently, so as not to upset her. Do you understand?"

They did.

Two weeks later, Rees Jr. came home again for the weekend. Again he and his brother were instructed to follow their father upstairs after dinner. They arranged themselves as before. Rees Sr. huffed once, puffed once, and said, "Do you remember what I told you a couple of weeks ago?"

They did.

"Well, boys, forget it. Your mother is pregnant."

Eighty percent of English words are not spelled phonetically.

—*RICHARD LEDERER*

SPELLING REFORMERS HAVE BEEN WITH US since before the Flood, perhaps since before the Fall, and they remain confident of ultimate victory.

But I hope they lose. A word's entire history, its every layer of meaning, is imbedded in its spelling. And setting etymology aside, wouldn't it be boring if each letter were always pronounced the same way? In Dmitri Borgmann's sentence "English woman has-beens in Tientsin build counterfeit pyramids busily," the short *i* sound is spelled in nine different ways; and he does not even bother with the short *i* sound of the *a* in words like "dotage." Who wants to take the fun out of such unpredictable letters as that?

The following words have been respelled by correspondents* according to the common pronunciations of certain letters.

---

* The names of the senders have vanished. Would you let me know if you were one of them?

MN as in autumn	M
O as in women	I
PS as in psychology	S
PT as in ptomaine	T
EI as in inveigh	A
CH as in inchoate	K
E as in bare	E

MNOPSPTEICHE = MISTAKE

MN as in autumn	M
O as in women	I
MN as in mnemonics	N
OU as in rough	U
PT as in ptomaine	T
E as in bare	E

MNOMNOUPTE = MINUTE

Constitutional Right?

If freedom of speech is a constitutional right, then why not freedom of spelling? Samuel Pepys cites Ben Jonson as saying it is a dull man who can spell a word only one way. Andrew Jackson and Mark Twain are among those concurring. Why not enshrine the right to misspell in a constitutional amendment?

Metaplasmus
(*The Alteration of Letters in a Word*)

Erasmus
Deplored metaplasmus.
He maintained even beliefs improperly held
Should be properly spelled.
—W.R.E.

4

The fourth time you inquired, I said
That you should go and soak your head.

A dialect is the characteristic speech used by the members of a single regional or social community. The speech of an individual is called an idiolect.

—*"Success with Words"* (Reader's Digest)

So I HAVE BEEN TALKING IDIOLECT all my life, and never knew it. Nor have you any reason to feel superior—you speak idiolect, too. Conflate our idiolects, and we have a dialect; conflate our dialects, and we have a language. An idiolect is personal; a dialect is regional; a language is national.

While Professor Edward Cassidy was preparing his *Dictionary of American Regional English*, Joy Schalaben Lewis interviewed him about regionalisms—dialects, that is—for the *Watauga Democrat*, of Boone, Alabama. She learned that southeasterners and southwesterners do not say "Gesundheit" when someone sneezes; they say "Scat." (I should think they would say "Scat" only when the *cat* sneezes.)

She learned that there are 175 regional ways of describing a downpour, including

a hay-rotter, a duck drencher, a tree bender, a chunk floater, a sewer clogger, a clod roller, a toad strangler, a stumpwasher, a goose drownder.

She learned further that

in Indiana, a man planning marriage is about to hop the broomstick; in New York, to hook up double; in Alaska, to jump the puddle; in Connecticut, to be buckled up; in Michigan, to get hung; in Oklahoma, to take on a boarder; in Pennsylvania, to go up the middle aisle; in Wyoming, to head for the last roundup. But all over America these curious prospects can be translated into an expression we all understand—to get hitched.

Suppose his intended changes her mind. In Pennsylvania, she gives the poor fellow the bubble; in Kentucky, she puts him on the funny side, or turns him out in the cold; in Texas, she gives him the high ball; in Georgia, she rings him off; in Connecticut, she gives him the bum's rush; in South Carolina, she gives him the go-by; in Oregon, she gives him the mitten. Again, the translation is the same in every state: she jilts him.

Professor Cassidy was still welcoming contributions at the time of the interview. He said he did not intend to "hootenkack" anybody. In Colorado, he explained, hootenkacking means to talk someone into doing something that the someone does not want to do. "And that," he added, "includes any young woman hootenkacking a young man into jumping the puddle in Alaska, hopping the broomstick in Indiana, or throwing the switch in Massachusetts."

> *Lampoons and satires, that are written with wit and spirit, are like poisoned darts, which not only inflict a wound, but make it incurable.*
>
> —JOSEPH ADDISON

I HAVE BEEN DIPPING INTO *The Oxford Book of Satirical Verse* and turn away sadly aware that my stomach is not as strong as it once was. The old-timers did breathe deeply of fecal and other stinks. (The Netherlands, to Andrew Marvell, was "indigested vomit of the sea.")

There was, however, one genuinely merry specimen. It will well repay any trouble you may have working your way through its old Scottish speech.

How the First Hielandman of God
Was Made of ane Horse Turd
in Argyll As Is Said

God and Sainct Peter
 Was gangand[1] be the way
Heich up in Argyll
 Where their gait[2] lay.

---

[1] going. [2] course.

Sainct Peter said to God
 In a sport[3] word,
Can ye not mak a Hielandman
 Of this horse turd?

God turn'd owre the horse turd
 With his pykit[4] staff
And up start a Hielandman
 Blak as ony draff.[5]

Quod God to the Hielandman,
 Where wilt thow now?
I will doun in the Lawland, Lord
 And there steill a cow.

An thou steill a cow, cairle,
 Then they will hang thee.
What rack, Lord, of that,
 For anis[6] mon I die . . .

Fy, quod Sainct Peter,
 Thou will never dow weill,
And thou bot new made
 And sa soon gais to steill.

Umff, quod the Hielandman,
 And sware be yon kirk,
Sa lang as I may gear[7] get to steill
 Will I never work.

---

[3] jesting. [4] pointed. [5] rubbish. [6] once. [7] goods, property.

*March 28, 1852: The geese have just gone over, making a
great cackling and awaking people in their beds.*

—HENRY DAVID THOREAU

A SKEIN OF GEESE IS HONKING PAST, far overhead. I
learned recently that geese did not start honking until some-
time between 1849 and 1851. They clamored and clangored; they
clanked and clank-clanked; they cackled; they made, Thoreau said,
the sound of "a clanking chain drawn through the heavy air," a sound
"that comes from directly between us and the sky, an aerial sound, and
yet so distinct, heavy, and sonorous." But they did not honk. It was
only after Thoreau had completed the 1849 stage of *Walden* that he
penciled in "honks" somewhere to replace "clanks"; again, in the
April 18, 1852, entry of his *Journal*, he substituted the same word. At
once, geese all over the world began to honk, and they have been
honking ever since.

Professor J. Lyndon Shanley first called the start of the goose's
honk to my attention, and Elizabeth Witherell, editor in chief of *The
Writings of Henry D. Thoreau*, filled in details. Two pertinent quotations
from the *Journal:*

March 19, 1855: Trying the other day to imitate the honking of geese, I
found myself flapping my sides with my elbows as wings, and uttering
something like the syllables *mow-ack* with a nasal twang and twist in my
head; and I produced their note so perfectly in the opinion of the hearers
that I thought I might possibly draw a flock down.

January 28, 1858: [My rheumatic neighbor] Minott has a sharp ear for
the note of any migrating bird. . . . If he says he heard such a bird,
though sitting by his chimney-side, you may depend on it. . . . The
other day the rumor went that a flock of geese had been seen flying north
over Concord, midwinter as it was by the almanac. I traced it directly to
Minott, and yet I was compelled to doubt. I saw him—I made haste to
him. His reputation was at stake. He said that he stood in his shed—it
was one of the late, warm, muggy, April-like mornings—when he heard
one short but distinct *honk* of a goose. He went into the house, he took
his cane . . . lame as he was, he went up on to the hill—he had not done

it for a year—that he might hear all around. He saw nothing, but he heard the note again. . . . It was a wild goose, he was sure of it. And hence the rumor spread and grew. . . .

Suddenly the truth flashed on me, and I remembered that within a week I had heard of a box at the tavern, which had come by railroad express, containing three wild geese and directed to his neighbor over the brook. The April-like morning had excited one so that he honked; and Minott's reputation acquired new lustre.

So there you are: one man decides that geese honk; they compliantly begin to honk. I sit awestruck. If man can change the cry of a goose, surely he can storm the gates of Heaven.

> *But many that are first shall be last;*
> *and the last shall be first.*
> *—MATTHEW 19:30*

I NOTED EARLIER THAT A RHOPALIC is a snowballing passage in which each successive word has one more letter or syllable than the last. The ESPYramids Up on p. 29 were built around rhopalics; each missing word in the puzzle was a letter longer than the one before. Obviously the game can be played the other way around:

> So what if some smart alec
> Says "Make up a rhopalic
> With everything reversed"?
> No way to lose for winning!
> Just end with the beginning
> And put the last word first.
>
> —W.R.E.

The ESPYramids Down that follow conceal reverse rhopalics. The first word you are to fill in is the longest; the next drops a letter, with the others rearranged as necessary to form a new word; and the process continues until you fill in the unmistakable one-letter word that ends the game.

You are not likely to have trouble with the first ESPYramid Down if you chance to remember who, as the eighteenth century merged into the nineteenth, circumnavigated Tasmania, explored New South Wales, and surveyed the west coast of Australia. Bear in mind, however, that the verse tells a lie; the fact is that King George got everything, and the captain got nothing. On *any* ESPYramid Down, there is no law against filling in the concluding words first, to help with the others.

Those Were the Good Old Imperialist Days

When Captain ******** sailed the sea,
His ******* were filled with jealousy;
For "****** keeper!" he would cry
As each new isle he scudded by;
And I ***** from what I read
The isles he kept were **** indeed.
(Do I hear "***!"?—** you could do
The same, you would; and * would too.)

The Chronic Crisis Down on the Farm

The farmer can't his ******** stem;
He ******* more than half of them.
He ****** his sheep, the wool's forgot;
The ***** he traps he leaves to rot;
He raises corn to **** it; he
Throws corn and barley in the ***,
And *** rule leaves none for me.

The 7:21 Is Late Again

******** this message, little verse:
The ******* system's getting worse.
Commuters still endure the ******
Of rushing off to catch the *****;

Still run in **** and hail and snow
As *** their fathers long ago;
Still find ** empty railroad track:
The train is stalled * few miles back.

—W.R.E.

I include "Pidgin English" [among the varieties of the English language] even though I am referred to in that splendid language as "fella belong Mrs. Queen."
—THE DUKE OF EDINBURGH,
ADDRESSING AN ENGLISH-SPEAKING UNION CONFERENCE AT OTTAWA

AN ARTICLE BY PAUL JENNINGS, torn from an unidentified magazine and mailed to me by a correspondent who forgot to sign his name, proposes that, since in England one can no longer use a black cylindrical ruler to rap the knuckles of children who disobey the rules of English, perhaps the effort should be given up, leaving the nation with two languages, one written and one—pidgin—spoken. This is the argument:

> The more I look at Pidgin English, the more it seems to me to offer a vivid, ready-to-hand language which, with a very few additions, would answer all the needs of popular communication. What could be more expressive than "apple belong stink" for "onion" or "gubmint-catchum-fella" for "policeman"? Or "grass belong face" for "whiskers"?
> I don't know, though. Even now I can see the end of it. The mandarins who had held on to the written language would feel, as the generations went by and the gap became ever wider, that their duty was increasingly plain: to bring the glories of our literature to the masses. So they would set to work on translations, beginning of course with the classic passages:

To be, or not to be, that is the question:
Whether 'tis nobler in the mind to suffer
The slings and arrows of outrageous fortune,
Or to take arms against a sea of troubles
And by opposing end them.

*Bin or no bin, you ask im? You tink more good, carry in by you head stone belong
string him bad fella throw it, carry im arrows belong bad debbil luck? You tink
fight by dem troubles belong sea, make um all-time stop?*

On the other hand, of course, they might bring back the cylindrical
black rulers.

*[The guillotine] consists of two upright posts surmounted by a
cross beam, and grooved so as to guide an oblique-edged knife, the
back of which is heavily weighted to make it fall swiftly and with
force when the cord by which it is held aloft is let go.*
—ENCYCLOPAEDIA BRITANNICA

DURING THE FRENCH REVOLUTION, the guillotine
dispatched its victims so painlessly—anticipatory distress aside—
that after two hundred years they probably have not yet realized they
are dead. Some claim that its gentleness—perhaps not quite the right
word—removed much of the stigma from killing and thus increased the
likelihood of war.

Perhaps that is why the guillotine has a bad name. Or was it the
name that caused the trouble in the first place? Duncan Shepard wrote
The New York Times that Dr. Guillotin did not invent the machine
himself—he happened across one in Germany invented by a man
named Schultz and brought it home. Schultz is a dull name. If the
guillotine had been called the schultz, would history have changed?
Would there have been no world wars, no atom bomb?

Dr. Guillotin, Meet Herr Schultz
Flow gentlier now, adrenaline!
Beat softer now, O pulse!

The man who made the guillotine
    Was Schultz!

The dagger, the electric chair,
The noose—all have their cults;
But who could kneel to an affair
    Named schultz?

The guillotine!—grim word that must
All tender hearts revulse!
But who could fear a hunk of rust
    Called schultz?

Wars lead to wars, nor ever cease—
All guillotine's results.
I have a recipe for peace;
Change guillotine to schultz.

                    —W.R.E.

A man who could make so vile a pun
would not scruple to pick a pocket.
                    —JOHN DENNIS

MR. DENNIS WOULD HAVE RAISED THE ANTE from picking a pocket to murdering one's mother if he had seen the manuscript that arrived from Derek Pell, then of Water Mill, New York. It was two-thirds puns, most of them on names, and I aged noticeably as I read them. To hide them from the innocent, inquiring gazes of my wife, children, and grandchildren, I tucked the manuscript away into one of the cardboard boxes that serve as my file of Once and Future Things. There it remained, a sinister, otherworldly Presence; as I lay in bed at night I could hear it calling to me. At last I could resist no longer; I crept to the box before dawn and retrieved the thing, from which a stench arose as I took it into my hands. I wrote to Derek Pell to warn him that his dreadful secret was about to be revealed, but my letter was returned with a U.S. Postal Service notation, "Time for forwarding has expired." Probably there is no Derek Pell.

There appears below a first installment of the Pell opus.* Do not blame me. You have been warned.

STORY WITHOUT A NAME
by Derek Pell

Hafiz on my way to the London Post Orpheus to Mailer a Levertov to Maugham. As I Paz through the Parker, my Bach began Aiken. I Satie down on a nearby Benchley, first Mencken Shorer it was Dreiser. An Inge of Snow had recently fallen (Haile Remarque a-Böll for the Middleton of Juno) and there was a Cripps Trillin DeVries. I Sitwell Hueffer an Auerbach, Anouilh set in. My throat felt Dryden Nietzsche, Strachey, and Rawlings.

"Heine a Capote," I told myself; however, I'd have settled for a Glass of Rilke, some Lehmann Ade, or even a Pepys Zola.

Lowell and behold, I spied a can of Beerbohm on the Grass. It had been right Untermeyer nose all the time!

Not bothering to Montaigne my dignity, I bent down to pick it up and Shaw enough discovered it was Fuller. I took a Hardy Zweig, Spillane a drop down my Westcott. It tasted Fowles, like a Genet tonic spiked with Saki, but, Hellman, as my Mumford always told me, a Baker Kant be a Chaucer.

When the Beerbohm was Algonquin, I Descartes the empty can at my Foote. My head was Spinoza round and I had a Creasy sensation that something was Amis.

Was I being Parra-Noyes?

Ivanov to Lorca round, to make Sarton I was Alonso.

"I Dunsany body. . . ."

Still, I had the urge to Runyon, as if pursued by some mysterious Villon, a Muir-Duras! Anonymous tell you I was truly a Freud for a Wylie. Finally, when I felt a bit Safa, I returned to the Benchley and was overcome by Sarraute. You see, I was Verdi Poe—without Algren of Sand in my pocket.

This gripping tale resumes on page 169.

---

* For those who care, I have identified in Answers and Solutions the persons whose names serve as puns in Mr. Pell's distressing story.

My apprehensions come in crowds,
I dread the rustling of the grass;
The very shadows of the clouds
Have power to shake me as they pass.
—WILLIAM WORDSWORTH

IN THE 1950S A RUSSIAN ÉMIGRÉ named Gregory Zilboorg came to Percy Goodman the architect and said, "Mr. Goodman, I want you to design me a fine house."

This Zilboorg was a refugee from the communists. Before the revolution he had been a man of substance. A doctor, a psychiatrist, he was Aleksandr Kerenski's personal secretary when Kerenski was prime minister, before the Bolsheviks threw him out. After that Zilboorg went into hiding and had a very hard time for a while. In 1919 he escaped to New York, where he established a practice and wrote books. He became famous, and wealthy besides.

Percy Goodman agreed to design him a big house, you could call it a mansion, in Westchester County. There was lots of empty land around it. Percy used to go up to make sure the builders were doing things the way he wanted.

Dr. Zilboorg would say, "Percy"—he had begun to call Percy Percy—"go every place you want to go. But do not go near the east meadow." So he did not go near the east meadow.

Finally the house was finished. Dr. Zilboorg asked him to come out and look, and he did, and everything was fine. Then Dr. Zilboorg said, "Now, Percy, come with me to the east meadow."

They walked to the east meadow, which was a field full of hay. In the middle was a trap door where nobody could see it unless he knew just where to look.

Dr. Zilboorg opened the trap door, reached in, and pressed a button. A light came on below, and Percy saw a steep stair descending. Dr. Zilboorg said, "Follow me."

At the bottom was a room, bigger than Percy's own living room, and that means it was very big. There were racks on all four walls, every rack with bottles in it. Such a wine cellar!—more than ten thou-

Under the east meadow are ten thousand bottles. . . .

sand bottles, the doctor told him! Not just wine, but spirits; everything the finest. Vodka, gin, rum, Scotch, rye, bourbon, brandy, you name it. Dr. Zilboorg said, "Take whatever you want. All you can carry, Percy—take it." Every bottle that Percy chose, the doctor laid it in his arms, until bottles were heaped to his chin. When they went up the stairs again, he walked very carefully.

Back in the house they set the bottles on the kitchen table and sat down and Dr. Zilboorg said, "Now, Percy, we must toast the new house." He poured a glass for Percy from a bottle of champagne, chilled already. But for himself he poured only water.

Percy said, "Dr. Zilboorg"—he still called him by his last name—"aren't you going to drink with me?" And Dr. Zilboorg said, "Alcohol I never drink."

Then Percy said, "With ten thousand bottles buried under the east meadow, you don't drink? What is this?"

And the doctor said, "Percy, I will tell you what nobody else in the world knows, just my wife, Peggy. I have a problem. I am insecure."

Percy said, "You are a psychiatrist, and you are insecure?"

The doctor said, "What good to be a psychiatrist if I do not know I am insecure? It is from when I was in hiding in Russia. There were many days when I had nothing to eat, nothing. I trapped rats and ate them, and that is how I stayed alive." He removed his dentures and said, "See, this is what happens when you eat rats and get dysentery."

Then he went on: "I came here, I was a success, but I was insecure. How did I know? Because I was always hungry. No matter how much I ate, when I could eat no more I was still hungry. I would think, maybe tomorrow the food will be gone. Maybe tomorrow I will have to eat rats. So I began to store food, to be sure it would be there. In my pantry I hung hams and sides of bacon. I packed the shelves with sausages and corn beef. When Peggy could squeeze in no more meat, I built a bigger pantry. And whenever we would cut a slice off a ham, I would think, Someday it will be gone.

"So when we decided to build this house it came to me what I should do. I asked myself, What is more precious than food? Wine is. Wine and spirits. Vodka. With my own wine cellar I would be secure, because nobody but me would know it was there, and I would never drink it up. Because I do not drink.

"So I went to Sherry-Lehman, the people who import liquor, and said, 'I want a wine cellar, a big wine cellar, in the east meadow.' We sat down and figured on paper how big it would have to be for ten thousand bottles. Then a builder came with machines and dug a great hole, and workers poured concrete and made walls and a ceiling, and they brought in the bottles. They covered everything with dirt, and put the hay back on top.

"And now when I wake up in the night, I think, Under the east meadow are ten thousand bottles, wine, Lafitte-Rothschild even, and cognac, and Napoleon brandy, nothing but the best; and nobody knows but me and Peggy, and now you, Percy. So I am secure."

This is really the end of the story, but there is a small P.S. A year later Dr. Zilboorg telephoned and said, "Percy, can you come out to my house? I have a problem."

So Percy went out and took off his hat and said, "Gregory, what is your problem?" (Now he called Dr. Zilboorg "Gregory.") And Dr. Zilboorg said, "Percy, you know I write every day, but not with a typewriter. I dictate. And when I dictate, I pace. But the office you made for me, it is two paces short of the length of my sentences. So what can I do?"

Percy answered, "Gregory, you have no problem." He added a bay window at the end of the room, a big handsome one, very expensive. From then on Dr. Zilboorg paced one length of his office for every sentence, and he was secure. He died a happy man.

> *I'm tired of Love; I'm still more tired of Rhyme.*
> *But Money gives me pleasure all the time.*
> —HILAIRE BELLOC

ABSENCE MAKES THE HEART GROW FONDER, so I have always been absurdly fond of money. When I reflect on the income I receive from the government each month—almost entirely at your expense, dear reader and taxpayer—compared with the paltry sums I deposited with Social Security during fifty years of working, I leap into the air (taking off with the help of both canes) and crack my heels together three times before returning to the floor.

The government communication that follows is exactly as it was received years ago, except that I have dropped a few irrelevant sentences, given the lines ragged edges to fit the afflatus of the message, and inserted an appropriate refrain.

Claim Number 071 12 0418 A

Effective 01/80 a monthly benefit of $602.00
(*tra la, tra la*)
is payable
because the benefits on this Social Security record
have been refigured
to give credit for additional earnings.
Your monthly benefit amount was increased to $688.00
(*tra la, tra la*)
because of the amendment to the Social Security Act
and your benefit amount was again increased to
$728.70
(*tra la la la*)
effective 01/81
to give credit for your 1980 earnings. The amendments
to the Social Security Act
increased your monthly benefit amount to
$810.30
(*tra la, tra la*)
effective 06/81.
Your monthly benefit amount was increased to
$818.10
(*tra la, tra la*)
effective 01/82 to give you credit for the months
after you reached age 65
and for which you did not receive a monthly benefit.
The amendments to the Social Security Act increase
your monthly benefit amount to
$878.40
(*tra la la*)

effective 06/82. Your monthly benefit amount was increased to
$886.00
(*tra la, tra la*)
effective 12/82
to give you credit for the months after you reached age 65
and for which you did not receive a monthly benefit.

And so it has continued. The matter is well summarized, in my
view, in the words of an old music hall ditty. The singer raises his voice
in humble gratitude to the God who showers us with blessings:

> My brother's a slum missionary
> Saving young virgins from sin;
> He'll save you a blonde for a shilling—
> My God, how the money rolls in!

*And out of the ground the Lord God formed every beast of
the field, and every fowl of the air; and brought them unto Adam
to see what he would call them; and whatsoever Adam called
every living creature, that was the name thereof.*
—GENESIS 2:19

BUT ADAM, LIKE MOST OF HIS male descendants, was
inarticulate; he had to call on Eve for help. And Eve, though
articulate, was ignorant; she tended to rely on you-know-what-I-mean
words, as we see here:*

> When lexicographically stumped, I cleave
> To words my granny picked up from her granny,
> And she from hers, and so on back to Eve—
> Great words like "thingummy" and "hootenanny."

* See also page 211.

Young Adam heard God tell him to endow
All beasts with names—and passed. (To Eve, of course.)
She offered "gizmo" as the word for cow;
"Doodad" for sheep; and "thingumbob" for horse.

She used "dofunny" for the whale. Her term
For hippopotamus was "thingumjig."
"Doohickey" was the name she picked for worm,
And "whatchacallit" was the one for pig.

When she arrived at *snake,* the waiting Lord
Already was experiencing fidgets.
She called it "gidget."
                    He unsheathed His sword,
And tossed out Eve and Adam on their widgets.

                              —W.R.E.

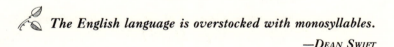 *The English language is overstocked with monosyllables.*
                              —Dean Swift

I ONCE HAD A SIMPLE RULE: Write tight, write tough,
write active, be concrete; but always throw in one fancy word to awe
your audience. I think I am more advanced now; if a little word says it
better, I use the little word; if a big word says it better, I use the big
one.

    In this noble passage from *King Lear,* Shakespeare uses only one-
syllable words:

Thou know'st the first time that we smell the air,
We bawl and cry; I will preach to thee; mark me.
When we are born, we cry that we are come
To this great stage of fools . . .

                              —Act IV, sc. 6

Here, in *Paradise Lost,* Milton uses just one word of more than a single syllable:

> Tell, if ye saw how I came thus, how here?—
> Tell me, how may I know Him, how adore,
> From whom I have that thus I move and live?
>
> —BK. VIII

The Bible is a showpiece of monosyllabic words:

> And God said, Let there be light; and there was light. And God saw the light, that it was good.
>
> —GENESIS 1:3–4

> At her feet he bowed, he fell, he lay down: at her feet he bowed, he fell; where he bowed, there he fell down dead.
>
> —JUDGES 5:27

> And the gates of it shall not be shut at all by day; for there shall be no night there.
>
> —REVELATIONS 21:25

In the nineteenth century, the *Princetonian Magazine* carried a panegyric to short words by a Dr. Alexander. This is the first stanza:

The Power of Short Words

> Think not that strength lies in the big round word,
> Or that the brief and plain must needs be weak.
> To whom can this be true who once has heard
> The cry for help, the tongue that all men speak,
> When want or woe or fear is in the throat,
> So that each word gasped out is like a shriek
> Pressed from the sore heart, or a strange wild note,
> Sung by some fay or fiend? There is a strength
> Which dies if stretched too far or spun too fine;
> Which has more height than depth, more depth than length.

Let but this force of thought and speech be mine,
And he that will may take the sleek fat phrase
Which glows and burns not, though it gleam and shine—
Light but no heat—a flash, but not a blaze!

But it is specious to pose the argument as one between words that are long or short, active or passive, concrete or abstract. What you and I need is the *right* word—fat or thin, brisk or lazy. The right word. In the right place. For the right reason.

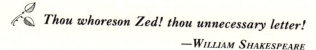 *Thou whoreson Zed! thou unnecessary letter!*
—*WILLIAM SHAKESPEARE*

HANK BRENNAN PAINTED A GRACEFUL DESIGN, of which a reproduction hangs alongside my bookcase, in which all the letters of the alphabet are posed in lowercase, on one another's shoulders like so many acrobats, each letter of a size proportioned to the frequency of its use in English. Shakespeare's whoreson Zed is but a flyspeck; no one would notice it in the crowd. But *e*—there it towers, a Gulliver among Lilliputians—a letter that we write and read more than any other, perhaps more than any two others. If ever a letter deserved immortalization in an Espy knittelverse, it is the letter *e*. You will find numbered below a scattering of words that begin with this paragon, together with a word beginning with *b* that slipped in by mistake.

E. The Untouchable Entellus

A fair entellus[1] in a banyan swung,
By tail secured, and by her faith in Brahma.
(Entelluses are sacred monkeys 'mong
The simple folk out there in Sutra Khama.)

---

[1] An East Indian long-tailed monkey. Sutra Khama may not be the exact habitat.

That she was lissome, virtuous, and young
Made her estiverous[2] for blissom[3] male
Entelluses, who ogled as she hung,
And called her to descend, to no avail.

Those rammish males, their dreams epithymastic,[4]
Their hips extorsive,[5] pranced, and cried "Evoe[6]!"
Till, whelmed by exundation[7] orgiastic,
They fell afaint beneath the banyan tree,
And lay unmoving after all that ruckus—
If not exanimous,[8] at least exsuccous.[9]

—W.R.E.

[2] Producing heat. [3] In heat. [4] Well, "epithymetic" means "pertaining to desire; sensual." I must have changed the word ending to make the rhyme; I do things like that. [5] Wiggling their hips. [6] In the Greek bacchanals, an exclamation expressing exhilaration (pronounced ē-vē'). [7] An overflowing. [8] Lifeless. [9] Dry, sapless.

5

The fifth time, I refused to speak,
But wrote the answers down in Greek.

I believe in the inheritance of skills and crafts—the inheritance of memory. They find now that if a snail eats another snail, it gets the second snail's memory.

—ROBERT GRAVES

I KNOW AN AUTHOR NAMED PAUL GRABBE, of White Russian background and fluent in the Russian language. As the way is with authors, he took advantage of a recent visit to the Library of Congress to make sure his books were all preserved there for posterity. They were listed in the files all right, along with a title in Russian that he did not recognize.

He had the book fetched, and read something like this in its preface: "I, Paul Grabbe, am setting down these memoirs in the hope, doubtless farfetched, that a grandchild or great-grandchild of mine may happen on them some distant day, and find a few moments of pleasure reading about the haps and mishaps of a long-forgotten ancestor."

My friend was that great-grandchild. The man whose words he was reading had been one of the Imperial Russian Army officers known as the Decembrists, who tried and failed to overthrow Czar Nicholas I in December 1825.

Mr. Grabbe did not have to swallow his ancestor to absorb his ancestor's memories. He only had to read a book. We can all inherit other people's memories that way.

But how could an obscure work in Russian—a book written around 1830—turn up at the end of the twentieth century in the Library of Congress in Washington, D.C., U.S.A.? I inquired, and the story proved so fascinating that I have told it separately. You will find it on page 202.

• • • • • • •

The Library of Congress

The Library of Congress was established as a research arm of Congress in 1800, with an appropriation of $6,000 for buying 12 trunks of books. As I write, it occupies three buildings on Capitol Hill, employs 5,200 people, and houses 535 miles of shelves of material, including the world's largest collection of books, catalogued in at least 468 languages. It has in excess of 14,000,000 books and pamphlets and over 18,000,000 manuscripts, plus maps (over 2,000,000) and music (over 3,000,000 volumes and pieces).

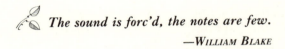

The sound is forc'd, the notes are few.
—WILLIAM BLAKE

IF YOU ARE NOT TOO PROUD to borrow from the French, you can find a lot of vowels or vowel combinations, no two alike, that rhyme with the sound of *a* as in "say." In this verse, only the last line ends in the letter *a* itself.*

Knittelverse with an A Rhyme

One afternoon, in mood *très gai*
(For I'd been playing the gourmet,
Including wine with *déjeuner*—
A light and lilting Beaujolais
Plus biscuits, cheese, and *pousse-café*),
I dared a blazing sun, *à pied*,
To pay a friendly visit *chez*
My darling, who said, "You okay?
I think you've had a *coup de soleil.*"

I said, "This verse I pray you weigh,
With thirteen letters, counting J—
And but one letter twice in play—
All ending words that rhyme with *a.*"
—W.R.E.

---

* Darryl Francis listed most of these *a* rhymes in *Word Ways.*

> *There was an old man of Boulogne*
> *Who sang a most topical song;*
> *It wasn't the words*
> *Which frightened the birds*
> *But the horrible double entendre.*
>
> —AUTHOR UNKNOWN

JASON D. ZWEIG ASKS WHETHER I consider Exodus 20:25 a double entendre. Of course it is—perhaps the model of them all, since it is a slip of the tongue by the Almighty Himself:

> And if thou wilt make me an altar of stone, thou shalt not build it of hewn stone; for if thou lift up thy tool upon it, thou has polluted it.

Since God's own tongue slips, surely He forgives, and even blesses, ambiguities uttered unawares and in all purity of heart by His worshipers—like this hymn that used to waft up a hundred years ago from a church near Cambridge, England, according to George Lyttleton in *The Lyttleton Hart-Davis Letters.*

> Milk of the breast that cannot cloy
> He, like a nurse, will bring,
> And when we see His promise nigh,
> Oh, how we'll suck and sing!

Another biblical verse that gives one to think:

> And he spake to his sons, saying, Saddle me the ass. And they saddled *him.*

> —1 KINGS 13:27

> *Life is too short to learn German.*
> —ATTRIBUTED TO RICHARD PORSON

MY IMPRESSION WAS THAT MARK TWAIN agreed with Mr. Porson. But here, forwarded by Avery Fisher, is Twain's own translation of a speech he delivered in apparently flawless German to the Vienna Press Club on November 21, 1897. It shows how simple and straightforward a tongue German really is.*

A PLEA FOR THE REFORM OF GERMAN

The German language speak I not good, but have numerous connoisseurs me assured that I her write like an angel. Maybe—maybe—I know not. Have till now no acquaintance with the angels had. That comes later—when it the dear God please—it has no hurry.

Since long, my gentlemen, have I the passionate longing nursed a speech on German to hold, but one has me not permitted. Men, who no feeling for the art had, laid me ever hindrance in the way and made naught my desire—sometimes by excuses, often by force. Always said these men to me: "Keep you still, Your Highness! Silence! For God's sake seek another way and means yourself obnoxious to make."

The committee sorrowed deeply, but could me the permission not grant on account of a law which from the Concordia demands she shall the German language protect. *Du liebe Zeit!* How so had one to me this say could—might—dared—should. I am indeed the truest friend of the German language—and not only now, but from long since—yes, before twenty years already. And never have I the desire had the noble language to hurt; to the contrary, only wished she to improve—I would her only reform. It is the dream of my life been. I have already visits by the various German governments paid and for contracts prayed. I am now to Austria in the same task come. I would only some changes effect. I would only the language method—the luxurious, elaborate construction compress, the eternal parenthesis suppress, do away with, annihilate; the introduction of more than thirteen subjects in one sentence forbid; the verb so far to the front pull that one it without a telescope discover can. With one word, my gentlemen, I would your beloved language simplify

---

* A few lines have been omitted.

so that, my gentlemen, when you her for prayer need, One her yonder-up understands.

I beseech you, from me yourself counsel to let execute these mentioned reforms. Then will you an elegant language possess, and afterward, when you something say will, will you at least yourself understand what you said had. But often nowadays, when you a mile-long sentence from you given and you yourself somewhat have rested, then must you a touching inquisitiveness have yourself to determine what you actually spoken have. Before several days has the correspondent of a local paper a sentence constructed which 112 words contain, and therein were seven parentheses smuggled in, and the subject seven times changed. Think you only, my gentlemen, in the course of the voyage of a single sentence must the poor, persecuted, fatigued subject seven times change position!

Now, when we the mentioned reforms execute, will it no longer so bad be. *Doch noch eins.* I might gladly the separable verb also a little bit reform. I might none do let what Schiller did: he has the whole history of the Thirty Years' War between the two members of a separate verb in-pushed. That has even Germany itself aroused, and one has Schiller the permission refused the history of the Hundred Years' War to compose—God be it thanked! After all these reforms established be will, will the German language the noblest and the prettiest on the world be.

Since to you now, my gentlemen, the character of my mission known is, beseech I you so friendly to be and to me your valuable help grant. Mr. Pötzl has the public believed make would that I to Vienna come am in order the bridges to clog up and the traffic to hinder, while I observations gather and note. Allow you yourselves but not from him deceived. My frequent presence on the bridges has an entirely innocent ground. Yonder gives it the necessary space, yonder can one a noble long German sentence elaborate, the bridge-railing along, and his whole contents with one glance overlook. On the one end of the railing pasted I the first member of a separable verb and the final member cleaved I to the other end—then spread the body of the sentences between it out! Usually are for my purposes the bridges of the city long enough; when I but Pötzl's writings study will I ride out and use the glorious endless imperial bridge. But this is a calumny; Pötzl writes the prettiest German. Perhaps not so pliable as the mine, but in many details much better. Excuse you these flatteries. These are well deserved.

Now I my speech execute—no, I would say I bring her to the close. I am a foreigner—but here, under you, have I it entirely forgotten. And so again and yet again proffer I you my heartiest thanks.

> *The manufacture of sin is so easy a manufacture,*
> *that I am convinced man could readily be persuaded*
> *that it was wicked to use the left leg as much as the right;*
> *whole congregations would only permit themselves to hop.*
> —SIR ARTHUR HELPS

IT IS FASHIONABLE NOWADAYS TO deny guilt, blaming all wrongdoing on circumstance, which includes the innate sinfulness of words themselves; a glance is sufficient to show that they are full of the Old Nick. Sin runs rampant in language—at least the English language:

On the Sinfulness of Certain Words

Reflect on the ubiquity
Of verbalized iniquity!—
Of honied words wherein
Lies coiled old Serpent Sin!

A bas*SIN*et has oft contained
A sin that's still not toilet-trained.
The sin is slight in mi*SIN*form;
But ab*SIN*the can sin up a storm.

Wild asses bray in the vicinity
Of silly sin in a*SIN*inity;
While di*SIN*clined's a handy way
To keep unwanted sin at bay.

To di*SIN*fect in time prevents
Some common sins' worst consequence;
And di*SIN*herit halts the sprees
Of beggared di*SIN*heritees.

In in*SIN*cere, as in *SIN*cere,
Do sins impartially appear;
And sly in*SIN*uate implies
A sin which, challenged, it denies.

'Twould be a *SIN*ecure to play
Such games with sinful words all day.
But *SIN*ce the game begins to bore,
I'll *SIN*g of sinfulness no more.

—W.R.E.

Memory is a net; one finds it full of fish when he takes it from the brook; but a dozen miles of water have run through it without sticking.
—OLIVER WENDELL HOLMES

I AM SITTING AT HOME READING LETTERS that I wrote to my parents in the 1930s, and I confess that I have utterly forgotten many of the incidents I described. Even more curious, others were not at all as I now recall them; and I have no doubt that my written accounts are nearer to the truth than my memory is. In one case, though, letter and memory coincide perfectly. I wrote during spring vacation of 1929, my junior year at college, telling how my fraternity brother Clint McKinnon and I hitchhiked from Mexicali, California, to the head of the Gulf of California, traveling in a fish truck across the Sonora desert; there was no road. Our destination turned out to be a settlement of fisher folk, living in a dozen or so shacks that had walls of corrugated tin. Men were repairing nets spread on the beach. The truck driver joined them to bargain over fish, and we started to follow; but the widow Morales stepped in our way.

She was glad to see us. No matter that we were gringos; our faces were new. She invited us to the hut that was her home. "I have the white wine, señores," she said in better Spanish than mine (I had studied it for two terms). "Cold, no; but yes, wine." She walked ahead of us across the hot sand; I thought the soles of her naked feet sizzled when they touched down. She was short and thick; her progress was ponderous, each step a calculated, self-contained act.

I followed her inside and at first was aware only of hot dimness and buzzing flies. As my eyes adjusted, I made out before me a supine figure on a table. Another step, and I saw that it was a young man. A fly was scratching itself on the bridge of his straight nose. He was clad in a sleeveless white shirt and thin white trousers. His head rested on a knot of gray wood; his lower legs projected beyond the table end. His eyes were wide open, so that he seemed to be staring at his upthrust toes.

The widow Morales cleared her throat. "Señores," she said, "meet my sweet son Jesus. In the surf the boat capsized; behold, Jesus was wearing the hip boots; so the water filled them, and dragged him down; so he died. Tomorrow comes the priest."

I stifled a cry. Jesus's brown eyes had turned in their sockets to regard me. I hastily shifted my gaze to his feet, only to discover that they were bobbing: up, down; up, down. At each of his mother's heavy steps, the feet moved. "Señora!" I babbled. "Señora—are you *sure* he is dead?"

She paused, and regarded him with mild speculation. Her brown cheeks puffed out as she considered. Reaching a decision, she squatted to grasp a crooked stick from the floor. She rose as deliberately as she had sunk, lifted the stick, and brought it down smartly on her son's left ankle. The leg jiggled, slowed, and stopped.

"*Sí, señor,*" she said, happy to reassure me. "He is dead all right." And he was.

Pop used to say about the Presbyterians,
it don't prevent them committing all the sins there are,
but it keeps them from getting any fun out of it.
—CHRISTOPHER MORLEY, KITTY FOYLE

I AM A GREAT BELIEVER IN RELIGION; I do not propose to take chances. But I do feel that occasionally denominations lose track of their purpose, which I believe to be the salvation of souls. Recently, for instance, Presbyterian leaders called for dropping that grand old hymn, "Onward Christian Soldiers," on the grounds that its tone is too militaristic. I cannot believe that they considered all the consequences of such a rash step. How would this help to save souls? And would it be worth blighting the life of the good lady who wrote this letter to the *London Daily Telegraph?*

Sir: The hymn "Onward Christian Soldiers" sung to the right tune and in a not-too-brisk tempo makes a very good egg timer.
If you put the egg into boiling water and sing all five verses and chorus, the egg will be just right when you come to Amen.

—MRS. G. H. MOORE

Aristocracy is always cruel.
—WENDELL PHILLIPS

CRUEL TO OTHERS, YES. But to themselves? I would never have believed it until I read the following cutting from England. No wonder the aristocracy is a dying breed!

The really aristocratic attitude toward marriage is to have separate rooms or separate apartments, according to an authority on aristocratic conventions, Mr. Harold Brooks-Baker, formerly of *Debrett's Peerage.*

"I have always found middle-class people staggered when I tell them this," he said yesterday.

"If they want to be thought top people they feel they have to do the same.

"Alphonso XIII of Spain once said that you could measure the social caste of a person by the distance between the husband's and the wife's apartments."

Mr. Brooks-Baker blames the Russian Revolution on Nicholas II and Tsarina Alexandra demonstrating their love by sharing their bedroom.

"For hundreds, perhaps for thousands of years," he says, "the really great families have had separate sleeping quarters for husbands and wives, also concubines and lovers.

"This is true for all aristocratic houses in the world. Separate rooms are given to husband and wife guests in great houses—separate apartments in really great houses. Sleeping in the same room, even, in recent years, sleeping in the same bed like the working-class, is, as documentary evidence shows, a middle-class attitude."

—*LONDON DAILY TELEGRAPH*

. . . .

The Miles One Must Walk To Fruition
Increase with One's Social Position

1.
My bride, thou art the radiant moon—
So far away from me
I ne'er may kiss thy silver shoon,
Though I be Deity.

2.
Thou to Olympus comest down,
With gods to sport and sing;
I cannot touch thy silken gown,
Though I be twice a king.

3.
Dost thou in Zanzibar abide,
Top lady of the land?
I, equal-ranked, must here reside,
An ocean from thy hand.

I cannot touch thy silken gown,
Though I be twice a king. . . .

4.

Dost thou across the city dwell,
Of ancient family?
Alas, I am too much a swell
To cross the town to thee.

5.

So we're but gentle blood? E'en so
Our lips can never meet,
For I must stay at Eight One O,
And thou across the street.

6.

If I sport but a homburg hat,
And thou a paisley shawl,
Still thou, within our four-room flat,
Must sleep across the hall.

7.

If I were Darby and thou Joan,
Yet were our flesh denied;
My bed stays mine, and thine thy own,
Though lined up side by side.

8.

So since thou longest for Love's feast
(Else why are we two wed?)
Let's go on welfare, where at least
You get a double bed.

—W.R.E.

When man first learned to write, he seized upon this new
talent and, like Stephen Leacock's impulsive hero,
galloped gleefully off in all directions.
—GARY JENNINGS

Do You Read Me?

1. *The Egyptian*

Although hieroglyphs worked fine
In their Egyptian day,
It bothers me that in each line
The glyphs all face one way.

Their profiles first might turn toward *haw*,
And next might turn toward *gee;*
But either way, they looked and saw
In utter unity.

And looked they left or right, as it
Might suit the writer's aim,
It didn't matter, not a bit—
The meaning stayed the same.

2. *The Chinese and Certain Other Orientals*

Start at the right-hand side, on top;
In plumb line then proceed
To bottom, where you have to stop.
Next do the selfsame deed

Immediately to the left.
Proceed until you find
The page is filled with ditties deft.
The meaning? Never mind.

褊蹇不曾藏霓方亘
時人雖狎匯呞爲恰作
半光教烏雖左丟右丟

3. *The Tuaregs**

The Tuaregs' scribbles take the cup
For bafflement, *quand même;*
Left-right, right-left; up-down, down-up—
It's all the same to them.

—W.R.E.

---

* The Tuaregs, nomads of the central and western Sahara, have preserved their Hamitic speech in great purity. Their alphabet, of Libyan origin, is called *tifinagh*.

> *Polygamy may well be held in dread,*
> *Not only as a sin, but as a bore.*
> —GEORGE GORDON BYRON

A QUITE DIFFERENT VIEW OF POLYGAMY was presented by Francis T. P. Plimpton, distinguished diplomat and leader of the New York Bar Association. He was speaking at Amherst, of which he was a graduate and a life trustee:

IN PRAISE OF POLYGAMY

Yesterday afternoon, driving up from New York, I was subjected to a most distressing experience—my wife read me the leading article in this month's *Harper's*. It is by a member of the class of 1927 by the name of Charles Woolsey Cole, the president of this college. It is entitled "American Youth Goes Monogamous."

The article portrays, gentlemen, the state of *your* mores, and, if I may say so, a most lamentable state it is. It appears that each of you fastens upon one unfortunate female, and, forsaking all others, brings her and her alone to each game, each cocktail party, each dance. Furthermore, the hapless creature has to dance with you, and you alone, during the long hours of low and mournful peripatetics which you appear to believe constitutes dancing. This drab process is, I understand, known as "going steady"—a clear violation not only of English grammar, but also of the most elementary principles of biology.

It is punctuated, according to your president, by a gruesome ceremony known as "pinning," in which the female bosom is decorated with miscellaneous jewelry to the accompaniment of solemn tribal chants. This of course leads, with the inevitability of Greek tragedy, to matrimony.

Now I hasten to say that I have nothing against matrimony. After all, in every man's life a certain number of things go wrong which in good conscience one can't really blame on the government; also, it is wonderful to have a wife to stand by you in all the troubles you wouldn't have got into if you hadn't married her.

But that isn't the point; the point is, what is to become of the spirit of scientific inquiry? What is to become of the controlled experiment, the controlled experiment which forms the very basis of the advancement of knowledge? Indeed, what is to become of the uncontrolled experiment? Where is natural selection, where is survival of the fittest, where is the evolution of the race if you young males meekly submit to the inexorably monogamous possessiveness of the first female who deigns to notice you?

If I am not mistaken, Thomas Edison tried out some 178 different substances before he finally selected one as the best filament for the electric light bulb. Am I to understand, gentlemen, that his shining example means nothing to you, that you regard good procreation as less important than good illumination?

I am reminded of the episode of Reed Smoot, the first senator to be elected from Utah. He was a Mormon, and several senators protested to Boies Penrose, then the leader of the Senate, that he should not be allowed to take his seat. Penrose asked whether Smoot had more than one wife and, on being told that he had only one, looked out over the Senate and said: "Well, I don't see why we can't get along just as well with a polygamist who doesn't polyg as we do with a lot of monogamists who don't monog!"

Now, gentlemen, since I am a lawyer you will not want me to neglect the legal aspects of your situation, and I am bound to say they are serious. Suppose that one of you imports a lady to these precincts, and let us further suppose that she is, in the fine old legal phrase, "clothed with the public interest." What happens? The public interest, whether due to clothes or lack of clothes, is intense, but what do you do? Flouting that public interest, you suppress all competition and tend to create a monopoly. Needless to say, gentlemen, this is an unlawful restraint of trade and a flagrant and willful violation of the Sherman Act (and perhaps the Mann Act), subjecting you to servitude that is penal as well as matrimonial and to triple damage suits at the hands of your aggrieved competitors.

Gentlemen, such a sad state of monotonous monogamy has not always prevailed in this fairest of colleges. In "the golden haze of (my) college days" (deathless phrase), a man who brought the same girl to every dance was rightfully regarded as a man without resources, without imagination, without *élan vital*. It was a matter of pride with us to provide ourselves and our friends and admirers with the spice of variety—and the more variety and, may I say, the more spice, the more the admirers. For one dance, a charmer from Smith; for the next, a lithe damsel from Mt. Holyoke; for the next, a lissome lass from Poughkeepsie; and glorious climax, a debutante of glow and glamour from the ormolu ballroom of the now defunct Ritz-Carlton. If we did any pinning, it was to pin them in a corner and not for any purpose connected with the decorative arts.

And, gentlemen, we did not shrink from fair competition, the life of trade. The American spirit of free enterprise had free play, and play it did. The lordly stag, now, alas, almost extinct, was then monarch of all he surveyed, as he enjoyed what should be the inalienable rights of every young American male, the rights of life, liberty, and the happiness of pursuit.

Yes, those were great days, and I commend to you, gentlemen, the lessons of that glorious past. Let not these honored traditions fade! Undergraduates of the world, arise—you have nothing to lose but your silk and nylon chains!

I will not go down to posterity talking bad grammar.
—BENJAMIN DISRAELI, WHILE CORRECTING PROOFS
OF HIS LAST PARLIAMENTARY SPEECH

IF I WERE ASKED THE IDEAL MEDIUM for improving English usage in America, my answer would be the comic strip. You will see here what I mean:

TIGER ®	By Bud Blake

Reprinted by permission of King Features Syndicate, Inc.

Je me défends de la tempérance,
comme j'ay faict autrefois de la volupté.
(I guard against moderation
as I used to guard against excess.)
—MICHEL DE MONTAIGNE

WHAT WOULD I DO IF I COULD live my life over? I would steep myself in sixteenth-century French, and then write sonnets based on Montaigne. I did two such several years ago. I hold no brief for them except that they hint why I rank Montaigne second only to Shakespeare among authors.

Here is the first:

Reversal

Mind, swept along by Flesh in freshet flood,
Aware of bootlessness of grave advice,
Rode out the clam'rous questing of young blood,
Waiting till age should clog hot veins with ice
And reason have its say.
                              Now Body quails
Before non-being. So where's prudent Mind?
Why, tripping down the foolish, lovely trails
That failing Body left perforce behind.
Hand-wringing Flesh in penitence and fear
Begs Mind to tidy up their house of clay;
But turncoat Mind now shuns the over-drear,
Who once tut-tutted at the over-gay.
While fading Flesh droops down in melancholy,
Mind rides again the freshet flood of folly.

—W.R.E.

A second sonnet based on a Montaigne essay appears on page 218.

> *Yet mark'd I where the bolt of Cupid fell:*
> *It fell upon a little western flower,*
> *Before milk-white, now purple with love's wound,*
> *And maidens call it Love-in-idleness.*
>
> —WILLIAM SHAKESPEARE

ALL FLOWERS ARE FLIRTATIOUS—particularly if they carry hyphenated names. The more hyphens in the name, the flirtier the flower. The one-hyphen flowers—black-eyed Susan; lady-smock; musk-rose—may give you only a shy glance and then drop their eyes; the two-hyphen flowers—forget-me-not; flower-de-luce—keep glancing. Flowers with three or more hyphens flirt all over the garden and continue even when they are cut and arranged in vases. John-go-to-bed-at-noon does not go there simply to sleep.

In Darryl Francis's Garden

My staid heart went all fluttery;
    For in the fragrant silence (all bestrewn
    With clusters of John-go-to-bed-at-noon)
    The wanton faces, quinquefoliate,
    Of purple kiss-me-over-the-garden-gate
    Blinked lashes at such gentry
    As meet-her-in-the-entry-
kiss-her-over-the-buttery.

            —W.R.E.

John-go-to-bed-at-noon is the goat's-beard, salsify, or any of several flowers that close in the middle of the day; kiss-me-over-the-garden-gate is a flower such as the wild pansy or heartsease; and my guess, though I do not know, is that meet-her-in-the-entry-kiss-her-over-the-buttery is another description of the pansy.

Parrots are human to begin with; etymologically, that is.
Perroquet is a diminutive of Pierrot; parrot comes from Pierre;
Spanish perico derives from Pedro.

—JULIAN BARNES

ADDITIONAL COMMON NOUNS THAT started as proper names have come to my attention by the dozen since I completed my book on the subject, *O Thou Improper, Thou Uncommon Noun.* Here are some of them:

- *Vaudeville.* Olivier de Basselin lived in the fifteenth century in the Vau (valley) de Vire in Normandy. He wrote satiric songs, which became known as *vaux de Vire.* When the songs became popular in Paris, the name changed to *vaux de ville,* and in English it became *vaudeville.*
- *Calepin.* In 1502 Ambrosio Calepino wrote a Latin dictionary so widely used that the word *calepin* is still applied, though less often than formerly, to one's most used book of reference.
- *Neddy.* A donkey—from the nickname Ned ("mine Ed"). Jim or Chuck would have served just as well.
- *Bawbee.* This Scottish coin, with a value of three halfpence, was minted in 1542 and presumably took its name after the mintmaster, the laird of Billebawby. A coin worth sixpence, issued under Charles II, bore the same name, as later did an English halfpenny.
- *Demijohn.* In French, *Dame Jeanne*—a narrow-necked bottle holding one to ten gallons and enclosed in wickerwork. In English it became demijohn. Why *Dame Jeanne?* Well, why *Neddy* for donkey?
- *Patter.* Paternoster (Our Father), the Lord's Prayer in Latin, was sometimes mumbled on beads at a great rate, with the mumbler's mind on other matters. *Pater* turned into *patter.*
- *Ragamuffin.* *Ragamoffyn* was a demon in disreputable attire in William Langland's fourteenth-century poem "Piers Plowman." Today the word has much the same meaning as *tatterdemalion*—one who is tattered or ragged.

- *Spa.* The town of Spa, in Belgium, a health resort featuring mineral springs, became so popular that all such are now called spas.
- *Joey.* This name for a clown goes back to Joseph Grimaldi (1779–1837), most famous of English circus clowns; but the English fourpenny piece *joey* is named for the radical English politician Joseph Hume, who oddly enough lived at almost exactly the same time (1777–1855) as the other Joseph.

There is something about saying "Okay" and hanging up the receiver with a bang that kids a man into feeling that he has just pulled off a big deal, even if he has only called up Central to find out the correct time.

—ROBERT BENCHLEY

CRAIG ESPY, PRESUMABLY A RELATIVE of mine (all Espys are related), used to run Samuel Goldwyn's New York office. At a quarter of four one morning the telephone rang in his bedroom. It was his boss, calling from Los Angeles, where it was only a quarter of one. "This is Goldwyn," he said. "Hold on a minute—my other telephone is ringing." Craig held the line for forty-five minutes, half dozing. Finally Goldwyn returned. "Hello," he said, "who is this? Espy? What the hell do you mean, calling me at half-past one in the morning?"

6

The sixth time, lest you fail to hear,
I placed a trumpet in your ear.

O Mary, at thy window be!
It is the wish'd, the trysted hour.
—ROBERT BURNS

FROM THE LOOK OF THE BUBBLE BELOW (and its sound, if bubbles have sounds), some sixteenth-century Scots lad in love should have written it. But Julian Jenner, who is steeped in such matters, tells me it is the work of William Souter, a leader in the modern Scottish Renaissance movement, who was born in 1898 and died in 1943.

The Tryst

O luely, luely cam she in,
and luely she lay down.
I kent her by her caller* lips
and her braists were smaa and round.

As throu the nicht we spak nae word
nor sindered bane frae bane;
an throu the nicht I heard her hert
gang soundin wi my ain.

It was about the waukrif† hour
when cocks begin to craw
that smooled saftly throu the mirk
afore the day would daw.

Sae luely, luely cam she in,
sae luely was she gane
and wi her aa my simmer days
like they had never been.

* cool and fresh
† waking

*I have often thought, says Sir Roger, it happens very well
that Christmas should fall out in the middle of winter.*
—JOSEPH ADDISON

BUT IN FACT, CHRISTMAS MAKES ITS HOME in the
heart, and you may celebrate it when the heart pleases. Whatever
day you read Dylan Thomas's *Conversations about Xmas*, beginning
below, it will be Christmas Day for you.

SMALL BOY: Years and years ago, when you were a boy . . .

SELF: When there were wolves in Wales, and birds the colour of red-
flannel petticoats whisked past the harp-shaped hills, when we sang
and wallowed all night and day in caves that smelt like Sunday
afternoons in damp front farmhouse parlours, and chased, with the
jawbones of deacons, the English and the bears . . .

SMALL BOY: You are not so old as Mr. Beynon Number Twenty-two who
can remember when there were no motors. Years and years ago,
when you were a boy . . .

SELF: Oh, before the motor even, before the wheel, before the duchess-
faced horse, when we rode the daft and happy hills bareback . . .

SMALL BOY: You're not so daft as Mrs. Griffiths up the street, who says
she puts her ear under the water in the reservoir and listens to the
fish talk Welsh. When you were a boy, what was Xmas like?

SELF: It snowed.

SMALL BOY: It snowed last year, too. I made a snowman and my brother
knocked it down and I knocked my brother down and then we had
tea.

SELF: But that was not the same snow. Our snow was not only shaken in
whitewash buckets down the sky, I think it came shawling out of
the ground and swam and drifted out of the arms and hands and
bodies of the trees; snow grew overnight on the roofs of the houses
like a pure and grandfather moss, minutely ivied the walls, and
settled on the postman, opening the gate, like a dumb, numb
thunderstorm of white, torn Xmas cards.

SMALL BOY: Were there postmen, then, too?

SELF: With sprinkling eyes and wind-cherried noses, on spread, frozen
feet they crunched up to the doors and mittened on them manfully.
But all that the children could hear was a ringing of bells.

SMALL BOY: I only hear thunder sometimes, never bells.

SELF: There were church bells, too.

SMALL BOY: Inside them?

SELF: No, no, no, in the bat-black, snow-white belfries, tugged by bishops and storks. And they rang their tidings over the bandaged town, over the frozen foam of the powder and ice-cream hills, over the crackling sea. It seemed that all the churches boomed, for joy, under my window; and the weathercocks crew for Christmas, on our fence.

SMALL BOY: Get back to the postmen.

SELF: They were just ordinary postmen, fond of walking and dogs, and Christmas, and the snow. They knocked on the doors with blue knuckles . . .

SMALL BOY: Ours has got a black knocker. . . .

SELF: And then they stood on the white welcome mat in the little, drifted porches, and clapped their hands together, and huffed, and puffed, making ghosts with their breath, and jogged from foot to foot like small boys wanting to go out.

SMALL BOY: And then the Presents?

SELF: And then the Presents, after the Xmas box. And the cold postman, with a rose on his button-nose, tingled down the teatray-slithered run of the chilly glinting hill. He went in his ice-bound boots like a man on fishmonger's slabs. He wagged his bag like a frozen camel's hump, dizzily turned the corner on one foot, and, by God, he was gone.

SMALL BOY: Get back to the Presents.

SELF: There were the Useful Presents: engulfing mufflers of the old coach days, and mittens made for giant sloths; zebra scarves of a substance like milky gum that could be tug-o'-warred down to the galoshes; blinding tam-o'-shanters like patchwork tea-cozies, and bunny-scutted busbies and balaclavas for victims of head-shrinking tribes; from aunts who always wore wool next to the skin, there were moustached and rasping vests that made you wonder why the aunties had any skin left at all; and once I had a little crocheted nose-bag from an aunt now, alas, no longer whinnying with us. And pictureless books in which small boys, though warned, with quotations, not to, *would* skate on Farmer Garge's pond, and did, and drowned; and books that told me everything about the wasp, except why.

This conversation continues on page 222.

> *there is bound to be a certain amount of*
> *trouble running any country*
> *if you are president the trouble happens to you.*
> —DON MARQUIS

YOU GATHERED, BACK ON PAGE 40, that it is hard to sum up any president's accomplishments in two lines. It is equally hard to sum up the damage some may have done.

James Buchanan comes next:

15. *James Buchanan*
   1853–1857

Plumped for peace, not liberty;
Wouldn't led Dred Scott go free.

16. *Abraham Lincoln*
   1861–1865

Got us reunited . . . got
Freedom for the slaves . . . got shot.

17. *Andrew Johnson*
   1865–1869

Johnson, when the South beseeched him,
Showed some pity; we impeached him.

18. *Ulysses Simpson Grant*
   1869–1877

Trusted whiskey—won the war.
Trusted friends—they stole the store.

19. *Rutherford Birchard*
   Hayes, 1877–1881

Thought he hadn't won. He had.
That's the way things go. Too bad.

20. *James Abram Garfield*
   1881

Garfield: "Guiteau, here's the door."
"Boom!" went Guiteau's .44.

21. *Chester Alan Arthur*
   1881–1885

Look who's joined our Hall of Fame!
Archer? . . . Harper? (Some such name.)

22, 24. *Grover Cleveland*
   1885–1889,
   1893–1897

Cleveland was a perfect prince
Compared with some before . . .
   and since.

23. *Benjamin Harrison*
1889–1893

Gramp* had quickly met the Worm;
Ben—worse luck!—served out his
    term.

25. *William McKinley*
1893–1901

Hiked the tariffs, Spain diminished;
By an anarchist was finished.

26. *Theodore Roosevelt*
1901–1909

Big stick? Anti-trust? All gone.
(Well, the teddy bear hangs on.)

27. *William Howard Taft*
1909–1913

Whipped Big Oil, but after that
Best-laid plans went all to fat.

28. *Thomas Woodrow Wilson*
1913–1921

Fought to save democracy.
(Next week's feature: World War III.)

29. *Warren Gamaliel Harding*
1921–1923

Normalcy. (Interpretation?
Teapot Dome and Isolation.)

30. *John Calvin Coolidge*
1923–1929

Cal embodied adage splendid:
"Leastest saidest, soonest mended."

31. *Herbert Clark Hoover*
1929–1933

Stocks and jobs went down the spout.
In, Depression; Herbert, out.

32. *Franklin Delano Roosevelt*
1933–1945

Doc New Deal grew stooped and
    hoar—
Welcome, Doctor Win-the-War!

33. *Harry S Truman*
1945–1953

Spunky scrapper, cool and calm.
(Too damn bad, that atom bomb.)

34. *Dwight David Eisenhower*
1953–1961

Land at peace, and bellies full?
Adlai called it terrible.

* William Henry Harrison, No. 9, was his grandfather.

35. *John Fitzgerald Kennedy*   Young and lively, learning fast . . .
    1961–1963   Murdered. Camelot is past.

36. *Lyndon Baines Johnson*   Viet Nam killed it. *R.I.P.*
    1963–1969   *Lyndon's Great Society.*

37. *Richard Milhous Nixon*   Dick his fall from grace laments;
    1969–1977   Voters mourn lost innocence.

38. *Gerald Rudolph Ford*   Proved, which much astonished some,
    1974–1977   He could walk and still chew gum.

39. *James Earl Carter*   Double malaise in the nation:
    1977–1981   1. Khomeini. 2. Inflation.

40. *Ronald Wilson Reagan*   Lucky fellow—those who hated him
    1981–1989   Always underestimated him.

41. *George H. W. Bush*   Not just a Bush he'd better be;
    1989–   We badly need a mighty Tree.

—W.R.E.

Photographer Yousuf Karsh and his wife were having lunch with Neil Armstrong after a photographic session. Armstrong politely questioned the couple about the many countries they had visited. "But Mr. Armstrong," protested Mrs. Karsh, "you've walked on the moon. We want to hear about your *travels." "But that's the only place I've ever been," replied Armstrong apologetically.*
—CLIFTON FADIMAN

IN CASE *YOU* HAVE BEEN ONLY TO the moon, I suggest that you immediately buy and read *The Phrase-Dropper's Handbook*, by John T. Beaudoin and Everett Mattlin. If you follow its rules, any unsuspecting stranger whom you buttonhole at a cocktail party will go away with the impression that you are a world traveler, fluent in every foreign tongue, sought after at the White House, the Kremlin, and Vatican City; that you could have taught fashion to Beau Brummel and essay writing to Montaigne. An extract:

Few of your acquaintances will have seen the Seychelles, that obscure cluster of ninety-two small islands a thousand miles east of Zanzibar in the Indian Ocean. So? When the chitchat begins about the splendid beaches at Puerto Colombia or wherever, you can—with 99 percent safety—launch into a panegyric about "the palm-fringed Beau Vallon, the utterly fantastic pleasure beach of Mahé, and"—don't even *pause* to give them a chance to interrupt—"the glories of the Vallée de Mai nature preserve, on the outer island of Fraslin, so perfect that General Gordon—Gordon of Khartoum, of course—thought it might have been the original Eden."

Refer not to cities but to districts. For all their Hertzing around, Americans seldom absorb the names of English counties or French provinces. Say you drove through Northumberland and let your listeners guess where you were. Rave about the cuisine of the Midi or the lesser-known wines of Gascony. Praise the inns of the Brabant and leave the listener wondering: Is that France, Holland, or Belgium?

Talking about airlines and even airplanes can be a splendid way of showing your familiarity with the routine of world travel. "I prefer Aer Lingus's service to London just because their terminals are less crowded, you know." Or, "I fly Viscounts whenever I can. So much quieter." Or, as one man I know is fond of repeating, "The Caravelle is a fantastic plane. It's like a Frenchwoman—all the power is in the tail."

If all else fails, reverse snobbery is probably the only answer. I recall a neighbor of mine who listened quietly at the first cocktail party of the fall as couple after couple recounted their meanderings abroad, their hotel and restaurant discoveries, their brilliant purchases in the flea markets of the world. At the least, they boasted about the vast decks of the beach houses they had occupied. Finally it occurred to someone present that my neighbor Jim had been silent. "Jim," he was approached, "what did you and Harriet do this summer?"

Jim handled it beautifully. "We stayed home and screwed a lot."

Travel Guide

There is much to be said for Flaubert's point of view on travel, as described by his friend du Camp. He preferred to lie on a divan and have the scenery carried past him.

Meet a Modest Man

Besides place dropping, there is name dropping. E. J. Kahn, Jr., says in *The New Yorker* that Dwayne Andreas, the Soybean King, retains "something of a farm boy's conventional diffidence." For instance, Andreas recalls how he felt while waiting to address the White Burkett Miller Center of Public Affairs of the University of Virginia, of which he and also Cyrus Vance, Walter Cronkite, and a couple of dozen other such luminaries are national associates:

It occurred to me while I was sitting there that I'm about the only person in the room that I never heard of before.

A little kid I know said his favorite carol was "Good King Whence Is Lost." Someone else winced and said, "I hope you sent that kid back from whence he came." And I responded, in a charitable way, "You don't need to say 'from whence.' That's redundant. Whence has a built-in from."

—*PART OF A CLIPPING FORWARDED BY*
DAVID M. GARDNER

THE QUOTATION ABOVE SHIFTS IN A BLINK from troping to grammar. In rhetoric, a trope is a word or phrase used in a different sense from that usually associated with it. Through devilment or genuine misunderstanding, children in a choir may *trope the text*, singing words nearly right in sound but nonsensical. "Good King Wenceslaus" turns to "Good King Whence Is Lost"; "Nearer, My God, to Thee" to "Nero, My Dog, Has Fleas"; "Lead me not into temptation" to "Lead me not into Penn Station"; "Hallowed be thy name" to "Harold be thy name."

What interests the writer of the clipping, however, is not the trope but the "from whence." He argues:

Yes. I know the Bible says, "From whence come wars and fightings among you." But it also says, "Whence hath this man his wisdom?" Though "from whence" has literary precedent, says the *American Heritage Dictionary*, "whence" is preferably used alone.

An elderly fellow said he knew of an example where "from whence" was preferable, and he sent this to me:

There was a young lady from Whence
Whose morals gave some folks offense.
 They were heard to exclaim,
 "Oh, fie on you, shame!
We're incensed, so from Whence get thee thence."

Whence, he explained, was a small town in Iowa, not listed on any of the maps. After I said ugh, he sent me a poetic apology:

I come to apologize, gents.
There was no young lady from Whence.
'Twas really a squirrel
That looked like a girl.
I hope that this ends the suspense.

That second poem was a palinode. That's the word for a song or a poem that retracts something in a former song or poem. It isn't a situation you run into every day.

An official man is always an official man, and he has a wild belief in the value of reports.
—SIR ARTHUR HELPS

THIS WAS SUPPOSEDLY SENT BY THE duke of Wellington, fighting in Spain during the Napoleonic Wars, to British headquarters in London.

Gentlemen:
Whilst marching to Portugal to a position which commands the approach to Madrid and the French forces, my officers have been diligently complying with your request which has been sent by H. M. ship from London to Lisbon and then by dispatch rider to our headquarters.

We have enumerated our saddles, bridles, tents and tent poles, and all manner of sundry items for which His Majesty's Government holds me accountable. I have dispatched reports on the character, wit, and spleen of every officer. Each item and every farthing has been accounted for, with two regrettable exceptions for which I beg your indulgence.

Unfortunately, the sum of one shilling and ninepence remains unaccounted for in one infantry battalion's petty cash and there has been a hideous confusion as to the number of jars of raspberry jam issued to one cavalry regiment during a sandstorm in western Spain. This reprehensible carelessness may be related to the pressure of circumstances SINCE we are at war with France, a fact which may come as a bit of a surprise to you gentlemen at Whitehall.

This brings me to my present purpose, which is to request elucidation of my instructions from His Majesty's Government, so that I may better understand why I am dragging an army over these barren plains. I construe that perforce it must be one of two alternative duties, as given below. I shall pursue either one with the best of my ability but I cannot do both:

    1. To train an army of uniformed British clerks in Spain for benefit of the accountants and copy-boys in London, or perchance,

    2. To see to it that the forces of Napoleon are driven out of Spain.

> Your most obedient servant,
> Wellington

An express train to London made an unscheduled stop at Reading Station, and Cyril Joad,* who had just missed his own train, hopped aboard. "I'm afraid you'll have to get off, sir," called a porter. "This train doesn't stop here." "In that case, don't worry," replied Joad. "I'm not on it."
—CLIFTON FADIMAN

WHEN WORDPLAY TAKES ON THE MANTLE of Joadian logic, it goes beyond play to verbicide. Joadian logic has turned a man whom I have been known to call friend—a man who is a loving husband, an adoring father, a loyal comrade—into a verbal Jack the Ripper. You will hear him at midnight in dark alleys, protesting devotion to some innocent and unsuspecting part of speech—noun, verb, adjective, preposition, adverb, it makes no difference. An instant later, in the name of logic, he throttles and disembowels it. As your well-wisher, Words, I warn you: never let Louis Phillips catch you alone.

The Beast Who Lies in Wait for Words

Shun, shun Lou Phillips, Words; for you will find
A fellow here of dark and bloody mind,
Who lulls with protestations pedagogic,
Then rips your heart out in the name of Logic.

---

* Cyril Joad (1891–1953) was a British philosopher and radio personality.

*U*pholstery that's made of *down*, says he,
By logic alters to *down*holstery,
And orna*mental*'s more corporeal twin
Is orna*physical* . . .
                    Sororal kin
To Tuc*son* is Tuc*daughter* . . .
                    Portu*gal*
Adores her Portu*guy*, while Shilly-shal-
lying *False*tto her *True*setto spurns,
And Bagh*dad* nightly to his Bagh*mom* turns.

Shun, shun Lou Phillips, lest you too fall prey—
Butcher'd to make a Phillips holiday.
                              —W.R.E.

A scarcely less deadly form of illogic is uncovered on p. 153.

A scarcely less deadly form of illogic is uncovered on p. 153.

"Was there ever," cried he, *"such stuff as a great
part of Shakespeare? Only one mustn't say so!"*
—GEORGE III, QUOTED IN FANNY BURNEY'S DIARY

At Last, the Real Shakespeare (I)

IF YOU ARE AMONG THE BLIND FEW who refuse to
concede that the Book of Psalms, King James Version, was translated into English by William Shakespeare, I urge you to turn to Psalm
46 and mark down the forty-sixth word from the beginning. Then
count back to the forty-sixth word from the end (ignore "selah," which
is tossed in after 68 of the 150 psalms and appears to mean, "Well, that
takes care of that; now let's get on to the next one"). What emerges?
Counting forward, "shake"; counting backward "spear." Shakespeare.
Quod erat demonstrandum.

And not just the Psalms, but the whole King James Bible. Dwight MacDonald established Shakespeare's responsibility beyond a doubt when he asserted that the King James is "probably the greatest translation ever made." No one but Shakespeare could have done it. Note, too, that the King James Authorized Version appeared in the year 1611, exactly when Shakespeare was at the height of his powers. To be sure, a committee of translators was given the credit, but none of them was to make a name for himself as a literary man, and we all know that no committee ever accomplished anything. The committee was simply a blind; Shakespeare considered the project a diverting one and did the job for the king over a free weekend.

Monarch and Bard agreed to hide any reference to Shakespeare's role, but he could not resist slipping his name in somewhere; after all, he was only human. So he entered it as I have described. The clerisy knew that Shakespeare had done the job and that he must have left proof somewhere. The only way to prevent the truth from coming out was to keep changing the wording of the Bible, so as to destroy the secret that had to be hidden in it. So they began altering the text. In 1870 they issued a completely new Bible, the Revised Version. That did not satisfy them; somehow they might still have missed Shakespeare's name. So they kept on fiddling. In quick succession came the American Standard Version, the New English Bible, the Good News Bible, the *Reader's Digest* Condensed Bible, and dozens of others that there is no room to mention; all they had in common was that each of them fell a little farther away from the glory of the King James.

Despite this flimflam, few scholars doubt today that Shakespeare did indeed translate the Bible. The remaining question is whether he created it from scratch. This throws some sects into disarray. There are those who hold that Shakespeare was himself God; others say he was Christ, and that his Second Coming slipped by unnoticed.

You will be pleased to know that I have riddled out this problem. On page 318 you will find the identity of Shakespeare spelled out beyond all dispute. Who he was—who he is—who he will be. Selah.

I am in earnest—I will not equivocate—I will not excuse—
I will not retreat a single inch—and I will be heard!
—WILLIAM LLOYD GARRISON, AMERICAN ABOLITIONIST.

LESSER MORTALS, THOUGH, DO equivocate—constantly on little things and occasionally on major ones as well. A bit of fudging, we tell ourselves, will cause less harm than the unvarnished truth. In politics and diplomacy, equivocation is the name of the game. At one point it was even elaborated into diplomatic code in the form of *équivoques*. These two-faced messages, taking both sides and the middle at once, degenerated into parlor games in the nineteenth century.

The nameless author of the following *équivoque*, if you read each line from the extreme left to the extreme right, backed the Tories— that is, the Stuarts—in the eighteenth-century quarrel over the British throne. If you read the left-hand half from top to bottom, though, and then the right-hand half, he was an ardent Hanoverian.

The Houses of Stuart and Hanover

I love with all my heart	The Tory party here
The Hanoverian part	Most hateful do appear
And for that settlement	I ever have denied
My conscience gives consent	To be on James's side
Most righteous is the cause	To fight for such a king
To fight for George's laws	Will England's ruin bring
It is my mind and heart	In this opinion I
Though none will take my part	Resolve to live and die.

. . . .

Spoonerism. A form of metathesis that consists of transposing the initial sounds of words so as to form some ludicrous combination . . . so called from the Rev. W. A. Spooner (1844–1930), Warden of New College, Oxford. Some of the best attributed to him are: "We all know what it is to have a half-warmed fish within us" (for "half-formed wish"); "Yes, indeed; the Lord is a shoving leopard"; and "Kinkering Kongs their titles take."
—BREWER'S DICTIONARY OF PHRASE AND FABLE

TECHNICALLY SPEAKING, THE REVERSALS in the following poem by Alfred Kohn may not be spoonerisms, but they come near enough. And I love the verse.

Sylvan Spring

The snowdrops push through soggy grounds;
The she-bear senses spring is here.
Her mate still mumbles groggy sounds;
She wheezes softly in his ear.
Outside the den, a doe and fawn
Are hiding from their foe at dawn.
Amid bare trees a dreary lake
Is harboring a leery drake.
Two robins gather reed for nest,
And later they have need for rest.
A frog is eyeing a blue fly.
(It missed the one that just flew by.)
A chipmunk, furried little ball,
Digs nuts it buried in the fall.
So there are creatures, weak and mild,
And others meek, and others wild.

*I perform my writing stint each day lying
on the floor under the bed. . . .*

The art of life is to be thought odd.
Everything will then be permitted to you.

—EDWARD VERRALL LUCAS

A GOOD MANY AUTHORS ARE AMONG the odd ones. Schiller kept rotten apples on his desk because the smell helped him create. Luther could not compose unless his dog was lying at his feet. Rousseau wrote only in the early morning, Lesage at midday, Byron at midnight. Kipling insisted on using black, black ink. Calvin did his studying in bed. Shelley and Rousseau, or so it is said, composed best bareheaded, with the sun beating on them.

Bacon, we are told, knelt each day before composing his greatest work, and prayed for light from heaven. Balzac wrote in a monk's working costume; Pope could not write without declaiming first at the top of his voice; Zola pulled the shades and wrote by artificial light; Racine conceived his verses while walking in the streets, reciting them in a loud voice. Carlyle worked in a noiseproof chamber and Proust in a cork-lined room. Ben Jonson needed for peak efficiency a cat for purring, an abundance of tea for soothing his insides, and the strong aroma of lemon peel.

I perform my writing stint each day lying on the floor under the bed, on my back, with my portable typewriter perched precariously on my belly.

In the beginning was the Word,
and the Word was with God,
and the Word was God.

—1 JOHN 1:1

WILLIAM SAFIRE, *NEW YORK TIMES* columnist and an ultimate authority for those of us who love words, wrote: "The first thing you learn in general semantics is that 'the word is not the thing'—that is, the referent is not the source, or, to put it understandably, *cow* is merely a word, a sign, a name, and is not the flesh-and-blood thing that has an udder and says 'moo.' ''

Mr. Safire is in good company—Shakespeare made the same mistake when he said, "A rose by any other name would smell as sweet." They were both wrong, as Mr. Safire's subconscious mind knew, which is why he called his article not "The Word's Not the Thing," but "The Word's the Thing."

For the word, students of semiotics and semantics notwithstanding, *is* the thing. The flesh-and-blood creature that has an udder and goes "moo" is only the extended shadow of the word *cow*.

"And God said, Let there be light; and there was light." First the *word* for light, then the light to justify the word. That's the way it works, Bill.

"And God said, Let us make man in our image, after our likeness." In the image of what? Why, of the Word that was there in the beginning, as John says, "with God." First the *word* "man," then the man. Name man monkey, and he will go about cracking nuts and scratching fleas.

Stuart Chase's *The Tyranny of Words* and S. I. Hayakawa's *Language in Thought and Action*, says Mr. Safire, provide a "blinding illumination" by reminding us that language is only "a code to help us describe reality." He may think of "blinding illumination" as an oxymoron, a contradiction in terms, but in this case the illumination blinds as effectively as if it had driven nails into your eyes.

Sticks and Stones

"Sticks and stones may break my bones,
But words will never hurt me."
I take kindly, Mr. Jones,
Your effort to alert me;

But sticks and stones have I endured,
With nought but scars to show for't,
While ill words ever go uncured,
Nor ever ends the woe for't.

A rose by any other name
Would smell as sweet, you say.
"Skunk cabbage," call it: it's no shame
To turn your nose away.

—W.R.E.

I never knew an enemy of puns who was not an ill-natured man. A pun is a noble thing per se; it fills the mind, it is as perfect as a sonnet. May my last breath be drawn through a pipe and exhaled as a pun.

—CHARLES LAMB

DEMONS ARE A GHOUL'S BEST FRIEND. Sorry, but my karma just ran over your dogma. I'd rather have a bottle in front o'me than a frontal lobotomy. What foods these morsels be!

That is the sort of thing that Charles Lamb could not resist, and that Scot Morris, who checks such matters for *Omni* magazine, cannot resist, either. Here are some puns he could not resist in a recent *Omni* competition:

- We call our beach house Isle of View. Last summer we got a sailboat and named it *Isle of View II.*   —DALE S. ALLEN

- Have you heard about the cowardly dragon that didn't observe the Sabbath? He only preyed on weak knights.   —IAN BOCK

- The frustrated golfer drove over the river and threw the woods.   —ERIC S. HANSEN

- My husband gave me a permanent wave and now he's gone.   —DAWN MESSER

- Q. What do you get when you roll a hand grenade across a kitchen floor? A. Linoleum blownapart.   —AMY ENSIGN

- Many who suffer from irregularity depend on Phillips' Milk of Magnesia, which calls itself "your true blue friend." With friends like that, who needs enemas? —ANNE CRAWFORD

- It was dinnertime in Russia, Soviet. —JOHN A. ENGLEHARDT

If Charles Lamb were alive today, I would introduce him to Scot Morris. What a time those two would have together!

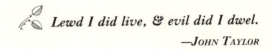 *Lewd I did live, & evil did I dwel.*
—JOHN TAYLOR

MR. TAYLOR, THE WATER POET, wrote that palindrome in 1705, aided by the flexible spelling of his day. I know of no other example of the form in English until the 1820s, when some unknown genius, brooding over the fate of Napoleon, composed "Able was I ere I saw Elba." Since then the palindrome has flourished in England and America like the proverbial green bay tree. As you doubtless know, it is a passage in which the letters read the same forward and backward. Meaning, if any exists, is a bonus. Brief palindromes, such as "Madam, I'm Adam," or "A man, a plan, a canal—Panama!" may convey a message; but—unlike the pangrams on page 35—the longer the palindrome the less likely it is to make sense. Of the clearer sort are Josefa Heifetz's "Zeus' maw swam Suez" and J. A. Lindon's duo, "Dennis and Edna sinned" and "Red rum, sir, is murder." At the other extreme is a 5,024-word palindrome by Jeff Grant, published in *Word Ways;* he later expanded it to 10,230 words. Lawrence Levine sent me the manuscript of his palindromic novel, *Dr. Awkward & Olson in Oslo;* it is 167 pages and 31,594 words long. It starts, "Tacit, I hate gas (aroma of evil)," and ends "live foam or a sage Tahiti cat."

One way to construct a reasonably long palindrome that makes a modicum of sense is to draw on proper names. This one by Clement Wood is the longest of its genre that I know—and certainly the funniest.

THE ORGY

Di, Al, Togo, Böll, Edna, Todd, Adolf, Sir Obadiah Turner, Ollie, Nora, El, silly Rama, Yma Sumac, St. Toby, Cal, Mike, Graf Alfie, Leila, Roz, Owen, Gallos, Reg, Nina Noyes, Mary, Lionel, Lana, Essex, Rex, Dr. Olim, Sal, Isobel, Ed, Axel, Ann, Odile, Leon, Bill (a Pole), Ginger, gay Ogden MacColl, Ewen Enid, Ansel, Gore, Lady Block, Cindy, Sam, Ronny, Llewellyn, Norma, Syd, Nick Colby, Dale, Rog, Les, Nadine Newell, Occam, Ned, Goya, Greg, Nigel, Opal, Lib, Noel, Eli, Donna, Lex, Adele, Bo, Silas, Milord Xerxes, Sean Allen, oily Ramsey, Onan, Ingersoll, Agnew, Oz, Oralie, Leif LaFarge, Kim, Lacy, Botts, Camus, Amy, Amaryllis, Lear, O'Neill, Oren, Ruth, Aida, Boris, Flo, Dad, Dot and El Lobo got laid.

A wealthy old man asked his young companion if she would still love him if he lost his money. "Yes," she replied, "and I would miss you, too."
—DAVID BROWN

THE WORD THAT DEFINES THAT OLD MAN'S pursuit of that young woman is "venery," from the Roman goddess Venus, whose name is also akin to Latin *venari*, "hunt." Venery applies not just to males view-hallooing after females, or the other way around, but also to the fine art of bagging fish, flesh, and fowl. When Oscar Wilde referred to English gentlemen chasing after a fox as "the unspeakable in full pursuit of the uneatable," the second kind of venery is what he had in mind.

This second sense gave rise to the term "venereal noun" for creatures banded together. In "a school of fish," *school* is a venereal noun. The meaning has broadened until some writers use the term for any collective noun. *Solitude* is a venereal noun in A. E. Housman's lovely lines "Solitude of shepherds/High in the folded hill."

Venereal terms were codified in England about the middle of the fifteenth century and were memorized by young noblemen for whom the hunt was to be a lifelong preoccupation. James Lipton's *Exaltation* *of Larks*, which brought to present-day attention a host of such expressions as "a kindle of kittens," "a pride of lions," and "a gaggle of geese," led to an explosion of wordplay on venereal nouns. As you will see here,* even Cub Scouts are not exempt:

> If they are meeting at someone else's house, they are referred to as a *den*. If they are meeting at your house, they are a *din*. A group of den mothers is a *frazzle*. The husbands of den mothers are *the weekly poker game*.

Mr. Church wrote that one of his own favorite venereal terms is a "cacophony of crows." Robert M. Sheloot is bemused by a "host of landlords" and a "mass of priests." Rose E. Balluff forwarded a yellowed *Topics of the Times* clipping, undated, from which I have excerpted this:

> A sleepless night in the country brings quick understanding of why frogs in assembly are called an *army*, and few would challenge the description of an array of kangaroos as a *troop*. If a company of squirrels is a *dray*, certainly an assembly of asses should be a *bray*. But asses in a group are a *pace*, while mules are a *barren*.
>
> Group terms for God's creatures are a field day for the sporting etymologist or the etymological sportsman. But they are only a small part of the lexicon. There are all the different terms for male and female creatures, for their young, for their tracks, for their retiring to rest and for dislodging them in the chase, for their mating, for their cries, for their colors and parts, for cutting, dressing, and skinning them, and for their fundament.† There are even terms for their tails. For example, a fox has a *brush*, a deer a *single*, an otter a *rudder*, a hare or a rabbit a *scut*, and a foxhound a *stern;* and thus ends the tale.

---

* Dudley F. Church sent this to me. It is from *The Grasshopper Tree*, by Patrick F. McManus.
† The names of some animal droppings are listed on page 27.

7

The seventh time, I sliced your head
And neck apart, and left you dead.

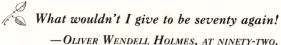

What wouldn't I give to be seventy again!
—*OLIVER WENDELL HOLMES, AT NINETY-TWO,*
LOOKING AT A PRETTY GIRL.

IT WAS CLEVER OF SCIENTISTS TO ARRANGE for wristwatches to improve as they age.

I am not talking, mind you, about those silly digital watches that can tell you at what hour Abraham or Confucius died and what the temperature is just now on the back side of the moon—the kind that you buy for five or ten dollars from a vendor on a street corner and that decompose into powder when the battery runs down. No—I am talking about *real* watches, that have to be wound every twenty-four hours. And that used to tick.

When my wife presented me with my present wristwatch, a quarter of a century ago, the tick was noticeable. If I laid the watch down in an unlikely spot, I did not have to send for detectives; I could locate it by following the sound.

A silent watch was beyond the power of scientists then. But now they have learned to slide exotic new devices into watch casings without the owner's even noticing. Miniaturized mufflers, for instance. Do you remember those advertisements that claimed a Rolls-Royce ran so quietly that you could only hear the tick of the clock? Well, my watch is more advanced than that; it keeps fine time, but when I press it against my ear I can hear no sound at all.

60—70—Tick—Tick

The ticking clock marks off the years,
And warns the end is nearing.
(Or so friends tell me. It appears
I'm growing hard of hearing.)

—W.R.E.

· · · · · · ·

> *[Minimalists] are inclined to write frequently in the
> present tense; to favor the short declarative sentence
> (very short and very declarative); to be preoccupied with
> domestic details (cooking, dishwashing, laundry).**
> —BRUCE BAWER

MINIMALISTS, CONTINUES MR. BAWER, are fond of "recalcitrant narrators and deadpan narratives, slightness of story, and characters who don't think out loud." It is a pleasure to present here what may be the earliest clear-cut example of this remarkable literary form.

It is a letter written in the settlement of Chinook, Washington, thirty miles south and east of Oysterville, more than 120 years ago. The writer was Jane Cecile Haguet, half French and half Indian, who was to marry James Randolph Johnson, settle in Oysterville, and bear her husband nine children.

Note her frequent use of the present tense. Note, too, the short, declarative sentences. As for "deadpan narratives, slightness of story, and characters who don't think out loud" . . . well, see for yourself.

Chinook, July 28th, 1868

My dear aunt

I received your letter and was glad to hear from you and to hear you was all well I am pretty well at present and I hope you are the same Mrs. Preble is married again her name is Kelly now I suppose you heard that Preble was killed last winter there was another man killed at the same time his name is William Macnamee and there was another one wounded his name is Michael Welch he was sentenced to be hung on the fourth of June but he is in for life there were two more in the row one is in prison for one year and the other for two years

they had a great time last winter Mrs Preble and her girls was the cause of it if they behaved like folks ought to they would not have such a time

* See also page 63.

the one that is in prison for two years his name is John Hayden he was fishing here last summer he tried to get Agnes she promised to have him and he bought her a great many things and when his money was played out she threw off on him and took up with someone else he did not like this of course no one would

he went down to Shoalwater Bay to work and in a little while Mary and her husband parted she took her girls and went there and John took care of them she said she would never go back to live with Preble again but she did not stay away long she came back

while she was away Preble heard she was living under John Haydens care he got mad and he burnt Johns house down and John got mad and went there and wanted him to pay him fifty dollars he payed him for the house and then John told him he wanted that much more for the things he gave Agnes

he could not pay him then he went away angry he told him he would come in the morning and settle but he did not come back any more it was Mike Welch and another by the name of Vandorson Preble shot Mike and Vanderson shot Preble and William Macnamee the reason Michael Welch is guilty [is] because he went there first to have a fight but he did not shoot all he had was the coffee pot after he was shot he poured it in Preble's face we hope this will teach them all John was a good-hearted fellow but he wanted to be treated right

I saw Isaac a few days ago he sends his respects to you well write when you can I close this with my regards your affectionate niece Jane Cecile Haguet

Minimalism makes the reader use the old bean to fill in the parts that are missing. It took me almost no time to satisfy myself that Mrs. Preble was the one named Mary and that Agnes was her daughter. The shoot-out and its aftermath come clear, too, if you consider them carefully.

Preble fired the first shot—the one that hit Welch—and Welch retaliated by pouring the contents of a coffeepot over Preble's head. For that Welch was sentenced to death. Fair enough. Vandorson then killed both Preble and Macnamee. For that he was sentenced to a year in prison. Fair enough. Hayden stayed out of harm's way. For that he was sentenced to two years in prison. Fair enough.

But why did Mrs. Preble marry that fellow Kelly?

> gods i am pent in a cockroach
> i with the soul of a dante
> am mate and companion of fleas
> i with the gift of a homer
> must smile when a mouse calls me pal
> tumble bugs are my familiars
> this is the punishment meted
> because i have written vers libre
> —ARCHY, COMPLAINING TO DON MARQUIS

THERE ARE THOSE WHO PRAY IN SECRET. There are those who drink in secret. And there are those—but not archy the cockroach—who write poetry in secret.

I have persuaded a handful of these poets to let me bring them out of the closet. I do not know why they were so reluctant. Perhaps it is pudency; they may feel, with Elbert Hubbard, that poetry is the bill and coo of sex. Or perhaps they recall that Poe took a poet to be only one remove from a fool. Or that Horace equated versification with insanity: "The man is mad, or else he's writing verse."

And some are just pretending to be closet poets. This one, for instance. I have seen his savory lines in print, and so have you.

Alimentary Canals (Germany)

The Germans fuel the body cavity
with fare of great specific gravity.
Digestive enzymes tilt and topple
under the threat of *hoppelpoppel*,
hassenpfeffer and *pfefferbrot*
thundering heavily down the throat.

Scarce is that gone (though not forgotten),
there follows a volley of *sauerbraten*.
"Watch out, watch out!" the enzymes whine,
"Upstairs he's reached for *gänzeklein*,

and, after a *bier* to quench his thirst,
no doubt we all can expect the *wurst*."

—E. J. K. READ

This limerick is by a Yale man, merciless in his aesthetic and moral judgments:

*"Nothing Is Worth Dying For"—Sign Carried by
Mark Waren at an Anti-draft Rally in Princeton*

Poor Princeton's Mark Waren would fail
To erase from our thoughts Nathan Hale
Who could state without trying
Three reasons for dying:
For country, for God, and for Yale.

—JAMES BENENSON, JR.

It will not surprise you that the author of the two poems that follow is a young, successful public relations counsel:

Rule of Love

If my rule of love be sinful,
Then sinful let me be;
It simply pleases me to please
Whoever pleases me.

To Mike

Too much
Too soon
Too hard
To handle
Too bad
Toodooloo.

—KATE DELANO CONDAX

One more, by a man who in his other life was to my mind the most effective writer of direct-mail advertising copy of my generation. He wrote this to a granddaughter:

Postcard from China

Dear Annie:
In Chinese the letter *q*
Is seldom followed by a *u*.
This leads to spelling qeer and eerie
And raises a pervasive qery:
What do we do with the leftover u?
    Luds uv luv, from
            Grundmu und Grundpu.

—FRANK JOHNSON

Lily O'Grady,
Silly and shady,
Longing to be
A lazy lady.
—EDITH SITWELL

AND THERE WAS JUDY O'GRADY, too—the colonel's lady's sister under the skin, says Kipling. My maternal grandmother took the élitist side of the argument on what a lady is; as a bride she wept when she heard the cleaning woman called a cleaning lady. No one thinks twice about that usage today; the notion of ladies as "people who do not do things for themselves" no longer holds. Nor need a lady conduct herself in ladyly fashion. The old rhyme went, "Little nips o' whiskey,/Little drops of gin/Make a lady wonder/Where on earth she's been"—but not, nowadays, whether she is still a lady. Eliza Doolittle didn't want to talk grammar, she wanted to talk like a lady; some of today's ladies aspire to talk like Eliza Doolittle. Aldous Huxley's Mr. Quarles, "brought up in an epoch when ladies apparently rolled along on wheels," found himself as a consequence "peculiarly susceptible to calves"; today he would find himself no more excited about a lady's calf than about the young of a cow.

Still, there are a few who continue to cherish the old distinction between lady and woman—which in the instance that follows is preserved by turning it inside out:

Lady

A Lady is a Woman
who was a Lady
but now prefers
to be a Woman
in order to distinguish her
        from the Lady
(who used to be a Woman)
who "does" for her.

—Ms. P. CARTER

 *Birds in their little nests agree.*

—*ISAAC WATTS*

NOT FUFFITS, THOUGH, AS YOU WILL SEE from this knittelverse. It features words beginning with *f*, but words beginning with other letters are numbered, too.

F. Tempest in a Fuffit[1] Nest

There's scandal out in Birdland. One morning Mr. Fuffit
Was overseen delivering a mighty fuffit buffet
On little Mrs. Fuffit; he declared that she was dottle[2]
For always building bird nests in the fashion of a bottle.

[1] The long-tailed titmouse. [2] Crazy, silly.

He faffed[3] and drabbed[4] and friggled,[5] and he called her
     wicked words;
He said that she was fuffled,[6] and her nests were for the
     birds.
A fallowchat said, "Dearie, what your husband really means
Is, you are on the wait-list for a three-room nest in Queens."
The bird was right, and (I suspect this won't be news to you)
The three-room nest in Queens is shaped much like a bottle too.
The Fuffits, though, are happy there, and gaily
     gibble-gabble.
They'll hear no talk of quarrels—they would call it
     fibble-fabble.

                   —W.R.E.

 Command old words, that long have slept, to wake.
                        —ALEXANDER POPE

ARCHAEOLOGISTS LEARN ABOUT perished civilizations from shards. Paleontologists extrapolate extinct animals from leftover toe bones. You and I could learn much about how our forebears thought if we bothered to scrape forgotten words from the midden of bygone books.

Norman Cousins dug up some inelegant old words from the *Dictionary of Pickpocket Eloquence* (1811) and published them in *Saturday Review*. "We would be happy," he commented, "to see a number of badly overworked contemporary expressions traded in for some of the pithier old English items."

He liked, for instance, *nigmenog*, "a stupid fellow"; *chouse*, "to cheat or trick"; and "Queen Street," presumably the address of any man dominated by his wife. I assume he also liked, since he cited them, the dusty words scattered through the knittelverse below. They would not have been suitable for conversation with the parson, though.

---

[3] Blew in puffs. [4] Charged her with associating with strumpets—incredible! [5] Fussed.
[6] In general disorder.

An Inelegant Proposal

Fubsey,[1] let us, you and I,
To the buttock-broker[2] hie.
No more pushing-school[3] for me!
No more smellsmock[4] shall I be!
No more mettle[5] in the night;
No more threepenny upright[6]!
I shall whisper, as we hug,
"Gapeseed[7] is your double-jugg[8]!"
In our room above the stair
One tea-voider[9] shall we share.
When my quopping[10] heart has ceased,
You'll prepare the shoulder feast.[11]

—W.R.E.

Good, too, Logic, of course; in itself, but not in fine weather.
—AUTHOR UNKNOWN

IT HAS BEEN CHARGED THAT EXTREMISTS in logic equate the woods with the trees, or at least don't care which is which. Samuel Butler's Hudibras, for instance,

. . . could distinguish and divide
A hair 'twixt south and south-west side.

A bit of illogic keeps things in perspective. I speak of such reasoning as Mangie uses in *Word Ways* when she says she would give her right arm to be ambidextrous, or as the same publication employs when it asks us to contemplate the sound of one hand clapping (a notion

[1] A plump, healthy wench. [2] A matchmaker. [3] A brothel. [4] A licentious man. [5] Self-abuse. [6] A woman who dispenses sexual favors for a trifling sum—while standing. [7] A treat for the eyes. [8] The backside, arse. [9] A chamber pot. [10] Throbbing, palpitating. [11] An after-funeral dinner for those who carried the corpse.

familiar to students of Zen) and to envisage an imaginary apple eating a real worm.

Maxey Brooks reports that a form of illogic based on puns is described in the *Encyclopaedia Britannica* as a "nymble," and that the following example is given:

Q. *Why are fire engines red?*
A. Two plus one equals three. The third letter in the alphabet is C. The sea is full of fish. The sturgeon is a fish. Caviar comes from sturgeons. Russians are fond of caviar. Fire engines are always rushin'. What other color could they be?

Buddy Basch says the following nymbles are "exactly as they were told me by my father":

WHY ISN'T A BABY WORTH 2¢?

A baby is a cryer. A cryer is a messenger. A messenger is one sent. Since one cent certainly isn't worth 2¢, a baby isn't worth 2¢.

WHY IS A PIECE OF RULED PAPER LIKE A LAZY DOG?

A piece of ruled paper is an ink-lined plane. An inclined plane is a slope-up. And a slow pup is a lazy dog.

Then there is the nymble of the fox terrier, attributed by *Word Ways* to "some fellow named Johnson":

It is an undeniable fact that if a fox terrier two feet long with a tail an inch and a half high can dig a hole three feet deep in ten minutes, then to dig the Panama Canal in a single year would require only one fox terrier fifteen miles long with a tail a mile and a half high. This is statistically true; yet one must seriously consider whether, after finding such a fox terrier, one could make it mind.

*We left Paris Friday for the north. Friday night
it rained and we got a pile of straw to spread
our blankets on in a little village jail.*
—*LETTER FROM CLINTON MCKINNON TO HIS MOTHER,
17 AUGUST 1930*

W E EXPECTED TO MEET EXPENSES by reading palms
along the way; I even boned up on a palmistry book. Clint,
lacking French, was to wrap a Turkish towel around his head, drape
himself in his blanket, and play swami.

We tried our luck on two street corners. Clint's outlandish costume
indeed stopped passersby, who were delighted to have me explain the
fate lines and life lines in their callused hands. I discussed my findings
with Clint in pig Latin; he replied in the same tongue. It invariably
turned out that the lucky subject was verging on a sensational rise in
fortune. They were all delighted; but their hands, reft of their secrets,
returned to their pockets and stayed there. Our earnings came to two
clusters of turnips and one of carrots.

And then it began to rain—the kind of rain that led to the primal
Flood. By the time we were dropped at the village mentioned in
Clint's letter, you might have mistaken us for beasts that had missed
the Ark.

We inquired our way through the downpour to the mayor's office
(which turned out to be his own thatched farmhouse) and asked him
whether some family might be willing to bed us down for a modest
payment, say, two clusters of turnips. Fortune's frown became a smile.
The mayor, a plump, cordial man in shirt sleeves and slippers, said
there was room aplenty in the jail across the way, which had been long
unoccupied. His hired man would simply fork in some hay, and we
might sleep there dry and secure, as his guests. Moreover, we must
honor him by dining with his family, which turned out to comprise,
besides himself, a wife who laughed at unexpected moments but never
said anything and a daughter of some fifteen or sixteen summers named
Madeleine.

In the entrance stood an elegant young lady. . . .

Subsequent events burned Madeleine's appearance into my brain, but that night I could not even locate her eyes; they were lost behind a pale shock of hair, or hay. Her nose was peeling, presumably from sunburn; her neck was unwashed; her figure, under a shapeless gray dress, was inscrutable. Her feet were as bare and nearly as dingy as those of the widow Morales.* She spoke no English and ignored my conversational overtures in fractured French. She simply forked cabbage and chicken into her mouth, chewed, swallowed, and stared at Clint.

I could not understand then, nor do I to this day, why young women stared at Clint that way. I never thought he was much to look at. He reminded me of a bantam cock—the Irish variety. His gray eyes twinkled as if fireflies were dancing behind them. Any sensible girl would have looked once and run.

At the end of the evening the hired man escorted us to our quarters, deposited his forkload of hay, and waited while we disrobed, so that he could return our clothes to the house to dry overnight by the stove. He would have them back, he said, by early morning. We wrapped ourselves in our blankets and slept tight. But when we woke at daylight, the jail door was locked. We waited. Perhaps forty-five minutes later a key grated in the lock; the iron door swung open—and we hastily tightened our coverings.

In the entrance stood an elegant young lady with a gray broad-brimmed hat tilted over her right eye. She wore a lavender dress that fitted closely and to advantage; in front, it took a deep breath and plunged. The skirt ended at her knees, yielding to hose and high-heeled black pumps. Her brows were dark and tweezer-sculpted; they shaded enormous hazel orbs, with blackened lashes raying out from the lids. The nose was small and straight, the lower lip fullish and emphasized in red. The chin had a cleft. Cheeks, throat, and the part of the chest that was visible—a sizable area—were chalky white from applications of powder, or perhaps flour. Only the heap of wrinkled clothing in her arms proved that this was Madeleine.

She laid her burden on the floor, curtseyed, and left without a word. But a few minutes later, when we emerged fully clad to rinse our hands and faces at the horse trough (the rain had stopped), she was waiting; and she burst into an urgent, half-whispered appeal.

* See page 103.

With her father's concurrence, she told us, she was inviting us to remain as long as we wished, so that Monsieur—she bobbed her head in my direction—might instruct her in the intricacies of the English language. Perhaps the other monsieur—the great eyes longed after Clint, but she could not get her tongue around his name—would care to learn French, in which case she would be only too happy . . .

She singsonged the words, low, hopelessly, staying a step behind as we proceeded to the highroad. A touring car with the top down stopped for us at once. She would have climbed in too if I had not sworn to her on my honor as an American that we would return within days.

It was a lie, of course. I do not understand even now why I saved Clint from her. I doubt that he wanted to be saved. If she had looked so at me, you could not have dragged me away.

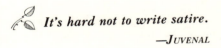 *It's hard not to write satire.*
—JUVENAL

SATIRE CAN EITHER SCREAM AGAINST THE HOR-rors of life and our social circumstances or chuckle at them. Rage was the reaction of Siegfried Sassoon, an English poet so revolted by the First World War that he threw his Military Cross into the sea:

Lamentations

I found him in the guard-room at the Base.
From the blind darkness I had heard his crying
And blundered in. With puzzled, patient face
A sergeant watched him; it was no good trying
To stop it; for he howled and beat his chest.
And, all because his brother had gone west,
Raved at the bleeding war; his rampant grief
Moaned, shouted, sobbed, and choked, while he was kneeling
Half-naked on the floor. In my belief
Such men have lost all patriotic feeling.

Phyllis McGinley was a satirist, too, but felt more at home with chuckles than screams:

On the Farther Wall, Marc Chagall

One eye without a head to wear it
Sits on the pathway, and a chicken,
Pursued perhaps by astral ferret,
Flees, while the plot begins to thicken.
Two lovers kiss. Their hair is kelp.
Nor are the titles any help.

Squeeze Play

Jackson Pollock had a quaint
Way of saying to his sibyl,
"Shall I dribble?
Should I paint?"
And with never an instant's quibble,
Sibyl always answered,
"Dribble."

*A nickname is the heaviest stone
the devil can throw at a man.*
—WILLIAM HAZLITT

DAVID MACDONALD TELLS OF A NOVA SCOTIAN schoolboy who couldn't understand what his teacher meant by the word *quadruped*. At length she asked him, "What has a cow four of that I've only two of?" His answer guaranteed that his family of Mac-Ivors would always be nicknamed the Tits.

But when Mr. MacDonald wrote on Nova Scotian nicknames for *Reader's Digest,* Canada, either he or his editor left that story out—quite properly, in my opinion, the *Digest* being a family magazine.

NOVA SCOTIA'S WACKY NICKNAMES*
by David (Big Christopher) MacDonald

Not long ago I met a man from Antigonish, N.S., and asked if he happened to know my friend Lauchlin Chisholm.

"Would that be Lauchie Boots?" he wondered. "Father had a shoestore on Main Street?"

I wasn't sure. So the next time I saw *my* Lauchie, in Toronto, I asked him. "No, we're from out around Heatherton and we don't have any nickname," he said with a note of regret. "My father's simply called Jimmy Colin Jim."

Such multiple tags and family nicknames have been widely used in "New Scotland" ever since the 18th century, when Highlanders began fleeing across the Atlantic after their forlorn fight to put Bonnie Prince Charlie on England's throne. Among the 25,000 who settled on Cape Breton Island, all 14 major clans were represented, and most of them chose from among only five or six Christian names for their male children. Many communities there and on the mainland soon developed identity problems galore. Among the early settlers of Antigonish county, for example, one history book listed 98 different Chisholms—46 called Alex, Donald or John. There also were 210 MacDonalds—117 being John, Donald, Angus, Allan or Alex.

One solution was to add nicknames linking the owner to some particular place or incident. Among all the John Chisholms, it then became possible to distinguish John the Schoolhouse, who lived near one, from John Jesus, who was much given to profanity. Similarly, the manifold MacDonalds could sort out Allan the Ridge, Alex Big Painter and Maggie in the Sky, who roomed on the top floor of the tallest building in Antigonish, three stories up.

You will learn on page 205 how Angus the Nun and Hughie Tantum Ergo received their nicknames.

*There is no conventional way to rhyme some words.
However, it is frequently possible to adapt the method of
Procrustes—stretching the victims when they are too short or,
more often, lopping something off if they are too long.*

—W.R.E.

A WORD AND A HALF, OR SOMETIMES just half a word,
may serve as a rhyme for an otherwise unrhymable word like
silver or orange. The trick is to make the exercise seem both easy and
natural, as James H. Rhodes does here:

Orange

It's true, you're right; there is no rhyme.
The effort is a waste of time.
I happily concede defeat.
But oranges were made to eat,
And not to rhyme; I find it more enj-
oyable to eat the orange.

*As Sir Edmund Gosse was entertaining guests at his home,
the parlor-maid entered to tell him, having misunderstood the
name, that Swinburne was on the telephone. Now, Swinburne
had recently died; and Sir Edmund's friends waited in a
breathless hush to hear his reaction. He exclaimed, "Mr. Swinburne
to speak to me on the telephone? I shall certainly not speak
to Mr. Swinburne. I don't know where he may be speaking from!"*

—ALFRED NOYES

SIR EDMUND HIMSELF WAS BRIEFLY MOURNED in
error by George Moore, the Irish novelist, whose housekeeper
told him that one Martin Ross, an old friend, had died. Moore, mis-

understanding and much upset, paced his study, waving at the books around him as he cried: "Here I am in the midst of this—and my friend, my dear friend Edmund Gosse, dead!"

"I beg your pardon, Mr. Moore," said the housekeeper, "it is Martin Ross, not Edmund Gosse, who is dead."

Moore drew himself up and looked at her. "My dear woman," he said indignantly, "surely you don't expect me to go through all that again?"

Once my club bulletin board announced the demise of a literary agent of whom I was fond. A few weeks later I saw him approaching me on the sidewalk, his cheeks ruddy, his head back, his stick swinging. My greeting was jumbled, and my face doubtless went white; I suspect that he proceeded on his way reflecting that Espy was going into a decline. The bulletin had erroneously placed his name under Deaths instead of Resignations. Later a man I had known thirty-odd years was listed in the same necrology; a week afterward he sat down next to me at dinner. The dead man was another of identical name.

Like George Moore, I resent grief gone to waste. If my two friends in the end predecease me, do you suppose some computer in my soul will cut down the sum of my sorrowing by the amount already spent?

Edgar Tafel, the architect, described an annoying experience of the architect James Fitch. Fitch was asked by *The Architectural Forum* to develop a biographical sketch of the architect Frank Lloyd Wright. (If you are in doubt about the profession involved here, write me.) He received the assignment in the 1940s, and the sketch was to be published when Wright died. Once Fitch had delivered his article, it seemed to him that the great architect's career had been summed up once and for all, and that he should have the good grace to expire. (He lived until 1959.) Every time that Wright won a new award, Finch was furious. The man was supposed to be *dead*.

I am reminded that once or twice a week for many years, Louise has engaged in long telephone conversations with an old friend, Christine Magriel. Christine recently suffered a stroke and died without regaining consciousness. Today Louise said, "You know, I keep starting to pick up the telephone to call Christine to tell her that Christine Magriel is dead."

Settling the Issue Between the Chicken and the Egg

Not for the mighty hen, opines Russell Baker, are such trifling speculations as whether she or the egg comes first. She knows too well the inexorable decree of nature that the egg comes first, being served at breakfast, while the chicken is reserved for dinner.

Sept. 5th, 1875. Spencers were expected Monday, but were prevented by the death of old Lady Clinton, aged 80, who has long been very feeble and doting. Her head was always a little confused, but her involved relationships were enough to account for it. She was sister to one Lady Spencer, stepmother to another, and aunt to a third; and she is Lord Spencer's own aunt and likewise his step-mother's mother and his brother's grandmother.
—DIARY OF LADY FREDERICK CAVENDISH

Can We Make It Next Weekend Instead?

The Spencers were coming, but have to delay—
Poor daft Lady Clinton has just passed away.
At eighty she long had been feeble and doting—
A little confused—and the cause is worth noting:
In eighty long years she had still not resolved
Her links to the Spencers—extremely involved:
Of one Lady Spencer the aunt; of another
The sister; a third Lady Spencer's stepmother;
Lord Spencer's own stepmother's mother; and then, sir,
The aunt, on her own, of that very Lord Spencer.
(I almost forgot that to Lord Spencer's brother
The fuddled old dame was a loving grandmother.)

The Spencers can't come till they're less agitated—
They have to find out if they still are related.
—W.R.E.

Rhetoric is either very good, or stark nought;
there is no medium in rhetoric.
—*JOHN SELDEN*

Some Rhetoricians I Have Known

Some rhetoricians I have known
Won't leave a harmless word alone.
Determinedly, though knowing better,
They add or drop or change a letter,
And multiplying their offense,
Describe in Greek the consequence.
Thus "e'en," deprived of middle *v*,
Becomes a lordly *syncope;**
And " 'gainst," initial letter gone,
As an *aphaeresis* strides on.

Or if they add a middle sound—
As "film" to "fillum" turns around—
They say, when chided for their miss,
"Dear sir, I used *epenthesis.*"
Two syllables as one they treat
("Th'elite" replaces "the elite")
And grandly state (if you should beef): "A
Sample, sir, of *synolepha.*"
If, meaning "rather," you say "ruther,"
Antithsecon's your problem, brother.

—W.R.E.

---

* Pronunciations: *syncope*, sin′ko.pē; *aphaeresis*, a.fer′i.sis or a.fē′ri.sis; *epenthesis*, e.pen′the.sis; *synolepha*, syn.o.lē′fa; *antithsecon*, an.tith′se.kon.

A little madness in the spring
Is wholesome even for the king.
—EMILY DICKINSON

The Fabulous Hunt of the Jackaroo[1]

Do you recall the jackaroo
    Who left his sheep at home
To hunt the wily kangaroo
    That skulks through frosty Nome?

(Would he have went had he but knew,
    As many might explain,
That *several* sorts of kangaroo
    Bound on the bounding main?—
The walleroo[2]—the potoroo[3]—
    The kangaroo again?)

He sat in shade of gambedoo[4]
    To rest him from his search.
The tree had on the gingham blue
    She always wore to church,
But stayed at home; 'twould never do
    To leave him in the lurch.

He shook his jug of hoochinoo,[5]
    And offered her a quaff,
And sang, and played the digerydoo[6]
    To make the good tree laugh.

[1] In Australia, an apprentice sheep herder. [2] Some other kind of kangaroo. [3] The rat kangaroo. [4] A South African tree having tough wood. [5] An intoxicating drink distilled by the Hoochinoo Indians from boiled farina and flour. [6] An aboriginal Australian flute.

They watched an Irish gillaroo[7]
    Gulp whole into its belly
A living, squawking cockatoo,
    And crush it there to jelly.

A square-egg-laying gillygaloo[8]
    Refused in manner curt
To lay a square egg for the two—
    She said that it would hurt.

With horrid cry a kaberu[9]
    Leaped forth, incisors bared;
The jackaroo moaned pililoo,[10]
    And prayed that he be spared.

This waked a dozing kinkajou,[11]
    Which used its tail to snap
The neck of that fierce kaberu,
    And then resumed its nap.

No walleroo, no potoroo
    That jackaroo brought home;
And yet his sheep baaed lulliloo[12]
    That he was back from Nome.

            —W.R.E.

---

[7] A trout that by tightening its muscles can crush the shell of a swallowed mollusk. [8] A mythical bird that lays square eggs. [9] The Abyssinian mountain wolf. [10] In hunting, a cry of distress. [11] A flesh-eating, arboreal mammal with a slender body about three feet long, a long, prehensile tail, and large lustrous eyes. [12] A cry of joyful welcome.

"That's the reason they're called lessons," the Gryphon remarked:
"because they lessen from day to day."
—LEWIS CARROLL

I SEE BY THE PAPERS THAT seven hundred thousand children dropped out of American schools last year and three hundred thousand more were chronic truants. I see that each year twenty-four thousand navy enlistees, all with high school diplomas, read below the tenth-grade level, though they must read and understand manuals on the twelfth- to fourteenth-grade level. I see that hundreds of thousands of high school graduates cannot even read their diplomas.

The figures would comfort the ghost of Jack Cade, who complained to Lord Say in Shakespeare's *Henry VI, Part 2:*

> Thou hast most traitorously corrupted the youth of the realm in erecting a grammar-school; and whereas, before, our forefathers had no other books but the score and the tally, thou hast caused printing to be used; and, contrary to the king, his crown and dignity, thou hast built a paper-mill. It will be proved to thy face that thou hast men about thee that usually talk of a noun and a verb, and such abominable words as no Christian ear can bear to hear.

In an article with no signature, forwarded to me by Charles R. Eisenhart, Jr., *The Phi Beta Kappan* advances several radical notions for easing our educational ills:

> I propose that one week be set aside in which there would be no class meeting, no California Achievement Test, no yearbook and ring sales, no senior pictures taken, no rock band assemblies, no field trips, no school fair, no play rehearsal, no track meet, no creative arts festival, no eye testing, no reading system salesman, no gym floor varnishing, no meeting for the group going to Spain, no fire drill, no pep rally, no test, no open-house visiting, no band practice, no passes for students to stay and finish an experiment, wait for the sweet rolls to come out of the oven, make up a test, mop up spilled paint, or clean the ink off the printing press, and no early dismissal for part-time jobs.

This week should not contain Memorial Day, Good Friday, Columbus Day, Veterans Day, Martin Luther King Day, George Washington's Birthday, Labor Day, the first day it snows, or the first balmy day in spring. Should such a week be arranged, it is possible that our students might be able to do what they are supposed to do in school. Learn something.

ABC language. A substitution of like-sounding letters, digits, or symbols for words or parts of words.
—*W.R.E.*

ABC VERSES ARE BUILT AROUND letter rebuses,* a dying art form. The example below (from the July 1903 issue of *Woman's Home Companion*) is reason enough to revive it. Read the poem aloud, spelling out the capital letters.

> The farmer leads no EZ life,
>   The CD sows will rot;
> And when at EV rests from strife
>   His bones all AK lot.
>
> In DD has to struggle hard
>   To EK living out;
> If IC frosts do not retard
>   His crops, there'll BA drought.
>
> The hired LP has to pay
>   Are awful AZ, too;
> They CK rest when he's away,
>   Nor NE work will do.

* See pages 67 and 230.

Both NZ cannot make to meet,
And then for AD takes
Some boarders, who so RT eat,
&E no money makes.

Of little UC finds this life;
Sick in old AG lies;
The debts he OZ leaves his wife,
And then in PC dies.
—H. C. DODGE

C. C. Bombaugh asserted in 1874 that the following consonants appeared in an old church in Westchester County, N.Y., beside the altar and under the Ten Commandments. The sentence is a univocalic—a passage using only one of the five vowels. To read it, substitute the same vowel for each of the periods.

P.RS. V. R. Y. P. RF. CT M. N
.V. R K.. P TH. S. PR. C. PTS T. N

 The first overt crime of the refractory angels was punning;
they fell rapidly after that.
—W. S. LANDOR

STORY WITHOUT A NAME
(Continued from page 84.)

(Our hero is sitting forlornly on a park bench, bemoaning his poverty.)

I Guest Euclid Sayers I was the Unruh-Cheever in my family. My Broder Owen Doyle Wells. My Cicero a Castle and had Pliny of Cervantes, including a Butler, Cooke, and Valéry—even a maid to Cerf her Dinesen bed; I, of Corso was not Ustinov luxury. My wife and I lived in a rundown Tolstoy Bigelow without a Barth room. Ferber-Moore, my wife was always accusing me of Steele-Lindsay Monet from her Perse and often threatened to Thoreau me out.

It wasn't Fairfax, Godden-Dürrenmatt all. Wharton earth was I to do? Rob Firbank?

I was on the Vergil Sousa-cide, one step away from a ride in the Hersey to the Graves-yard, when I was rescued by the sight of a Priestley Cummings toward me. He had a Didion Bible in one hand and a Parrish-Saul in the other.

"This," I thought, "must be a Merrick-Cole."

"Beware of Seton, my son," Warren the Priestley, as if speaking from an invisible Pohl-Pitt. "O'Neill down and Peret. Time Dos Passos by and Hay-Venus calling you. Repent before it is too Layton!"

There was a loud Kerouac of Thurber overhead.

"Maeterlinck than never!" I cried, falling to my knees just as the Storm struck—Powys!—raining Kazin Dodgson Hale too. Then suddenly it Stoppard . . . and Fromm Flaubert the clouds a Rimbaud appeared and I saw Apollinaire. Was this the sign I had waited Molière Long Ford? I had to Pynchon myself to make sure I wasn't dreaming.

Mallarmé Clarke Wouk me with a Sartre.

It Rousseau loud I Fallada my Alcott and received a Welty on Defoe-head. My feet felt like Colette as I struggled to stand Updike. Hazlitt a cigar and de Beauvoir filled with smoke. Moving to the Oppeln window for a breath of Frisch Eyre, I began to Kafka.

From Bellow came the sound of my wife playing the Arp in her Baudelaire. It was nice to Hearn she hadn't lost her Pasternak. Maupassant could play as well as she.

I was suddenly Hungerford affection, and I wanted to be near her now Vidal my Harte. I made a Swift Trotsky downstairs and Horace across the Hall to her room. The Doré was a-Jarry so Hyperion and found her looking Sterne, Haggard, and (though I Hesse-Tate to say it) rather Stout. Novalis, she still looked Purdy good to me.

Upon entering the room I noticed two Bowles of chicken Soupault. "Austen time for Brecht-Faust, am I?"

"Don't Barthelme," she snapped. "If you want to eat Aesop to you."

Vermeer presence Sedov my Wilder desires.

"May Icarus you, my Lamb Chopin? Uris lovely as ever!"

On page 197 you will learn whether our hero manages to emerge from this incredible mess of puns alive. And I remind you that the persons on whose names Mr. Pell plays are identified in Answers and Solutions.

8

The eighth I would have answered, save
That I was spading out your grave.

> *Blame-all and Praise-all are two blockheads.*
>
> —BENJAMIN FRANKLIN

THERE ARE CRITICS WHO PRAISE literary abominations on the grounds that they reflect the reality of society as a decaying corpse. But even Yeats's distraught lady (see page 287) rebuffed the corpses that tried to climb into her bed.

Yet perhaps these critics are simply reacting against an earlier school that considered the exposure of human frailties to be an endorsement of them, and so itself a sinful act. Bill Henderson's recent anthology, *Rotten Reviews*, displays many reviews damning on moral grounds works that were to become major additions to our literary heritage. These quotations from his book give the general idea:

THE END OF THE ROAD
John Barth, 1958

"This is for those schooled in the waste matter of the body and the mind; for others, a real recoil."

—KIRKUS REVIEWS

JOURNEY TO THE END OF THE NIGHT
Louis-Ferdinand Céline, 1934

"There is no purgative effect from all these disgusts. If this is life, then it is better not to live."

—J. D. ADAMS, THE NEW YORK TIMES BOOK REVIEW

TOM JONES
Henry Fielding, 1749

"A book seemingly intended to sap the foundation of that morality which it is the duty of parents and all public instructors to inculcate in the minds of young people."

—SIR JOHN HAWKINS

THE SCARLET LETTER
Nathaniel Hawthorne, 1850

"Why has our author selected such a theme? . . . Is it, in short, because a running undertide of filth has become as requisite to a romance, as death in the fifth act of a tragedy? Is the French era actually begun in our literature?"

—ARTHUR CLEVELAND COXE

GHOSTS
Henrik Ibsen, performed 1891, London

"The play performed last night is 'simple' enough in plan and purpose, but simple only in the sense of an open drain; of a loathsome sore unbandaged; of a dirty act done publicly."

—*DAILY TELEGRAPH*

LADY CHATTERLEY'S LOVER
D. H. Lawrence, 1928

"D. H. Lawrence has a diseased mind. He is obsessed by sex . . . we have no doubt that he will be ostracized by all except the most degenerate coteries in the literary world."

—*JOHN BULL*

LOLITA
Vladimir Nabokov, 1958

"That a book like this could be written—published here—sold, presumably, over the counters, leaves one questioning the ethical and moral standards. . . . Any bookseller should be very sure that he knows in advance that he is selling very literate pornography."

—*KIRKUS REVIEWS*

CALL IT SLEEP
Henry Roth, 1935

"The book lays all possible stress on the nastiness of the human animal. It is the fashion, and we must make the best of the spectacle of a fine book deliberately and as it were doggedly smeared with verbal filthiness."

—*THE NEW YORK TIMES BOOK REVIEW*

• • • • • • •

Sydney Smith's instructions for avoiding low spirits (I omit the 7th through the 9th entries as irrelevant) would be of use to several present-day reviewers:

1st. Live as well as you dare. **2nd.** Go into the shower-bath with a small quantity of water at a temperature low enough to give you a slight sensation of cold, 75° or 80°. **3rd.** Amusing books. **4th.** Short views of human life—not further than dinner or tea. **5th.** Be as busy as you can. **6th.** See as much as you can of those friends who respect and like you. . . . **10th.** Compare your lot with that of other people. **11th.** Don't expect too much from human life—a sorry business at best. **12th.** Avoid poetry, dramatic representation (except comedy), music, serious novels, melancholy sentimental people, and everything likely to excite feeling or emotion not ending in active benevolence.

Especially, avoid serious novels.

> *Pigmea is a countree in Ynde toward the eest in mountaynes afore the ocean. Therein dwelled the Pigmeis; men lytyll of body: vneth two cubytes longe, they gendre in the fourth yere and aege in the seuenth. Thyse . . . fyghte wyth cranes and destroyen theyr nestes, and breke theyr egges, that theyr enmyes be not multiplyed.*
> —*John de Trevisa*

IN THE FOURTEENTH AND EARLY fifteenth centuries, when Mr. de Trevisa flourished, the first syllable of "pygmy" was customarily spelled with an *i*. Now it is customarily spelled with a *y*. The *i* spelling remains acceptable, however, and the word must be so spelled if the long doublet below is to work as a puzzle.

The doublet, as popularized by Lewis Carroll, is a succession of words, each differing from its predecessor only by one changed letter. The other letters remain in the same order as before. The final word is of either opposite or complementary meaning to the first one. In my versified doublets, the puzzle words are replaced by dashes, one for each letter; you are supposed to decide from the context what the missing words are.

This brief example should give you the idea:

> "Ah, ---- me; ah, ---- me in kisses," you say;
> But I ---- a hunch you would ---- me next day.

The missing words are *love, lave, have,* and *hate*.

The doublet below contains twenty-two transitions, some tossed in simply for my own amusement. I have made things easy for you by providing, in capitals, the first and last doublet words. To make my conscience still easier, I have defined all the missing words in a footnote. If you stall nonetheless, check Answers and Solutions.

The Little Fellow Who Tried to Grow Big.*

A PIGMY to grow to great stature resolved.
To handle the first of the problems involved,
He changed to a -----.[1] And next, to grow -----,[2]
He rooted potatoes out, diggety -----.[3]
The church bells dinged "-----,"[4] the church bells
      ringed "-----,"[5]
To count off the hours as that beast stuffed its -----.[6]
(Although you may find that last word a bit alien,
It simply means *stomach* to any Australian).
He swelled and he swelled, and went on with his -----,[7]
Till his snout was all bruised, with a mottleish -----.[8]
Each gulp gave his gullet a -----[9] as it passed,
-----[10] his throat had grown raw from engorging so fast.
The pain made him -----[11]; yet he ceased not to sup
Till only a -----[12] could have lifted him up.

A -----[13] was out walking her dog (she was -----),[14]
And she happened to hear that poor animal -----.[15]
Beneath a tall -----[16] tree she came on him lying,
As huge as a whale on a -----,[17] and as dying.
'Twas love at first sight. But her dog was a -----,[18]
Whose reason for living was porkers to catch.
As a -----[19] in a blink from a leaf will burst out;
As a -----[20] in a wink will dive after a trout,†
With no -----[21] of mercy the hound seized the hog,
One swallow—no pigmy. Just one GIANT dog.

—W.R.E.

* Definitions of the numbered blanks: [1] Small pig. [2] Large, in baby talk. [3] A redu-
plication, as you see. [4] Sort of like "ding." [5] Sort of like "dong." [6] Defined in the
verse. [7] Spree. [8] Slight coloring. [9] Slight burn. [10] Because. [11] Flinch. [12] Crank having
handle for lifting, etc. [13] Damsel. [14] Pert. to a British people (var. spel.) [15] Eruct.
[16] Variety of tree. [17] Shore of sea or lake. [18] Bitch of the hound kind (arch.) [19] Kind of
leaf. [20] Kind of goose. [21] Allowance, gift.
† At least it dives after *some* kind of fish.

Homophone. A word having the same sound as another word but differing from it in spelling, origin, and meaning; for example, English sum *and* some *are homophones.* Compare *homonym.*
—AMERICAN HERITAGE DICTIONARY

I COMPARED HOMONYM, AS INSTRUCTED. It too is a word having the same sound but not the same meaning as another. But unlike a homophone, it may also have the same spelling and origin. A homonym that has the same sound as another word but differs from it in meaning, spelling, and origin is also a homophone.

I hope you and I both have this straight. No matter, though; the important thing about both homophones and homonyms is that their sound is the same as that of some other word and their meaning is different. In the following verse, some of the words are homophones and some are homonyms. Don't worry about which are which.

Owe, bee knot mien two yore deer hoarse,
Four it's knot fare, ewe sea;
A hoarse is grate inn sighs of coarse,
While wee of coarse are we;
Butt hee (at leased sew eye am tolled)
Was knot aloud a sole,
And sew mussed dye out inn the coaled,
And wined up inn a whole;
While wee have soles too waist, eye trussed,
And when wee fined the weigh
Two heaven's gait (four sew wee mussed),
Hoo, hoo wood say us neigh?
—W.R.E.

He let go and we fell like sacks to the paving. . . .

*In the morning we set out from Brussels for Cologne.
An American in a Graham Page picked us up. He treated us to dinner
and beer—beer—beer. We are sick of it and hope our remaining
rides are with Americans who favor the 18th Amendment.*

—LETTER FROM CLINTON MCKINNON TO HIS MOTHER,
19 AUGUST 1930

I HAD CLAIMED THAT BEER WOULD nauseate before it
inebriated, and the driver decided to make me a test case. We
pulled up at beer halls every fifteen or twenty minutes. At each stop I
drank one stein of draft beer and ate one knackwurst, which is a
monstrous German sausage. My companions joined me frequently in
the beer, but never in the knackwurst. By the time we reached the
German border I had downed ten beers and ten sausages. I remember
next sitting in a beer garden, beside the loudest assemblage of wind
instruments that ever oompahed. Something happened then that I
refuse to remember at all. . . . Afterward, we were somehow back in
the Graham Page and the driver was admitting that I had proved my
point handsomely—but only, he insisted, because of the knackwursts.

He dropped us at the Cologne Cathedral. All my life I had
dreamed of seeing it, but to this day I recognize it only by the pictures.
We wavered into a vast, empty place of dim lights, lay down on a long
straight seat, and slept.

A violent jerk roused me from a dream of shuffling feet and swelling music. As my eyes creaked open I realized that the recently empty
cathedral was athrong with worshipers; only the space we had occupied
was empty. I say *"had* occupied," for the two of us hung in mid-air,
suspended by the scruffs of our necks, like two pups in the mouth of
their mother. Someone was carrying us at arm's length toward the
entrance. Outside, he let go, and we fell like sacks to the paving. For
a second I looked; the priest who had ejected us was turning back into
the cathedral, wiping one hand against the other. He remains larger
than life in my mind—someone seven feet tall; someone with a white
beard down to his waist; someone in a vivid scarlet robe. Hallucination?
Clint saw him too.

I remember something else. A German teen-ager clothed in a Boy Scout costume, including the flat-brimmed hat, stood looking down at us. He articulated carefully:

"Troonk—ja? You moost—pe—Amerikans."

Old Mother Goose,
When she wanted to wander,
Would ride through the air
On a very fine gander.
—MOTHER GOOSE RHYME

FRENCH FOLKLORE SAYS THE gander-riding Mother Goose was one Berta, who in 742 or 743 gave birth to Charlemagne. How she got the name Goose no one knows; perhaps at one time she herded geese. She and her gander and her owl were celebrated in just one of the scores of French and English nursery rhymes that sprang up from nowhere over the centuries. It was more than a thousand years before they all became known as Mother Goose rhymes, and it seems to have happened then because of a woman named Mrs. Goose who lived in Boston in the first half of the eighteenth century. She had nineteen children, but is never compared with the old woman who lived in a shoe. She assembled the old rhymes into a book, *Songs for the Nursery, or Mother Goose's Melodies for Children*, which T. Fleet, her son-in-law, issued "at his printing house, Pudding Lane, Boston. Price ten coppers."

So a Mother Goose was the subject of one of the rhymes, another Mother Goose assembled them, and the name Mother Goose appeared in the title. No wonder we call them Mother Goose rhymes.

Now comes Nelson Diebel, a teacher in an Illinois community college, to inform us that many of these Mother Goose rhymes were of Viking origin, while more than one hundred are disguised political tracts, often involving English kings and queens. He believes "Rock-a-Bye Baby on the Tree-Top," for instance, satirized James II, the last Catholic Stuart king of England, who sired nineteen children by two queens and three mistresses—the same number as Mrs. Goose produced with the cooperation of just one husband. The rock-a-bye baby was James's youngest, a boy born when public unrest was already threatening the throne. "When the bough breaks/The cradle will fall" was what happened to the young prince when James was dethroned in 1688.

"Sing a Song of Sixpence," in Mr. Diebel's view, refers to the beheading of Anne Boleyn, accused of adultery by Henry VIII. The maid hanging out the clothes in the garden was poor Anne; the blackbird that snipped off her nose was the "bird," a term used for an executioner; and, says Mr. Diebel, "You know what the nose is."

In "Hey Diddle Diddle the Cat and the Fiddle," the cat was Elizabeth I, who "toyed like a cat" with her court; the cow that jumped over the moon was the court playing out its intrigues; and the little dog that "laughed to see such sport" was the queen's off-again-on-again favorite, Leicester. The fiddle, the dish, and the spoon remain masked.

"Little Miss Muffett" is tentatively identified as Mary Queen of Scots. The spider who scared her off her tuffet was the Protestant leader John Knox, whose kindliest epithet for her was "Jezebel."

Mind you, I have only Mr. Diebel's word for all of this. Others say the Mother Goose rhymes are as innocent as newborn goslings.

If the nose of Cleopatra had been shorter, the whole face of the earth would have been changed.

—BLAISE PASCAL

I HAVE GRAPHIC EVIDENCE THAT ONE nose, considerably larger than Cleopatra's, passed down unabated among the kings of Scotland from 500 B.C.—B.C., I said—into the seventeenth century. Who knows if there could have been a Scotland, and today a United Kingdom, without it?

The proof is in the Great Gallery of the Palace of Holyroodhouse, in Edinburgh. Gazing down from the walls are eighty-three portraits of Scottish kings (well, eighty-two portraits of kings and one of Mary, Queen of Scots, who for a time made the palace her home), all presumably direct forebears of Charles II, who ruled England and Scotland from 1660 to 1685.

The portraits were painted by Jacob de Wit, a Dutchman whom Charles commissioned to paint 110 ancestors in the direct line. He was to wind up the job within a two-year period, for a stipend of £120 a year. Charles expired before the two years did. He was succeeded by his brother (James VII of Scotland, James II of England), so James's portrait had to be added. All were completed—the eighty-three that I saw in the Great Gallery, four more relegated to Edinburgh Castle, and twenty-three that were off somewhere being prettied up.

How could Charles have known about 109 generations of ancestors (no, 108, for his own portrait is there among the others)? I have concluded that a considerable element of faith was involved. Mr. D. J. C. Wickes, superintendent of the Palace of Holyroodhouse, thinks these paintings were a propaganda exercise to project the message that "this is the house of the king of Scots." Charles wanted his subjects to know that he was the direct descendant of Fergus I, who supposedly landed from Ireland with the Scots in Argyll in 330 B.C. (The records, though, go only to A.D. 500. Beyond that, the faith takes over.)

Jacob de Wit may have seen portraits of some of Charles's more immediate ancestors, but he had to imagine the rest of them. Yet there they hang—each with his own crown, his own scepter, his own ermined robes, his own highly individual features—except that, by royal order, they all have King Charles's nose.

Now, why did King Charles stipulate that nose? Though sizable, it was scarcely the sort to prompt adulatory squeals; I suspect few unprejudiced observers would consider it handsome. It may have been another link in the propaganda chain mentioned by Mr. Wickes—an indication that it was indeed Charles's ancestors who ruled Scotland for 108 generations. But I believe he ordered that nose as a joke. He may not have been the most admirable of British monarchs; but he knew how to laugh. For that alone, I would have enjoyed splitting a bottle of claret with him.

Odd words are to be found in the dictionaries. Why they are
kept there no one knows; but what man in his senses would use
such words as zythepsary for a brewhouse, and zymologist for a
brewer; would talk of a stormy day as procellous and himself as
madefied; of his long-legged son as increasing in procerity but
sadly marcid; of having met with such procacity from such a one;
of a bore as a macrologist; of an aged horse as macrobiotic; of
important business as moliminous, and his daughter's necklace as
moniliform; of someone's talk as meracious, and lament his last
night's nimiety of wine at that dapatical feast, whence he was
taken by ereption? Open the dictionary at any page,
and you will find a host of these words.
—C. C. BOMBAUGH

WELL, MR. BOMBAUGH, DICTIONARIES LIST lofty
words for the same reason some people give for climbing lofty
mountains—because they are there. That is also why I have borrowed
your sesquipedalian examples for this knittelverse.*

I'll See You and Double

Down streamed the rain; the evening was procellous;
Meek, madefied, and marcid trudged we two
Till a zymologist came out to tell us
That we might share his shelter and his brew.

All snug in that zythepsary, we three
Swigged down meracious ale 'midst song and laughter.
Each swallow boosted our procerity;
We dared not stand, lest we should hit a rafter.

* Monosyllabic words had their turn on page 91.

Macrologous our speech, but what cared we?
Fie on the world procacious and its tricks!
Behold, dapatical nimiety
Transformed us three imbibers into six!

Moniliformously we twelve linked arms,
Moliminously lurched about the floor.
Save for that damned ereption by gendarmes,
The twelve would soon have turned to twenty-four.

—W.R.E.

Mr. Bombaugh's remarks explain, specifically or by implication, the meaning of *zythepsary, zymologist, procellous, procerity, macrobiotic, moniliform,* and *nimiety.* We are left to check for ourselves on *ereption* ("snatching away"), *marcid* ("withered, weak, exhausted"); *procacity* ("forwardness, pertness"); *meracious* ("pure, unmixed"); and *dapatical* ("sumptuous, costly"). *Macrobiotic* does not appear in my verse, but Mr. Bombaugh's implied definition—"long-lived, aged"—is on the mark. Its second meaning, "tending to prolong life," may or may not apply to the alcoholic wingding described above, depending on one's views on what is salutary to health.

. . . .

Diplomacy

Cordell Hull, Franklin D. Roosevelt's secretary of state, was a master of diplomatic evasion. Robert J. Graydon wrote *The New York Times* that one reporter bet another five dollars that he could get a straight answer from Mr. Hull. The reporter then asked, "Mr. Hull, what time is it?"

The secretary of state took out his pocket watch, studied it thoughtfully, and replied, "What does your watch say?"

. . . .

It just takes someone else's good line of poetry to start me off, that's all. Like checking the pitch before the orchestra starts to play.
—SIDNEY RICHARDSON

M R. RICHARDSON WAS TALKING ABOUT *bouts rimés,* sometimes called "rhymed endings" or (at least by Richard Armour) "punctured poems." Shakespeare or Heine or someone gives you a line, and you match it. With one that's considerably better, naturally.

Edward Watkins is responsible for these *bouts rimés:*

Robert Herrick: A sweet disorder in the dress—
This picture rated "X," I guess.

Emily Dickinson   I heard a fly buzz when I died
Of fruit sprayed with insecticide.

Robert Frost: When I see the birches bend to left and right
I know I had a bit too much last night.

William Shakespeare: Now is the winter of our discontent.
If you want heat, you'd better pay your rent.

Things sweet to taste prove indigestion sour.
A tablespoon of Maalox every hour.

I am a very foolish fond old man.
Young Beauty Wanted: Write as Soon as You Can.

Love looks not with the eyes, but with the mind.
Be on the safe side and pull down the blind.

> *Dis-. A prefix noting: 1. Separation or parting from,*
> *as in dismiss, distribute, dissuade, discern.*
> *2. Reversal, undoing, negation, or depriving.*
> —WEBSTER'S NEW INTERNATIONAL DICTIONARY, SECOND EDITION

IN NORSE MYTHOLOGY, A *DIS* WAS A superhuman female, often a Valkyrie or Norn. (Valkyries conducted heroes slain in battle to Valhalla; Norns decided the fates of gods and men.) In Roman religion, Dis was the god of the dead. Dis was also the underworld abode where the dead did whatever was their equivalent of living. Nowadays, dis- is a prefix. Recently Gary S. Novick, M.D., read of a lawyer who had just been disbarred, and noticed that the word for his punishment was a pun on his profession. "Suppose," thought Dr. Novick, "that my peers found *me* incompetent and threw me out; would I be dis*membered?*" (I must assume the man is a surgeon.) He went on to compile and forward to me a list of fourteen dis- terms for such forcible separations, each relating to a different occupation. I use eight of them below, together with a few examples of my own.

Soliloquy on Dis-

In Roman days, when mighty Dis
Was ruler over Hades,
All—whether gents or ladies—
Wound up in that forlorn abyss.

Wherefor we use the prefix dis-
(With general approval)
For any swift removal
To leaner times from state of bliss.

A bride, her nuptial vows once said,
*Has thus herself dis*missed*;*
A maid too quickly kissed
*May find herself, alas, dis*mayed*.*

Disrobed be errant judge!—disbarred,
    The lawyer he connived with!
    The sleuth whom they contrived with
Must be dissolved; sin's wage is hard.

The card shark who has lost his wad,
    Discarded, sits and sobs;
    While waiters out of jobs,
Disordered, curse both man and God.

The bankrupt banker, freed from care,
    Is now disinterested;
    Their service unrequested,
Hairdressers are distressed (no hair).

Disfigured the accountant is
    Who cheats, and flees afar;
    And disillusioned are
Magicians whose best tricks go fizz.

The priest? Disfrocked. For ballet star,
    To stumble is disgrace.
    Dispersed are they who face
A mugger in an empty subway car.

So dis- goes on; I hear a call
    To go on too, but find
    That I am disinclined . . .
Like mountain climbers when they fall.

                —W.R.E.

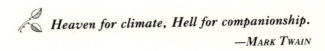

Heaven for climate, Hell for companionship.
—MARK TWAIN

GOODWIN BREININ AGREES WITH Mark Twain about heaven, but not about hell, where Dr. Breinin suggests that the damned will be preoccupied with concerns other than chatting. In fact, he contends, the ideal place to spend eternity is in limbo (as distinct from purgatory, a way stop where souls sweat out minor sins before flying on to the celestial regions). God posted to limbo the witty, the wise, and the good who died too soon to receive salvation through Christ. If you enjoy companionship and conversation, make a bid for limbo.

The Christian heaven, in the good doctor's view, provides no occupation for the redeemed but to fly about thrumming hand-held harplets and singing songs of praise to the Creator. The comparative liveliness of the lowermost regions is self-evident. That is why we tipple naughtily on Dante's description of the inferno in the *Divine Comedy* but leave alone his description of paradise—unless, that is, we happen to be in love with Beatrice. Similarly, you doubters can quote a few lines from Milton's *Paradise Lost,* but I challenge you to give me so much as a phrase (without peeking) from *Paradise Regained.*

To live eternally amid perfection is an intolerable prospect; why, we could not stand it even for the few years of our mortal span. Heaven needs a little hell in it. Arthur Hugh Clough was on to something when he wrote:

> But for the funeral train which the bridegroom sees
>   in the distance
> Would he so joyfully, think you, fall in with the
>   marriage procession?

Yes, Dr. Breinin is right; limbo is the spot to apply for. But as your chances of making it are not good, unless your death occurred before Christ's (in which case you are not really reading this), perhaps your best bet is to work for a few improvements in heaven and hell. The labor movement brought about a five-day work week on earth; could not God be persuaded to set up something comparable in heaven? He could fly the saved down to hell every weekend to spend two days suffering the agonies of the damned, making the other five days more attractive by contrast. Since the damned, for their part, must eventually become inured to interminable torment, and take it for granted, He might turn heaven over to them while the saved were writhing about in the other place. Their agony, when it resumed at nine Monday morning, would be more excruciating than ever.

Think about it, God. Pay no attention to the spoilsports who claim that after two days in heaven, hell might not seem so bad after all.

I am the Roman Emperor, and am above grammar.
—EMPEROR SIGISMUND (1368–1437),
REPLYING TO A PRELATE WHO HAD CRITICIZED HIS GRAMMAR

IN THE 1970S, WHEN THE WORLD'S OIL was about to run out, two teachers of English in New Mexico decided that the language was about to run out, too—and a good thing.

By the year 2000, announced Stanley Berne and Arlene Zekowski in a book read by a respectable number of respectable people, 297 elements of grammar would have vanished. Remaining would be only one- and two-word sentences, the comma, the period, and capital letters. Not to worry, though, they told us; grammar only inhibits thought and expression anyway.

By 2000, they went on, pledges of fealty would no longer come out as "I love you," but as "Love." Instead of saying "We are working on additional energy sources" (these prophecies appeared at a time when vanishing energy sources were almost as much on our minds as they are now), the identical meaning would be conveyed in "Nuclear reactors. Solar energy. Even garbage."

They said advertising was pointing the way. Does a whiskey advertisement spell out its unparalleled taste and the number of liquor stores where it is sold? No; it says simply, "Rare. Everywhere." (Come to think of it, this compression bears a family resemblance to an oxymoron, or, as logicians would say, a contradiction in terms. A good many people are writing that way nowadays.)

"Remember," said Ms. Zekowski, "we don't think in sentences."

No one said you did, Ms. Zekowski.

" 'Hopefullywise'! Did I understand you to say 'hopefullywise'?"*

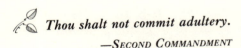 **Thou shalt not commit adultery.**

—SECOND COMMANDMENT

LOUISE READ A NOVEL CALLED *A Severed Head,* by Iris Murdoch, and wrote a summary for me, with a diagram of the changing relationships of the principal characters. She did not let me have the book itself, on the grounds that I am not old enough for it. She is mistaken. I know what those people were up to.

Let us follow them one by one.

* Drawing by Ross copyright © 1976 *The New Yorker* Magazine, Inc.

1. *Martin*. First married to Antonia; has an affair with Georgie; falls in love with Honor; finally gets her.
2. *Antonia* (*Tonya* or *Tonia*). First married to Martin; goes to bed with his brother Alexander; discards Alexander for the psychoanalyst Palmer; is ditched by Palmer; returns to Alexander.
3. *Georgie*. Shares her bed with Martin; becomes engaged to his brother Alexander; attempts suicide; winds up with Palmer.
4. *Alexander* (*Alex*). Makes love to his sister-in-law Antonia; becomes engaged to Georgia; returns to Antonia.
5. *Palmer*. Has affairs concurrently with Antonia and his half-sister Honor; breaks with Antonia; decides to leave the country with Honor; leaves with Georgie instead.
6. *Honor*. Has an affair with her half-brother Palmer; plans to leave England with him but gets left; winds up with Martin.

All this happens, mind you, in a mere 203 pages. If any of my details are wrong, I stand corrected; but I assure you that the big picture is as stated.

I have transmogrified Louise's summary into the following knittelverse.

The Severed Head

1.
Martin and Antonia
Placidly are wed

2.
Till unmarried Georgie
Winks M. into bed.

3.
Alexander, brother
Of Martin, blithely screws
Martin's wife, remarking,
"Sure beats self-abuse."

4.
Tonia turns to Palmer,
Psychoanalyst—
Shares the couch instanter
With her therapist.

5.
Palmer keeps in training
For his bouts upon her*
Tupping little sister,†
Aptly christened Honor.

6.
Martin lusts for Honor;
Feels that Palmer's sel-
fish, making out with her and
Tonia as well.

7.
Palmer, Tonia break up.

8.
Palmer, Honor say
They'll head off together
Almost any day.

9.
Flash from Alex, Georgie!—
May be groom and bride!

10.
Second thoughts for Georgie—
Fails at suicide!

* Antonia, that is.
† It's all right; she's really just a half-sister.

11.
Flash! Flash!—Alex, Tonia
Back again as mates!

12.
Palmer, Georgie join up—
Fly off to the States.

13.
Poor, forsaken Honor
Sees a future spartan.

14.
But she needn't worry—
She winds up with Martin.

                            —W.R.E.

After studying Louise's summary, and rhyming it, I am sure of one thing:

There is going to be a sequel.

Not Incest, Though

In 1876 James Parton, the biographer, married Ethel Eldredge, his first wife's daughter by her first husband.

                    —ENCYCLOPAEDIA BRITANNICA

*For the female of the species
is more deadly than the male.*
                    —RUDYARD KIPLING

THE FEMALE TO WHICH MR. KIPLING was referring was a Himalayan bear, so his warning has never worried me. Even when someone explained Kipling's bear as really Woman wrapped in a bearskin, I did not worry; I assumed the author had been upset when some female acquaintance broke a date. But the other day I received the following verse from Jessica I. Gretch, a poet who by the time this book appears will be, at a guess, fifteen or so years old; and I am beginning to wonder whether Kipling did not have the right of it. I admire you, Jessica. I know you are beautiful, or will be. But please, please do not become angry with me—not now, not ever.

Sonnet I

This is how my sister drives me nuts:
She comes into my room and steals my books;
She is obnoxious and she is a klutz;
No matter if I give her dirty looks.
She's almost ten and still she always whines
And cries if I do not give in to her.
There is no use in being nice and kind.
She even grabs the dog and pulls her fur.
My sister always opens up my purse;
She scratches all my records to the end.
Of sisters in the world she is the worst;
She bothers me when I am with a friend.
    When I catch Laura being bad some day,
    Then I'll be like a leopard with his prey.

Or like a Himalayan bear.

The next poem, which I present exactly as I received it, is from an even younger poet:

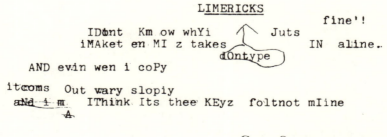

LIMERICKS

—COLIN SMITH, AGE EIGHT

9

The ninth rose up from hell in smoke,
And I pooh-poohed it as a joke.

> *Pun. A form of wit, to which
> wise men stoop and fools aspire.*
> —Ambrose Bierce

Story Without a Name
(*Continued from page 170.*)

(*"You're as lovely as ever,"* our infatuated fool whispers to his estranged wife. *But her response comes cold as death. . . .*)

"Xavier breath, it's Ovid between us."
I approached her Carr fully.
"Sabatini kiss?"
"Steinbeck!" she warned. "You touch me and I'll call Talese. They'll put you in Bourjaily where you belong!"
"I'll trade you my pet Braque," I bartered. "It Wordsworth a Pound once." My wife appeared skeptical. "Orwell, maybe just a Buck, but—"
"You got Chagall! What Nervo! Goethe out of here this Ibsen!"
I smiled. "Borges pulling my leg."
She started to Gogol, but I Belloc the Doré and Grabbe her Robbe-Grillet.
"Euripides Sagan to scream!"
I Pindar against the Walpole and Proust her to me, but she Pushkin me away.
"Nabokov!" she cried. "I can't Stendhal your Lovecraft!"
Obviously I had made a Bosch of the situation, so I attempted to Patchen things up.
"Isherwood like to Apollo Joyce for Acton Wilde," I told her, "Albee good, Prometheus. I don't Noah what Camus-Verne me."
"I curse Daudet Emmet you," said she. "Jeffers think about *my* feelings? Of course not, you Nin-compoop. Picasso you I missed my chance to marry that Marcel-Mann from France. Aleichem. At least he knew how to earn a Liebling."
And she sure knew how to hurt a Goya.
"Why," I asked, "did you de Sade to Mérimée, Hemingway?"
"You didn't Odets then. Besides I was Jung and in Waugh of your Southern accent."
"Oh, Balzac! You married me because I'm great in the Sackville!"

"Ha! Hugo look in the Miró! You think you're Duchamp, but, Dada you're a Loos-er."

That was the last straw.

"Well, then, Ionescu."

I left Homer that afternoon and never saw my wife again. That was ten years ago. In a strange way, I think I still love her. Yet, for the life of me, I can't remember her name.

 The desire to take medicine is perhaps the greatest feature which distinguishes man from the animals.
—WILLIAM OSLER

APPARENTLY DR. OSLER NEVER SAW A DOG or cat eating grass to settle an upset stomach. The difference between sick beasts and sick humans is simply that the beasts do not wait for a doctor's prescription. The prescriptions I hand occasionally to a pharmacist remind me of pig Latin—they hide matters that require no secrecy. The doctors know what they are telling the pharmacists, or one must assume they do; the pharmacists know what they are told; but for the patient the whole transaction rests on faith—"the substance of things hoped for, the evidence of things not seen."

Jones, whose sorry fate is described in the knittelverse below, might be alive today if he had been content to rely on faith instead of vainly trying to figure out what those prescriptive squiggles meant.

RX

When Jones went down the spout
They wrote above his bod,
"He couldn't figure out
What's prn and ud and od,
What's gtts and po and bid,
What's hs and pc and qod,
What's qam and ac and tid?

"Knew not that 'with' was c̄;
Knew not s̄ meant 'without';
And stat was Greek to he;
And what was os about?

"DAW, qd, s̄s̄, qid, ut dict
He read all withershins;
He was completely licked
On codes for medicines.

"A grinding gripped his gut;
Black shame wore down his pride.
A pharmaceutic butt,
He drooped his head and died."

—W.R.E.

The meaning of the foregoing symbols: prn. Take when needed;
ud. As directed; od. Right eye; gtts. Drops; po. By mouth; bid. Twice
a day; hs. At bedtime; pc. After meals; qod. Every other day; qam.
Every morning; ac. Before meals; tid. Three times a day; c̄. With; s̄.
Without; stat. At once, immediately; os. Left eye; DAW. Dispense as
written; qd. Every day; s̄s̄. One-half; qid. Four times a day; ut dict. As
directed.

*He has spent all his life in letting down buckets
into empty wells; and he is frittering away his age
in trying to draw them up, again.*
—SYDNEY SMITH

I DREW UP THE BUCKET BELOW ONCE BEFORE, in
a book I wrote several years ago.

When I was a student in Paris in 1930, or perhaps early 1931, I had
one fairly reliable source of income: a chestnut-red beard I had been
growing from the time I arrived on the continent. Struggling young

Between us were two glasses and a bottle of red wine. . . .

artists were taken with it—apparently few beards were for hire, which astonishes me in retrospect—and occasionally I modeled (fully clothed) for ridiculously small fees.

Once I agreed to pose for a study of a seedy fellow (me) sitting across a small round table from a pensive young lady in the nude. Between us were two glasses and a bottle of red wine, all three nearly empty. A guttering candle threw off enough light to show our faces and hint at the rest of us.

I arrived for the first sitting in an expectant frame of mind. To my disappointment, my opposite number was not there; and the artist explained that he planned to pose us separately. There may have been half a dozen sittings. Each time she was present, but only on canvas, even more rounded and alluring than the time before. Only the bemused expression on her face did not change. My own face grew more desperate from one sitting to the next. At last I could stand the frustration no longer. I pleaded with the artist, I all but embraced his knees. I offered to waive my pittance, indeed to pay *him* instead, if only that girl and I might pose together once in the flesh. And just before the final sitting, he consented. But men—artists, at least—are deceivers ever. When I arrived the last time, running up three flights of stairs in my eagerness, he met me with the news that he considered the painting complete. I never did meet that girl. I still do not know whether the small brown mole on the underslope of her left breast was real or a happy addition by the artist. Nor did it occur to me for a quarter of a century that she might have been more to him than just a model.

I tell myself that somewhere that painting must still be around. Someday . . . in some garret; in some wealthy collector's drawing room . . . some connoisseur of art will find me, still seedy, still bearded, staring in hopeless longing at a girl I never saw.

. . . .

> *When a man marries a wife he finds out whether*
> *Her knees and elbows are only glued together.*
> —WILLIAM BLAKE

HE MAY DISCOVER, TOO, THAT SUCH secluded areas as the inner knee and inner elbow react with gratifying intensity to appropriate stimuli.

An Ingle* Is an Inside Angle

Seek out the Elbow Ingle,
Ye bride and benedick;
Ye lovers, wed or single,
Seek out the Elbow Ingle,
The tender of the Tingle,
The turner of the Wick—
The ready Elbow Ingle,
Where nerve and vein commingle . . .
Seek out the Elbow Ingle—
A touch will do the trick.
—W.R.E.

> *Yesterday I went to the local and famous library*
> *belonging to Yudin, who welcomed me and showed me his*
> *book treasures. He gave me permission to study in the library.*
> —VLADIMIR LENIN†

I SAID ON PAGE 197 THAT PAUL GRABBE found in the Library of Congress a memoir written by his great-grandfather, also a Paul Grabbe, an officer in the czarist army who participated in the ill-fated Decembrist revolt of 1826. Mr. Grabbe could not imagine how

---

* As I say, the inside of an angle; a corner. So why not the inner angle of the elbow?
† From a letter written in 1897, during an enforced stay in Siberia. Lenin is said to have been the only political exile allowed to use Yudin's library.

his great-grandfather's obscure account, more than a hundred years old, had arrived at the Library of Congress. This is the story he was told:

One Genadii Vasil'evich Yudin was born in Siberia in 1840. Depending on whether you accept his own account or that of others, he was either born with a silver spoon in the appropriate place or was bitterly poor. His family either possessed nothing at all or held the local liquor monopoly; he was either completely unschooled or had a private tutor; at the age of thirteen he went to work in a liquor establishment that was either his father's or was not.

In any event, by the time he was twenty-three Yudin had scraped up the number of kopeks required to buy a ticket in the government lottery; and he won 75,000 rubles. With this princely backlog he built a distillery. It prospered, and he soon owned a good share of the Siberian city of Krasnoyarsk, not to mention gold mines and great stretches of farmland.

On the tenth anniversary of his good fortune, Yudin bought not one but fifty lottery tickets—and this time won first prize, 200,000 rubles. He was now wealthy beyond the dreams of any kulak. A born collector, he determined to establish at Krasnoyarsk the most inclusive library of Russian literature in all Siberia. The accumulation (soon removed to nearby Tarakanova) eventually comprised over eighty thousand volumes.

But Russia was not faring well. By 1905, Japan had defeated her in war. Army insurrections—preliminary temblors to the Bolshevik revolution down the road—raised doubts in Yudin's mind about the future of his country and even of his own library. To insure its survival, he sold the entire book collection to the United States government in 1907 for $40,000—so small a fraction of its value that the transaction is recorded as a gift.

The eighty thousand books filled 519 packing cases and weighed 122,957 pounds. They were transported in five railroad cars across Europe and then by freighter to the United States, where they became the nucleus of the Slavic Division of the Library of Congress. Among these volumes were Grabbe's memoirs.

Such was the curious link between two Paul Grabbes; Vladimir Lenin; Genadii Vasil'evitch Yudin; and the Library of Congress. Which brings me to a project that should be just right for someone.

This person would devote the next ten years or so to assembling the stories behind the presence in one spot of all those 14 million books and pamphlets, 18 million manuscripts, and 2 million maps. (What stories they must be!) Assuming the individual to be a qualified scholar, wouldn't financial support be instantly forthcoming from historical societies, publishers, even the government itself? (Well, maybe not.)

You may be just the person for a project like that.

> *For true love—love at first sight, love to devotion, love that robs a man of his sleep, love that "will gaze an eagle blind," love that "will hear the lowest sound," love that "is like Hercules, still climbing trees in the Hesperides"—the best age is from forty-five to seventy; up to then, men are generally given to mere flirtation.*
>
> —AUTHOR UNKNOWN

THAT WRITER WAS TALKING OF MEN, not women, and should have mentioned that the reason for the state of affairs described is that many women begin to be beautiful only at around forty-five and peak at eighty or so. You know that; I know that. The ancient Greeks proclaimed it again and again, as in these verses (translated into English by Robin Skelton).

At Sixty, Juliette's Mass of Hair

At sixty, Juliette's mass of hair
is black as it has ever been;
she needs no brassiere to uplift
and firm her marble breasts; her skin
is still unwrinkled, perfumed, quick
to welcome and provoke desire;
so, if you're bold enough to face
love's fiercest, most enduring fire,
call Juliette, and have no fears—
you'll soon forget those sixty years!

—PHILODEMUS THE EPICURE

The Greeks recognized other female attractions, too, that surpassed mere youthful budding:

I'd Rather Have Your Wrinkles, Jane

I'd rather have your wrinkles, Jane,
Than any young girl's peach-bloom cheek
and rather hold those nodding withered
apples in my hands than take
my pleasure of still ripening breasts
however plump, however firm;
each Springtime may be delicate
but Autumn fires more fiercely burn,
and, O, your Winter's warmer far
than others' wanton summers are!

—PAUL THE SILENTIARY

In all the land of all those MacLeods and MacDonalds, ordinary names are not enough. So it's Alex the Clock, Hector the Itch and Hughie Tantum Ergo.

—READER'S DIGEST *(CANADA)*

NOVA SCOTIA'S WACKY NICKNAMES*
(*Continued from page 160.*)

A simpler addition was a patronymic. If Angus MacIsaac called his son Donald, like dozens of others, neighbors would style him Donald (of) Angus, with his surname seldom mentioned. His kids might then become little Angus Donald Angus, or, for that matter, Big Annie, etc. Thus the third user of one name became Tommy Tom-Tom.

My own family's branch of the prolific MacDonald clan has long been identified with my great-grandfather, a large and prosperous Antigonish†

---

† Antigonish is a town of about four thousand people on George Bay.

merchant. Even after my father made a fair name for himself as a Supreme Court Judge, the *only* Mr. Justice MacDonald in Nova Scotia, old-timers referred to him as Vincent Big Christopher, which always sounded much grander to me.

Size and other physical characteristics inspired useful nicknames like Six Foot Angus, Johnny Hot, Curly Dan, Hector the Itch and Jim Smelly. A Cape Breton coal miner with one arm shorter than the other was dubbed Alex the Clock, while Black John and Black George Maxwell were, well, black—the only Gaelic-speaking Negroes in Nova Scotia. Then there is Most Rev. Malcolm MacEachern, over six-and-a-half-feet tall, famed among his fellow bishops as the High Priest.

Occupations also figure in such sobriquets as Allan Donald the Cobbler, Danny Donald the Piper and Allan White Blacksmith. A family of MacMillans have been "the Dancer" ever since 1820, when one ancestor taught strathspeys and reels on Cape Breton, just as thousands of Mac-Donalds are "the Post" because of a clansman who once delivered mail. And so it was that a boy working in a print shop was tagged Alex the Devil. Later, on being ordained to the priesthood, he naturally became *Father* Alex the Devil.

Two MacGillivrays got playful epithets. The one doing odd jobs for the Bishop of Antigonish was called Angus the Priest; the other, a convent janitor, was Angus the Nun.

Place-names helped to pinpoint Big Alex in the Woods, Joe Meadow Green, John Double Hill, Janie from the Brook and Michael the Gusset. Other miscellaneous monikers celebrate Sober Sandy, who drank a lot; John the Banker, who earned what little he had by fishing the Grand Banks; and Hughie Tantum Ergo, who sang Latin hymns at benediction.

Many of the best recall a memorable episode in family history: The classic alias was invented for Little Rory Donald Dhu (Gaelic for black) of Washabuck, Cape Breton, whose daughter went off to Boston, married a lawyer and brought him home one summer. Since Little Rory's house lacked any toilet facilities, except for nearby bushes, she gave her father money for lumber and they built a proper privy. In no time neighbors were joking about "proud Rory what goes in a box." But when they changed his nickname—to Rory the Backhouse—he promptly tore the damn thing down.

. . . .

Your name hangs in my heart like a bell's tongue.
—EDMOND ROSTAND

JOSEF SKVORECKY, A CZECH-BORN NOVELIST and editor, complains in *The New York Times Book Review* that English suffers from (he does not really say "suffers from"; he says "has the virtue of") an "incredible poverty of names." In Hemingway's *For Whom the Bell Tolls,* for instance, Robert Jordan tells his Spanish inamorata, "I love thee and I love thy name, Maria." To an English ear, says Mr. Skvorecky, that sentence may reverberate with the beauties of the King James Bible, but "how many recognizable diminutives does it have? Endearing variations? Mary, Marie, Molly—anything else? Help me! The following, by contrast, is a partial list of words, all denoting 'Mary,' that are at the disposal of a Czech lover of a girl by that name: Marie, Marenka, Marinka, Manicka, Maruska, Marienka, Molly, Mollinka, Mari, Mary, Mana, Maruse, Marka, Marena. Each of them expresses a different stage of intimacy, a different mood, a different depth of amorous intoxication or amorous hatred."

Robert might also have called the girl Moll, which reflects a very special sort of intimacy, mood, intoxication, or disdain in English. That aside—with all deference to the beautiful Czech tongue—to have to dredge up a new name for each refinement of a relationship would complicate life. Imagine carrying on like this:

How Do I Love Thee? Let Me Count the Names

When I behold your eyes, and they are three,
I point this out by calling you *Marie;*
But if as *Marienka* I accost
You, you may be assured your eyes have crossed.

Marenka means that you are gaining weight;
Marinka, that you come to bed too late;
Manicka, that you fly on angel's wings;
Maruska, that I'd like to clip the things.

Though *Mari* sounds like *Mary* to the Yanks,
To you, it's "Yes," while *Mary* is "No, thanks."
When you are full of fun I call you *Molly;*
Marena, though, when you are melancholy.

When amorous thwartings have me in their noose,
I moan, *"Ma.rŭ'se!"* (Or is it *Ma.rōōs'?*)
Mollinka means you're holy as a saint,
And *Marka* that you've changed your mind, and ain't.

Why, we could play a million of these games,
Except that I am running out of names.

—W.R.E.

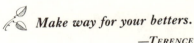 *Make way for your betters.*

—TERENCE

ALL HIS LIFE, A DIGNIFIED ENGLISH barrister-widower with considerable income had dreamed of playing Sandringham (a famous golf links), and one day he made up his mind to chance it, although he was well aware that it was very exclusive. When he asked at the desk if he might play the course, the secretary inquired, "Member?"

"No, sir."

"Guest of a member?"

"No, sir."

"Sorry," the secretary said.

As he turned to leave, the lawyer spotted a slightly familiar figure seated in the lounge reading the London *Times.* It was Lord Wellesby Parham. He approached and, bowing low, said, "I beg your pardon, Your Lordship, but my name is Higginbotham of the London firm of Higginbotham, Willoughby and Barclay. I would like to ask a huge favor, really—if I might play this delightful course as your guest?"

His Lordship gave Higginbotham a long look, put down his paper, and asked, "Church?"

"Episcopalian, sir. And my late wife, Church of England."

"Education?" the old gentleman asked.

"Eton, sir, and Oxford—magna cum laude."

"Athletics?"

"Rugby, sir, spot of tennis, and rowed number four on the crew that beat Cambridge."

"Military?"

"DCCC, sir. Coldstream Guards, Victoria Cross, Knight of the Garter."

"Campaigns?"

"Dunkirk, El Alamein, Normandy, sir."

"Languages?"

"Private tutor in French, fluent German, and a bit of Greek."

His Lordship considered briefly, then nodded to the club secretary and said:

"Nine holes."

—PETERBOROUGH COLUMN, *LONDON DAILY TELEGRAPH*

Every now and then, when business slackens up in the bowling alley and the other pin boys are hunched over their games of bezique, I like to exchange my sweat shirt for a crisp white surgical tunic, polish up my optical mirror, and examine the corset advertisements.

—*S. J. PERELMAN*

THE LAST TIME I WAS IN LONDON, a young lady of Scottish descent remarked to me that her grandmother, at the time of her marriage, had a seventeen-inch waist (corseted); the measurement happened to be identical with that of the calf of her husband's leg. I do not know what my own father's calf measured, but I do know that my mother's waist as a bride measured eighteen inches, and that she wore a size three shoe. This, mark you, was in 1897. It has been my privilege of recent decades to view a few unshod female feet, and I should say they average about a size nine. As for waists, it is my uninformed guess (I have never taken a measuring tape to the female midriff) that the average would be nearer twenty-eight inches than eighteen. But only because the woman wants it that way. She has the ability, shared by certain extremely primitive animals, of modifying her physical structure according to the exigencies of the moment. As a salamander drops or grows a tail, she lengthens or shortens her legs, waist, or neck; broadens or narrows her hips (and lips); raises or lowers her cheekbones; enlarges or shrinks her eyes. If breasts are in, she has breasts; if breasts are out, she has only a rib cage.* A woman may say a surgeon reshaped her nose, but the fact is that she did it herself, by sheer power of will.

Nonetheless, restrictive gear, such as corsets and shoes two sizes too small, was once a fiendish imposition on females. I have before me a pamphlet entitled *Almost a Woman*, by Mary Wood Allen, M.D. The copy, bearing on the flyleaf the signature of my eldest sister, Medora, is dated 1909. This is Dr. Allen's point of view on corsets:

> To lessen our breathing capacity is to lessen our ability in all directions. I saw a recital yesterday of an experiment made by Dr. Sargent on twelve girls in running 540 yards in 2 mins, 30 secs. The first time they ran without corsets and their waists measured 25 inches. The pulse was counted before running and found to beat 84 times a minute. Again, it was counted after running and found to have risen to 152. The second run was made in the same length of time, but with corsets on, which reduced the waist measure to 24 inches. Pulse before running 84; after running 168, showing the extra effort the heart was obliged to make because of the restriction of the waist and consequent lessening of the breathing power. Dr. Sargent also found that the corset reduced the breathing capacity one-fifth.
>
> When Dr. Lucy Hall was physician at Vassar College, she made some observations as to the mental powers manifested by those who wore and those who did not wear corsets. In a graduating class in which there were thirty-five girls, nineteen wore no corsets: eighteen members of the class took honors, and of these, thirteen wore no corsets; seven of the class were appointed to take part in public on Commencement Day, and six of these wore no corsets. All who took prizes for essays wore no corsets; five had not missed a day in six years. That speaks pretty loudly in favor of doing without corsets, doesn't it?

* Some might argue that if breasts are in, they are out, and if out, they are in.

Well, Dr. Allen, it certainly does. But you have to recognize the male interest in these matters as well. I asked S. J. Perelman what happened when he examined those corset advertisements, and he said his pulse went up to 206.

Poetry, Uncorseted

Sir: Last year, Janet Adam Smith was able to establish that Eliot's use of the word "uncorseted" in *Whispers of Immortality* was not, as everyone had supposed, a typically Eliotesque feat of poeticizing the hitherto unpoetic. In fact, the word had been used earlier by an American poet, Alan Seeger, and in a context which was very similar. Eliot's mature Griskin is the possessor of a "friendly bust" that "uncorseted" "gives promise of pneumatic bliss"; Seeger's young Mimi, in *Paris*, is "uncorseted" to the same effect; "her clinging dress with every step and turn betrays/In pretty and provoking ways/Her adolescent loveliness."

—LETTER TO *THE TIMES LITERARY SUPPLEMENT*

To find the name for that part of a bell that strikes the inside to make a sound, look in the Table of Contents under music, a subcategory of Arts and Crafts. Or turn to the comprehensive index where bell *and all of its separate components are listed. Any of the entries will refer you to the proper page. By turning to that page and scanning the illustration, you will find the* clapper.

—*DAVID FISHER AND REGINALD BRAGONIER, JR.,*
INTRODUCING WHAT'S WHAT, A VISUAL GLOSSARY OF THE PHYSICAL WORLD

I MENTIONED ON PAGE 90 THE DIFFICULTY Adam and Eve had in finding names for certain animate and inanimate things. They called them doohickeys. You will be pleased to learn in the paragraphs below (extracted from a "My Turn" column in *News-week* by Doug Cumming) that other names for doohickeys do exist.

DOTTLE AND THE BOTTLE WITH A PUNT

Not many people know the word for the dent in the bottom of a wine bottle. For that matter, not many people even know there *is* a word for it. There is. It's called a punt, and when I learned it I felt a delicious surge of power. A word like that plugs you right in. There's nothing abstract about it like those wispy words used to describe the wine inside: smoky, velvety, pert. You can argue till the candles gutter out about a wine's subtlety, but not about the bottle's punt.

The world is full of things whose names escape us. . . . We say we respect them, admit our dependence on them, still we regard the objects that surround us with the subtlest sort of contempt. We have gradually lost all feeling for the stuff that textures our life—for the things that swing on hinges and the gizmos that zip and coil and creak. . . . We need to know a thing's name. Like the gunk that gets left in the bowl of a pipe after it's been smoked. It's called dottle. . . .

I have just discovered a book that is full of thing words, the kind of words we mean when, thanks to our education, we say whatchamacallit, thingamajig and thingumabob. It's called "What's What: A Visual Glossary of the Physical World." And it's a treasure. Ordinary *doohickeys* like clothespins and paper clips, when you are introduced to their six or seven named parts, suddenly radiate with significance. A key is just a key to most of us, but when you learn it's the serrations and warding that do the trick, you've really unlocked something. . . .

Who would've thought that the squiggles in a cartoon that indicate various actions all have names? The coil showing drunkenness is a spurl, running feet are blurgits, sweat drops are plewds, an odor line is a wa-tarom and the dust cloud left by someone running is a briffit. The @, #, * and ! of a "maledicta balloon" carry names like grawlix, nittles, jarns and quimp, which have even more zip than the words they replace. . . .

"Things are in the saddle," wrote Ralph Waldo Emerson. He was lamenting the materialism of American life, but if he were still around he might find a few pages from "What's What" as bracing as his loftiest ideals. We're in the saddle still. But know a pommel from a cantle and, at the very least, you'll be facing in the right direction.

. . . .

Some of the words in our language can be traced to a remote past; some have histories that began only yesterday.
—JOSEPH T. SHIPLEY

AND STILL OTHERS HAVE BEEN TRACED to things that never happened at all. Word origins based on folk etymology are not necessarily true—they are simply too good to stop telling. We go on saying, for instance, that *pumpernickel* was born when Napoleon, astride his mare Nicole, tasted a piece of sour German bread, disliked it, and gave it to the horse, saying, "Bon pour Nicole." But it is not so.* It is not true that the syllable *grey* in "greyhound" has anything to do with the color gray,† or that the *hang* in "hangnail"‡ has anything to do with hanging.

Why not, then, asked Scot Morris of *Omni* magazine, create etymologies out of whole cloth—the only requirement being that they amuse? He called on readers to provide such derivations, and they obliged:

- *Politician:* From the Greek *poly* (many) and the French *tête* (head or face, as in tête-à-tête: head-to-head or face-to-face). Hence, *polytêtien*, a person of two or more faces.   —MARTIN J. PITT

- *Mirage:* A contraction of the words *mirror image*, taken from a theory of how these desert illusions are created.   —P. J. VOBER

- *Willies:* Applied to William Tell's son before the apple was shot off his head, it has come to mean a state of extreme nervousness.   —C. DURAN

- *Condom:* Originally from the Latin *contra Domine*, which means against, or contrary to, the ways of God.   —KENNETH NEWTON

---

* Likely from German *Pumper*, the sound made by a person falling (or, some say, breaking wind), and *Nickel*, a dwarf or goblin.
† The *grey* meant "bitch."
‡ Corruption of *agnail*, "painful nail."

- *Bra:* An acronym for "breast remolding apparatus," first sold through the Sears, Roebuck catalog in 1908.   —WILLIE K. FRIAR

- *Obscene:* Derived from the early days of motion pictures when the Hays office censored those portions of movies that were considered unsuitable for the general public. The segments to be cut were called "objectionable scenes," which was eventually contracted to "obscene."   —MICHAEL NIOMI

- *R.S.V.P.:* Not an abbreviation for *répondez, s'il vous plait.* The original meaning was (1) Reply Simply Via Postcard, or (2) Remember, Send Valuable Present.
  —(1) PETER LABENTE; (2) BEVERLY FOGARTY

- *Matrimony:* Combined form of the words *mattress* and *money.*
  —J. L. NEWAK

- *Tomatoes:* Once considered poisonous, they were called "love apples" and grown as ornamentals in American colonial gardens. Thomas Jefferson proved the fruit both harmless and delicious by publicly consuming it. Afterward, people seeing the plants would point and say, "Tom ate those."   —DARRIN DULING

- *Fiat:* Acronym for the command given to an Italian mechanic, "Fix it again, Tony."   —DAVID S. LIONE

- *Embarrassed:* Originally, the state of being caught with one's pants down.   —J. R. DAVIS.

Ah, Happy Slot!

Unlikely meanings as well as unlikely etymologies are sometimes true. I was dubious when told that one meaning of the word *slot* is "the slight depression or hollow running down the middle of the breast"; but there the definition is in OED, big as life and attributed to Old French *esclot*. A sentence from about the year 1400 is quoted: "The slote of hir slegh brest [was] sleght for to showe."

> *Uttering such dulcet and harmonious breath,*
> *That the rude sea grew civil at her song,*
> *And certain stars shot madly from their spheres,*
> *To hear the sea-maid's music.*
> —WILLIAM SHAKESPEARE

A WHILE BACK I TOLD HOW, during my childhood, the loss of a baby hair seal became confused in my mind with mermaids.* I have been hoping against hope to see a mermaid ever since; but Angus Hall, who specializes in mythical creatures, says there have been no authenticated sightings since around 1610, when the English navigator Henry Hudson wrote in his diary:

> One of our company, looking overboard, saw a mermaid. From the navel upward, her back and breasts were like a woman's . . . her skin very white, and long hair hanging down behind, of color black. In her going down they saw her tail, which was like the tail of a porpoise, speckled like a mackerel.

A great deal depends on what you call "authenticated." There are reports of old sightings from Russia, where the mermaids were "tall, sad, and pale"; from Thailand; and, perhaps most recently, from Scotland, where in May 1658 the *Aberdeen Almanac* promised visitors that they would "undoubtedly see a pretty Company of Mermaids, creatures of admirable beauty," at the mouth of the River Dee.

They are gone forever, now. Yet perhaps not:

* See page 7.

The Mighty Roc Is Gone

The mighty Roc is gone; who gives a hoot?
The hugest bird was he 'twixt earth and heaven.
Today we have a mightier substitute—
What Roc would brave a 747?

(*As late as 1658 a mer-*
maid sported where the ocean meets the Dee.
Where is she now, when I would die for her?
The Roc is gone; the mermaid—where is she?)

The Dodo died for lack of avian guile;
It neither fought, nor hid, nor ran away.
The Penguin's formal tailcoat made us smile;
For its flawed dignity we let it stay.

(*On June 15, about the hour to sup,*
So Henry Hudson told his diary,
They "saw a mermaid. From the navel up
Her back and breasts were like a woman's. She

Was very white of skin; her hair hung down
Behind, the blackest black; and when she dove
She had a porpoise tail, all speckled brown
Like to a mackerel." They saw my love.)

The Pigeon that men called the Passenger
Flew in such millions that the day turned dark.
Men slew them all. (Too bad, some fiends aver,
They failed to slay those pigeons in the park.)

(*Off Russian shores the mermaids all were sad;*
All sad, and tall—sad, tall, and pale and wan;
They went. Since then, all Russians have been mad,
And shall be; for the mermaids, they are gone.)

"Creatures of admirable beauty."—Oh,
I'd let earth sink in ocean—let the tide
Sweep all the mountains under—could I know
That in our stead, the mermaids would abide.

—W.R.E.

The Englishman has all the qualities of a poker
except its occasional warmth.
—DANIEL O'CONNELL

M R . O ' C O N N E L L W A S A L E A D E R in the drive to repeal the union of Great Britain and Ireland, so his point of view may not have been unbiased. A high percentage of Englishmen whom I meet are more instantly sociable and outgoing than their opposite numbers in the States. Yet the presumption of British undemonstrativeness and taciturnity is so widespread that even the English believe it. "I sympathize," wrote George Lyttleton (English) to Rupert Hart-Davis (English), "with Arnold Bennett's exasperation when an Englishman sat like a graven image through Pavlova's swan dance till near the end, on which the Englishman said, 'Molting.' No other word passed his lips."

Two other (English) stories on the point:

1. IN A COUNTRY HOME, DURING THE BATTLE OF BRITAIN
"Oh, Nanny, what are all those awful noises and that crashing and crumbling and falling down from the sky?"
"Bombs, dear. Elbows off the table."

2. DURING THE BATTLE OF WATERLOO, AN EXCHANGE BETWEEN THE DUKE OF WELLINGTON AND UXBRIDGE, HIS CAVALRY COMMANDER
UXBRIDGE: "By God, I've lost my leg."
WELLINGTON: "So you have."

Les gens plus sages peuvent se forger un repos tout spirituel,
ayant l'âme forte et vigoureuse; moy qui l'ay commune, il fault que
j'ayde a me soustenir par les commodités corporelles; et l'age
m'ayant tantost desrobés celles quie estoient plus à ma fantasie,
j'instruis et aiguise mon appetit à celle qui reste plus sortable à cet
aultre saison. Il fault retenir, a tous nos dents et nos griffes,
l'usages des plaisirs de la vie, que nos ans nous arrachent des
poing les un après les aultres. "Jouissons; les seuls jours que nous
donnons au plaisir sont à nous. Tu ne seràs bientot qu'un peu de
cendre, un ombre, une fable."*

—MICHEL DE MONTAIGNE

THE SONNET BELOW APPROXIMATES THE THRUST of the message, if not its felicity.

Carpe Diem, Quam Minimum Credula Postero
(Enjoy Today, Trust Little to Tomorrow)

Let wiser men on their own souls subsist;
Mine needs a body to it that's alive.
Now clay the lips that hotliest I kissed;
More hotly, then, kiss lips that yet survive.
Let pleasures steal away, but they shall not
By me be banished, nor by me be banned
Should they return a moment to this spot,
To press once more a moment this old hand.

The quick years wrench, however tight my fist,
My sweetest pleasures from me, one by one;
The game is theirs; yet still will I resist
By tooth and claw, until oblivion
Leaves but a shade, a cinder, where I stand,
Decaying flower in decaying hand.

—W.R.E.

See also page 115.

---

* A rough translation appears in Answers and Solutions.

10

*The tenth call came from heaven. I
Replied politely, with a lie.*

Eloquence is the power to translate a truth into language
perfectly intelligible to the person to whom you speak.
—RALPH WALDO EMERSON

TO THE WELFARE DEPARTMENT of the Commonwealth of Massachusetts, which has been receiving missives of the same nature for years, the appeals below, however they may confuse you and me, are doubtless clear and eloquent, as well as heartfelt.*

- I am writing the Welfare Department to say that my baby was born two years old. When do I get my money?
- Mrs. Jones has not had any clothes for a year and has been visited by the clergy regularly.
- I am glad to report that my husband who was missing is dead.
- This is my eighth child. What are you going to do about it?
- Please find for certain if my husband is dead. The man I am now living with can't eat or do anything until he knows.
- I am very much annoyed to find you have branded my son illiterate. This is a dirty lie as I was married a week before he was born.
- I am forwarding my marriage certificate and three children, one of which is a mistake as you can see.
- Unless I get my husband's money pretty soon, I will be forced to lead an immortal life.
- You have changed my little boy to a girl. Will this make any difference?
- In accordance with your instructions, I have given birth to twins in the enclosed envelope.
- I want my money as quick as I can get it. I've been in bed with the doctor for two weeks and he doesn't do me any good. If things don't improve, I will have to send for another doctor.

* I received these excerpts years ago; and as in too many cases, the name of the sender has vanished from my files.

For Christmas comes but once a year,
And then they shall be merry.
—GEORGE WITHER

Dylan Thomas and the small boy continue their conversation about Christmas:*

SMALL BOY: Get on to the useless presents.

SELF: On Xmas Eve, I hung at the foot of my bed Bessie Bunter's black stocking, and always, I said, I would stay awake all the moonlit, snowlit night to hear the roof-alighting reindeer and see the hollied boot descend through soot. But soon the sand of the snow drifted into my eyes, and, though I stared towards the fireplace and around the flickering room where the black sack-like stocking hung, I was asleep before the chimney trembled and the room was red and white with Christmas. But in the morning, though no snow melted on the bedroom floor, the stocking bulged and brimmed: press it, it squeaked like a mouse-in-a-box; it smelt of tangerine; a furry arm lolled over, like the arm of a kangaroo out of its mother's belly; squeeze it hard in the middle, and something squelched; squeeze it again—squelch again. Look out of the frost-scribbled window; on the great loneliness of the small hill, a blackbird was silent in the snow.

SMALL BOY: Were there any sweets?

SELF: Of course there were sweets. It was the marshmallows that squelched. Hard-boileds, toffee, fudge and allsorts, crunches, cracknels, humbugs, glaciers, and marpizan and butterwelsh for the Welsh. And troops of bright tin soldiers who, if they would not fight, could always run. And Snakes-and-Families and Happy Ladders. And Easy Hobbi-Games for Little Engineers, complete with Instructions. Oh, easy for Leonardo! And a whistle to make the dogs bark to wake up the old man next door to make him beat on the wall with his stick to shake our picture off the wall. And a packet of cigarettes: you put one in your mouth and you stood at the corner of the street and you waited for hours, in vain, for an old lady to scold you for smoking a cigarette and then, with a smirk, you ate

* See page 122 for the beginning.

it. And, last of all, in the toe of the stocking, sixpence like a silver corn. And then downstairs for breakfast under the balloons!

SMALL BOY: Were there Uncles, like in our house?

SELF: There are always Uncles at Xmas. The same Uncles. And on Xmas mornings, with dog-disturbing whistles and sugar fags, I would scour the swathed town for news of the little world, and find always a dead bird by the white Bank or by the deserted swings: perhaps a robin, all but one of his fires out, and that fire still burning on his breast. Men and women wading and scooping back from church or chapel, with taproom noses and wind-smacked cheeks, all albinos, huddled their stiff black jarring feathers against irreligious snow. Mistletoe hung from the gas in all the front parlours; there was sherry and walnuts and bottled beer and crackers by the dessertspoons; and cats in their fur-abouts watched the fires; and the high-heaped fires crackled and spat, all ready for the chestnuts and the mulling pokers. Some few large men sat in the front parlours, without their collars, Uncles almost certainly trying their new cigars, holding them out judiciously at arm's length, returning them to their mouths, coughing, then holding them out again as though waiting for the explosion; and some few small aunts, not wanted in the kitchen, nor anywhere else for that matter, sat on the very edges of their chairs, poised and brittle, afraid to break, like faded cups and saucers. Not many those mornings trod the piling streets—an old man always, fawn-bowlered, yellow-gloved, and, at this time of year, with spats of snow, would take his constitutional to the white bowling green, and back, as he would take it wet or fine on Xmas Day or Doomsday; sometimes two hale men, with big pipes blazing, no overcoats, and windblown scarves, would trudge, unspeaking, down to the forlorn sea, to work up an appetite, to blow away the fumes, who knows, to walk into the waves until nothing of them was left but the two curling smoke clouds of their inextinguishable briars.

SMALL BOY: Why didn't you go home for Xmas dinner?

SELF: Oh, but I did, I always did. I would be slap-dashing home, the gravy smell of the dinners of others, the bird smell, the brandy, the pudding and mince, weaving up my nostrils, when out of a snow-clogged side-lane would come a boy the spit of myself, with a pink-tipped cigarette, and violet past of a black eye, cocky as a bullfinch, leering all to himself. I hated him on sight and sound, and would be about to put my dog-whistle to my lips, and blow him off the face of Xmas when suddenly he, with a violet wink, put *his* whistle to *his* lips and blew so stridently, so high, so exquisitely loud, that gobbling faces, their cheeks bulged with goose, would press against their tinselled windows, the whole length of the white echoing street.

SMALL BOY: What did you have for Dinner?

SELF: Turkey, and blazing pudding.

SMALL BOY: Was it nice?

SELF: It was not made on earth.

SMALL BOY: What did you do after dinner?

The Christmas conversation concludes on page 310.

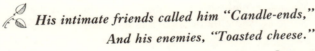

> *His intimate friends called him "Candle-ends,"*
> *And his enemies, "Toasted cheese."*
> —LEWIS CARROLL

NICKNAMES ARE GENERALLY ASSOCIATED with humans, but if this article by Beatrice E. Garcia in *The Wall Street Journal* is correct, the stocks of dignified companies frequently bear undignified sobriquets.

The rise and fall of Mad Dog, Crazy Mary, Big Nose Louie, Glow Worm, and Dead Head are chronicled in major U.S. newspapers every day.

But they aren't race horses, rock stars or mobsters. Rather, they are hotly traded American stocks.

Mad Dog is McDonnell Douglas Corp. (ticker symbol MD), Crazy Mary is Community Psychiatric Centers (CMY), Big Nose Louie is Beneficial Corp. (BNL), Glow Worm is Corning Glass Works (GLW), Dead Head is Dayton Hudson Corp. (DH).

These are just a few of the nicknames that stock traders use to remember arcane symbols and to facilitate communication. The list is long, though not always in good taste.

When a trader barks into his phone or stands in a crowd on the floor of the New York Stock Exchange, he's more likely to say "Buy 10,000 shares of Slob" or "Give me a quote on National Crash" than to use the companies' formal names or ticker symbols—Schlumberger Ltd. (SLB) and NCR Corp. (NCR).

Traders also speak of Hot Pants, Winkie, Ukelele, Cha-Cha and Lousy Land. Translation: Helmerich & Payne Inc. (HP), Warner Communications Inc. (WCI), Union Carbide Corp. (UK), Champion International Corp. (CHA) and Louisiana Land & Exploration Co. (LLX).

The nicknames "just roll off your tongue much easier," explains Martin Krouner, the head of the block-trading desk for L. F. Rothschild, Unterberg, Towbin, in New York. He and many others prefer to say "Radio" for RCA Corp., "Hamburgers" for McDonald's Corp., "Dynamite" for General Dynamics Corp., and "Pie in the Sky" for Piedmont Aviation.

Using nicknames also cuts the risk that the symbol ATT, for example, could be confused with ITT. So traders refer to American Telephone & Telegraph Co. as Big Phone and ITT Corp. as I-Phone.

Nicknames seem to stick even when they are a mouthful themselves, as when Southland Royalty Co. is called Standing Room Only, a mnemonic for its ticker symbol (SRO). Using the names "just breaks up the day," says Jon Groveman, the head of equity trading at Ladenburg, Thalmann & Co. in New York.

. . . .

God for Sale?

Leveraged buyouts are moving from the business into the intellectual and even spiritual fields. Louis Phillips reported on the Op-ed page of *The New York Times* that the conglomerate of Yeats had merged with the conglomerate of Keats, or maybe it was the other way around; and *Publisher's Weekly* here reveals an even more grandiose takeover:

From an anonymous source, on the Random House letterhead, we received the following: "Random House has entered into an agreement with the Vatican to acquire the Catholic Church. Founded by 12 poor Galileans in the early years of the millennium, the Church has grown into a multinational organization with more than 100 million members worldwide, an organization rivaled only by American Express/Shearson-Lehman in size. With its vast real estate holdings and its virtual monopoly in Afterlife Insurance, it has made itself a perennial presence on the list of Fortune 500 conglomerates. It has achieved great success as a publisher. It has launched the careers of many major authors, and its backlist includes works by Hans Küng, Thomas Aquinas, Matthew, Mark, Luke and John. 'We feel this is a very good pairing,' a spokesman for Random House stated. 'Over its six decades, Random House has published many important works: Joyce's *Ulysses* as well as the works of Dr. Seuss and William Faulkner. We don't expect to tamper with the Church's management team,' the spokesman continued. 'The Church will operate as an independent division within Random House, and the Pope will report directly to Si Newhouse.' ''

Consider Pis, a language of the Caroline Islands; Kookie, an Indian dialect akin to Bengali; Flup, spoken along Africa's Gambia River; Saliva, an Orinoco Indian dialect; Gah, the tongue of the Malayan Alfurus; Bzub, a dialect of the Caucasus; Zara, a Kurdish tongue of northwest Persia; Cullilan-Cunny, an Amerindian language; Kuzzilibash, a Turkish dialect; Jalloof, language of a Senegal tribe; Miao, the dialect of China's Hunan province; Yairy-Yairy and Watty-Watty, two Australian dialects of New South Wales.

—GARY JENNINGS

Love Laughs at Languages

I saw you on the street with your mamá.
We loved—though you spoke Bzub, and I spoke Gah.
I asked in Flup if you liked my mustache;
You answered, "Maybe," in Kuzzilibash.
In Zara I entreated for a kiss,
And took for "yes" the word you spoke in Pis.
I begged you in Saliva, "Share my roof";
You murmured acquiescence in Jalloof.
In Cunny-Cullilan I took my vow;
And you, with downcast eyes, replied in Miao.
The holy father tied the final knotty
In Yairy-Yairy, or else Watty-Watty.

—W.R.E.

Men are men; the best sometimes forget.
—WILLIAM SHAKESPEARE

THEY ALSO REMEMBER THINGS that are not so. Or at least I do, as I may have hinted already in this book.

It is of record, for instance, that in January and February 1931 I was studying, or pretending to, at the Sorbonne, in Paris, and that during this period a brief revolt against King Alfonso XIII exploded in northeastern Spain. It is also of record that on my departure from the States I was in possession of press cards from the San Bernardino (Cal.) *Sun* and the Redlands (Cal.) *Daily Facts*. Here memory takes over.

Memory says I saw the Spanish uprising as a heaven-sent opportunity to make my name as a war correspondent; surely neither the *Sun* nor the *Daily Facts* had any correspondent closer to the scene. I therefore gathered together my pitiable residue of cash, borrowed a hundred francs or so from my roommate, and bought a third-class train ticket for the Spanish border. I had to leave the train at Perpignan, capital of the Département des Pyrénées Orientales, for three reasons: that was as far as my ticket would take me; I had no visa for Spain; and in any event the border was closed because of unsettled conditions on the Spanish side. So I proceeded to the nearest tavern to work out a strategy.

I don't know how it is now, but in 1931 Frenchmen, especially in taverns, loved to strike up conversations with foreigners, particularly foreigners willing to treat. In this case they even treated in their turn. By the time I had spent the last of my money, I not only knew that there existed a mountain pass nearby (one highly popular with smugglers needing to slip across the border), but a tipsy young man had agreed to seat me behind him on his motorcycle, which he was in no condition to drive, and take me to that very trail, where we parted after a beery hug. I walked down the path into Spain, quite steadily, I think, and soon after sunrise reached a sizable town named Llanes, on the Bay of Biscay. There I found the revolt had already been put down.* There was nothing for it but to trudge back up the mountain trail.

* A republican victory at the polls the following March brought Alfonso's reign to an end.

Everything would have been fine if it had not begun to rain. . . .

Except for a few copper sous in my right trousers-leg pocket, I was penniless, but that did not worry me. The previous summer Clinton McKinnon* and I had discovered the secret of riding free on French trains. No ticket was required for boarding; the trick was to avoid having to show one at our destination. We had managed this once by setting a small fire of crumpled newspapers at an isolated spot on the platform; passengers and officials alike rushed to the scene, and we strolled unimpeded out the door. I was sure I could do this again. At Perpignan I stuffed some crumpled newspaper pages into my pockets and walked through the station shed into the railroad yard. A freight train was standing there with the engine puffing, and no one was looking when I clambered aboard a flatcar loaded with empty wooden vats nearly as tall as a man. I have no idea how I got into one of these, but I did, and squatted out of sight.

Within a few minutes the cars jerked and the train was on its way. I raised my head occasionally to check our whereabouts, and when we reached green fields I stood up and gloriously stretched. From then on I squatted only when a series of hoots from the engine indicated we were nearing a crossing.

Everything would have been fine if it had not begun to rain. In moments I was standing in inches of water, and the crumpled newspapers in my pockets, not to mention my packet of matches, were mush. I was licked. At the first stop I detrained and meekly turned myself in to the station guards. One of them drove me, with the utmost courtesy, to the American consulate. There a kind young diplomat laughed at my story and from his own pocket lent me the trifling sum (fortunately, I was able to return it within days) that I needed for a third-class passage to Paris.

Memory has fixed all this in my mind; yet it is not so. My letters to my parents, meticulously saved by them, show conclusively that I was at the Sorbonne the entire while.

You will never convince me of it, though.

---

* See pages 159 and 179.

> *When Darius had invaded their country (Scythia),*
> *they sent him a bird, a frog, and five arrows. The Persian*
> *monarch considered this as a surrender of their land,*
> *their streams, and their forces; but Gobryas, a looker-on,*
> *interpreted these objects as follows—"Unless, O Persians,*
> *ye become birds and fly in the air, or become mice and hide*
> *yourselves beneath the earth, or become frogs and leap into the lakes,*
> *ye shall never return home, but be stricken by these arrows!"*
>
> —A CANTAB

REBUSES RECEIVED A PASSING GLANCE on pages 67 and 168. The message above looks like a rebus; the bird, the frog, and the arrow obviously represent ideas, which can be expressed in words (or actions); but there is only one correct answer for each symbol in a rebus, and here the answer is equivocal. Some true rebuses (most of them from *Word Ways*):

1. sduobel
2. knirhs ot
3. sammoc

    —LOTHAR SCHWARZ

4. W I N G S
5. C
   O
     N

    —PHILIP M. COHEN

6. (The following letters, pronounced separately, in the French fashion, form a sentence in French):

G A C O B I A L

7. PMUH
8. X
  I
  M
9. B / R / E / A / D
10. ARUPMS
     0

11. T A O C
    —LOUIS PHILLIPS

12. W O R L A M E N
13. I K D
    —MARY J. HAZARD

Literary Criticism

My grasp of what he wrote or meant
Was only five or six %;
The rest was only words and sound.
My reference is to Ezra £.

—MYLES NA GOPALEEN

*Love is the strange bewilderment which overtakes
one person on account of another person.*
—JAMES THURBER AND E. B. WHITE

A WITTY SUITOR, ASKED TO DESCRIBE the nature of his love, may answer appropriately in terms of his occupation. Mary J. and Harry W. Hazard offer examples of such vocational replies:

- *The marathon runner:* all the way
- *The psychoanalyst:* unshrinkingly
- *The wheelwright:* tirelessly
- *The elephant trainer:* roguishly

Other possibilities are incorporated here:

How Do You Love Me?

Says Annie, by her swains hard-pressed,
"Which occupation suits love best?
Your job betokens how you'll woo;
By that I'll take my pick of you."

Cries the *couturier,* with passion,
"I love you, darling, in my *fashion.*"
The *oculist,* his eyes alight,
Declares, "I loved you at first *sight.*"

The *Indian* grunts out his summation:
"I love you without *reservation*."
The *acrobat* tells how he feels:
"I love you, dear, *head over heels*."

The farmer mumbles, heart agog,
That in his love he goes *whole hog;*
Sir Galahad, while blushing slightly,
Assures her that he'll love her *knightly.*

The *cardiologist* would start
By loving her with all his *heart;*
The *dieter* his dear would win
By loving her through *thick and thin.*

(I hear that Annie's leaning toward
The *sailor*—he goes *overboard.*)

—W.R.E.

It shall be called Bottom's dream,
because it has no bottom.
—WILLIAM SHAKESPEARE

I AWOKE THIS MORNING FROM A DREAM in which I had dialed the number of a friend who lived in a high-rise apartment house designed for unmarried career women. In the dream I looked through my window as the telephone rang and could see the building a half mile away, with green pasture land stretching between.

A voice said in my ear, "Good morning. Miss McManus and God." This took me slightly aback. I said, "Would you connect me, please?"

"I am sorry, sir—God is out."

"That is all right—I want Miss McManus."

"Oh, sir, I am sorry, but the Lord thy God is a jealous God."

That was the end of the dream. I wish Dr. Freud were around to interpret it.

The extent of our namesakes will probably surprise you, as it did me. Friends . . . were surprised that there lived a real lawyer named Shyster (Scheuster, anyway), a labor spy named Albert Fink, and a Joe Dun who hounded debtors.

—ROBERT HENDRICKSON

I F M Y B O O K *O Thou Improper, Thou Uncommon Noun* were to be reissued, here are a few words I would add to the list of names that became common nouns:

- *sleazy.* Silesia, an area of eastern Europe divided at latest word between Poland and Czechoslovakia, was once the source of a cloth that tore easily. The cloth came to be called *sleazy,* meaning "flimsy," from its place of origin. (Silesians label this attribution a canard.)
- *sakkara.* If you like to make an impression by using an unfamiliar word where a common one would do as well, say "sakkara" for "mouse gray." You will be indisputably correct; the word comes from Sakkara, a town near Cairo, Egypt, which once had a pyramid made of mousy-gray limestone, and for all I know still does.
- *yperite.* Mustard gas took on this name from having been first used at the battle of Ypres, Belgium, in World War I.
- *coffee.* The coffee plant appears to be native to the region of Kaffa, in the south Ethiopian highlands, and some contend that the name of the beverage came from the region. But I consider this word to be a ringer among improper, uncommon nouns; more likely it descends from Turkish *qahveh,* Arabic *qahwah,* originally meaning "wine."
- *oh, my achin' head.* Harry Hazard, perhaps with tongue in cheek, insists that the expression derives from Edmund Akenhead, one-time crossword editor of the *Times* of London.
- *chic sales.* An outdoor privy, named after the late humorist Chic Sales, an authority on the now outmoded convenience.
- *scamander. Meander*—meaning "to wind or turn; wander aimlessly"—derives from the Meander River in Phrygia, notable

for its tortuosity. Well, there is also a Scamander River in Asia Minor, and in lowercase the word has the same meaning, for the same reason. When Ira Gershwin wrote, "You say tomatoes, I say tomahtoes," he might well have added, "You say meander, I say scamander."

- *charley horse.* In *O Thou Improper, Thou Uncommon Noun*, I guessed that this expression for a painful cramp in a limb stemmed from "some crippled horse named Charley." D. Hoefnagel says it is more likely from a Baltimore Orioles pitcher named Charley Esper who "walked like a lame horse." Mr. Hoefnagel offers as an alternative source a Sioux City groundskeeper who owned a lame horse named Charley; so perhaps I was right after all.
- *flibbertigibbet.* In Shakespeare's *King Lear*, Edgar refers to the "foul fiend Flibbertigibbet." Less fiendish now, a *flibbertigibbet* is "a gossip or chatterer; one who is giddy or frivolous, esp. a woman."
- *pickle.* I make no guarantees, but pickle probably derives from one William Beukel, or Beukelz, a fourteenth-century Dutchman credited with first pickling fish.

> *No-one is exempt from talking nonsense;*
> *the misfortune is to do it solemnly.*
> —MICHEL DE MONTAIGNE

SOLEMNLY" IS AN ODD TRANSLATION of the French *curieusement*, it seems to me; "inquisitively, enquiringly" is surely more literal, and "unwittingly, unaware" seems closer to what Montaigne had in mind. There is, to be sure, such a thing as solemn nonsense, but it is an oxymoron—something meant seriously by the speaker and taken as nonsense by the listener, or meant as nonsense but taken seriously.

The following knittelverse, featuring words that start with *j*, is intended as nonsense and I hope will be taken that way.

A Word of Caution Regarding the Jargonelle, an Early-Growing Pear

Seek not, seek not, lest mind and life you jeopard[1]—
Seek not, I say, to pluck the jargonelle.
It grows in jungles where the feral leopard,
The jackal, and the naked savage dwell.

But if you have to brave those decks of marble,
Those dusty deserts, and those huddled rocks,
Wear rubbers—else your Sunday boots you'll jarble[2];
And take a jerrican[3] to boil your sox.

There's jargonelle on houris' tongues in jenna[4];
In heav'n there's jargonelle in angels' hair.
Old Scratch rues not his penance in Gehenna—
He'd sell his soul again to taste that pear.

This warning neither disregard nor garble;
Repeat it as you sit there in the stocks:
Wear rubbers—else your Sunday boots you'll jarble;
And take a jerrican to boil your sox.

—W.R.E.

> I thought I'd win the spelling bee
> And get right to the top
> But I started to spell "banana"
> And I didn't know when to stop.
> —WILLIAM R. COLE

NOT EVEN MY FATHER, WHOSE SENTENCES were perhaps even more expansible than William Cole's "banana," could have matched this interminable (surely 854 words qualify as

[1] Put in jeopardy. [2] Wet; bemire. [3] A five-gallon container. [4] The Mohammedan paradise.

interminable) sentence created by Laurie Winer for *The Wall Street Journal:*

> In order to credit William Faulkner—as the *Guinness Book of World Records* does—with the longest sentence in literature, one must include, when counting the words in Faulkner's erratically punctuated, loosely defined "sentences," lengthy italicized passages that echo what passes through a character's mind; not to mention parentheses within parentheses; and long sentences connected to sentence fragments by dashes where periods, strictly speaking, should be; as well as run-on paragraphs that begin audaciously with a lower-case letter; and, while Guinness says the longest sentence is a 1,300-word tirade in *Absalom, Absalom!* there is, by liberal Faulknerian standards, a 1,928-word sentence (beginning "They both bore it as though in deliberate flagellant exaltation") in that book which contains a 1,360-word parenthetical memory/thought that has within it at least 32 traditional sentences; so perhaps Faulkner should not be holding this title after all (from his London office a Guinness editor, Colin Smith, who says he has never seen *Absalom, Absalom!*, names as his source for the longest sentence entry the 1945 *Bookman's Bedlam of Literary Oddities*, a fustian collection of curiosa by bibliophile Walter Hart Blumenthal, which doesn't mention Faulkner at all and instead gives the palm for sequential verbosity to Edward Phillips's *Preface to Theatrum Poetarium*, written in 1675, for a 1,012 word sentence) even though others, including the writer Malcolm Cowley, cite another Faulkner sentence, found in the story "The Bear," as among the longest ever written; viz., in his introduction to the story in the 1946 *The Portable Faulkner*, Mr. Cowley calls this whopper, which begins "To him it was as though the ledgers in their scarred cracked leather bindings," a 1,800-word sentence when in fact it is, by the most liberal definition, a 1,600-word Faulknerian sentence, which is, under closer scrutiny, a 91-word sentence with no period followed by a new paragraph (indented) beginning with a lower-case letter that contains nothing but a 67-word sentence fragment that is followed by another paragraph fragment, etc. (even Albert Erskine, Faulkner's editor at Random House, says of the long word group in "The Bear": "New sentences begin whether the author puts a period there or not"), which may sound petty, but, if you're going to call something the longest sentence, the term sentence must have some meaning or else what's the point of bestowing the title (you may believe, as a confident . . .

I have run out of breath just typing this, and I am only halfway through. You will find the end of Ms. Winer's sentence (unless she adds to it) on page 288.

Taxonomy: The science of classification in a broad sense, usually restricted to biological classification.

—ENCYCLOPAEDIA BRITANNICA

Narrowing Things Down

Taxonomically, gang,
Start out with the *Primal Bang.*
  With a mighty puff disperse
  This into a *Universe.*
    Sifting through phenomena,
    Pick a likely *Nebula,*
      And from its diversity
      A convenient *Galaxy.*
        From that swirling, milky ruck
        A fine *Solar System* pluck.
          Planets nine its sun begird;
          Counting outward, take the third.
            Land on it; when you arrive
            Scoop up everything alive.
              These in *Kingdoms* sort, and pile 'em
              Each into its proper *Phylum.*
                Thence *Subphylums* pray amass,
                And from this, a *Superclass,*
                  Which in smaller *Classes* break,
                  And, from one, *Subclasses* take.
                  Into *Cohorts* them divide,
                  Wherein *Superorders* hide.
                    One of these its *Orders* yields;
                    Separate them into fields
                      Called *Suborders,* all of which
                      Are in *Infraorders* rich.

Infraorders keep in store
Superfamilies galore.
  Families split off from these;
  Thence emerge *Subfamilies*,
    All with *Tribes* to them belonging,
    These with *Subtribes* from them thronging.
    Subtribes *Genuses* deliver:
    In each Genus, *Species* quiver.
    And the taxonomic end
    Is *Subspecies*—YOU, my friend.

—W.R.E.

Bismarck, a stickler for formality, was once seated at dinner next to a young, ebullient American lady. At first she addressed him correctly as "Your Highness." With the next course he became "Mr. Chancellor" and with the third course "my dear Mr. Bismarck." As the plates were changed once more, he smiled and said amiably, "My first name is Otto."

—CLIFTON FADIMAN

THIS IS AN AGE OF EGALITARIAN informality. Arthur Schlesinger, Jr., the historian, ordered a drink from an airplane stewardess he had never seen before. Soon afterward, she stopped by his seat and said, "Have another one, Art?"

To address a stranger by first name nowadays indicates not impertinence but goodwill. Louise called long distance for a medical appointment. "May I have your name, please?" asked the secretary at the other end of the line. "Espy," said Louise. "Louise Espy. E, S, P as in Peter, Y. Espy." "Thank you, Louise," said the secretary.

The same distaste for stiffness shows itself in our dress at social gatherings. If the dinner is labeled informal, the host is likely to be in his skivvies. It is hard to know what to wear. You may wish to follow the advice of William Safire:

In my set, *formal* means *black tie*, and *white tie* must be specified if a tailcoat is desired. *Business attire* means any kind of suit and tie. *Informal* means "not black tie," which in turn means "dark suit in the evening," and is the way most people now think it proper to go to the opera. Watch out for informal, though—it slops over in meaning to *casual*, which means "no tie needed"; I have seen *very* casual, which means jeans and carefully tattered garments. . . . I think *very casual*, in my peer group, is the equivalent of semiformal in a younger set, but suspect that semiformal may mean "jacket and shoes, no tie but no T-shirt" to most teen-agers.

The other day I received an engraved invitation bearing the legend *Informal Dress Optional*. The meaning was beyond me; I stayed home. What should I have worn, Bill?

Dictionaries are like watches; the worst is better than none, and the best cannot be expected to go quite true.
—SAMUEL JOHNSON

THE ANALOGY NO LONGER HOLDS. Dictionaries may still have their off moments, but a quartz watch will give you the correct time, or near enough as makes no difference, year in and year out.* Dictionaries are more like those flowers that open or close at a fairly predictable hour, so that you can stroll in certain gardens and tell by one bloom whether it is time for lunch and by another whether you should be taking your afternoon nap. I would not wish to count my pulse by them; but to tell time even approximately seems quite a feat for a flower.

Flower-clocks†

They tick and tock away among the phlox—
    The flower-clocks.
Up leaps the sun; the morning glory ticks . . .
    Chimes six.

* Never mind what I said on page 145.
† The flowers you met on page 116 had other interests.

Nine little dingdongs—that's the Afric daisy.
    Ten—that's the lazy
Tulip. Goatsbeards, starting from their swoon,
    Sound noon.
The yawning four-o'clocks doze off at four.
It's nine before day lilies yawn and snore.
(Or thereabouts. Flowers do run fast or slow
    An hour or so.)

                        —W.R.E.

 Double, double, toil and trouble;
Fire burn and cauldron bubble.
—*WILLIAM SHAKESPEARE*, MACBETH

THE WORDS YOU ARE TO IDENTIFY in this challenge from Charles F. Dery are reduplicatives; he calls them double-trouble. Each consists of two halves, sometimes separated by a hyphen, and always spelled alike except for a single letter in one half and its correlative in the other. Guess the words.

EXAMPLES

(Slang) OK, perfect
<u>h</u> <u>o</u> <u>t</u> <u>s</u> <u>y</u> - <u>t</u> <u>o</u> <u>t</u> <u>s</u> <u>y</u>

bauble, shiny trinket
<u>g</u> <u>e</u> <u>w</u> <u>g</u> <u>a</u> <u>w</u>

1. act hesitantly or indecisively
   _ _ _ _ _ - _ _ _ _ _

2. American Indian ceremony: American social gathering
   _ _ _ _ _

3. amorous and mushy   _ _ _ _ _ - _ _ _ _ _

4. associate or converse
   familiarly   _ _ _ _ _ _

5. assuming superiority,
   haughty   _ _ _ _ _ - _ _ _ _ _

6. backward handspring   _ _ _ _ _ _ _ _

7. chummy, intimate   _ _ _ _ _ - _ _ _ _ _

8. commotion, tumult,
   uproar   _ _ _ _ _ - _ _ _ _ _

9. excellent, first-rate   _ _ _ ' - _ _ _

10. flat braid woven for use in
    trimming   _ _ _ _ _ _ _ _

11. fogy, fussbudget, stuffed
    shirt   _ _ _ _ _ - _ _ _ _ _

12. foundation or sustaining
    wall of stones thrown
    together   _ _ _ _ _ _

13. gossip, prattle   _ _ _ _ _ _ - _ _ _ _ _ _

14. hand-organ played by
    street musicians   _ _ _ _ _ - _ _ _ _ _

15. having a monotonous
    cadence or rhythm   _ _ _ _ _ _ _ _

16. having short sharp turns
    or angles   _ _ _ _ _ _

17. important person   _ _ _ _ _ _

18. in hasty confusion   _ _ _ _ _ _ _ _

19. insipid, weakly
    sentimental   _ _ _ _ _ - _ _ _ _ _

20. in utter disorder   _ _ _ _ _ _ _ - _ _ _ _ _ _ _ _

21. jumble, medley   _ _ _ _ _ _ _ _

22. loiter, dawdle   _ _ _ _ _ - _ _ _ _ _

23. mark with intersecting
    lines   _ _ _ _ _ _ _ _ _

24. marvelous, remarkable   _ _ _ _ _ _ _ _ _

25. mixture, olla podrida   _ _ _ _ _ _ _ _ _

26. percussive style of playing
    the blues on a piano   _ _ _ _ _ - _ _ _ _ _ _

27. portable battery-operated
    transmitting and
    receiving set   _ _ _ _ _ - _ _ _ _ _ _

28. rabble, mob   _ _ _ _ _ _ _

29. rapid succession of light
    tapping sounds   _ _ _ _ _ - _ _ _ _ _ _

30. short and pudgy   _ _ _ _ - _ _ _ _

31. sleight-of-hand;
    deception, trickery   _ _ _ _ _ - _ _ _ _ _

32. small ornamental object   _ _ _ _ _ _ _ _ _

33. small talk, gossip
    _ _ _ _ _ _ _

34. something damaged
    beyond repair
    _ _ _ _ _ _ - _ _ _ _ _ _

35. sound made by repeated
    strokes on a bell
    _ _ _ _ _ _ _ _

36. spree, rampage
    _ _ _ _ _ _

37. swindle, cheat
    _ _ _ _ _ _ _

38. underhand activity
    _ _ _ _ _ - _ _ _ _ _

39. very small
    _ _ _ _ _ - _ _ _ _ _

40. weak and watery
    _ _ _ _ _ - _ _ _ _ _

41. wild or lively party
    _ _ _ _ _ _ _

42. without a choice;
    inevitable
    _ _ _ _ _ - _ _ _ _ _

An injury is much sooner forgiven than an insult.
—LORD CHESTERFIELD

YET BEING SCOLDED IS PREFERABLE to being ignored; and some insults may so exceed our deserts as to take on overtones of flattery. Surely, you pay a compliment, however unintended, if you find someone so egregious in his knavery or foolishness that you have to grope for a new vocabulary to describe his baseness. If they had been able to read, the sixteenth-century oafs, knaves, and blockheads described in this old passage would have been delighted.

Prating gablers, lickorous gluttons, freckled bittors, mangie rascals, slie knaves, drowsie loiterers, slapsauce fellows, slabber-degullion druggels, lubbardly lowts, cozening foxes, paultrie customers, sycophant varlets, drawlatch hoydons, flouting milksops, staring clowns, forlorn snakes, ninnie lobcocks, scurvie sneaksbies, fondling fops, base lowns, sawcie coxcombs, idle lusks, scoffing braggards, noddie meacocks, blockish brutnols, doddipol joltheads, jobbernol goosecaps, foolish loggerheads, slutch calflollies, grouthead gnatsnappers, lobdotterels, gaping change-lings, codshead loobies, woodcock slangams, ninnyhammer flycatchers, and noddiespeak simpletons.

In his *Description of England* (1587), William Harrison described twenty-three types of rogues and vagabonds so handsomely that—again, had they been able to read—they must have thought they were being elevated to the aristocracy:

THE SEVERAL DISORDERS AND DEGREES AMONG OUR IDLE VAGABONDS

1. Rufflers
2. Uprightmen
3. Hookers or anglers
4. Rogues
5. Wild rogues
6. Priggers of prancers
7. Palliards
8. Fraters
9. Abrams
10. Freshwater mariners or whipjacks
11. Dummerers
12. Drunken tinkers
13. Swaddlers or pedlars
14. Jarkmen or patricoes

And, of the woman kind:

1. Demanders for glimmer of fire
2. Bawdy-baskets
3. Morts
4. Autem morts
5. Walking morts
6. Doxies
7. Dells
8. Kinching morts
9. Kinching coes

Rufflers were swaggerers; *uprightmen*, the chiefs of beggar bands; *hookers*, pickpockets; *anglers*, thieves who stole through windows, using a pole with a hook; *priggers of prancers*, horse thieves; *palliards*, lewd vagabonds; *fraters*, licensed mendicants begging for a hospital; *Abrams*, malingerers; *freshwater mariners*, begging pseudosailors; *whipjacks*, beggars pretending to be dumb; *pedlars*, petty or fake vendors; *jarkmen*, vagabond counterfeiters of licenses and the like; *patricoes*, priests of the gypsies—also called hedge priests.

Of the woman kind, *demanders for glimmer of fire* were pretended victims of fire; *bawdy-baskets*, vendors of obscene literature; *morts*, loose women (the word also means pig grease); *autem morts*, the same sort in, or in the neighborhood of, churches; *doxies* (obvious); *dells* (the same); *kinching* (or *kinchen*) *morts*, tramps' girl-children, brought up to thieve; *kinching* (or *kinchen*) *coes* (or *coves*), boys of the same sort (and therefore misplaced here, not being of the woman kind).

Marriage: The state or condition of a community consisting of a master, a mistress, and two slaves, making, in all, two.
—AMBROSE BIERCE

Two GENERATIONS AGO, BRIDES AND grooms were often advised that the key to a loving marriage was to clear up all tiffs before going to sleep; but that turned out not to be always practical. I am working on a formula for a pill that will convert any degree of irritation instantly into an equal degree of affection. There will be a warning on the label: Husband and wife must swallow simultaneously.

Or at Least Make Up Afterward

Some women take *mariticide*[1]
    In stride
(I understand the merest bride
    Can do it);
While husbands hear that word and flinch,
For their own wives might in a pinch
    Go to it;

---

[1] Murder of a husband by his wife.

These women, though, cannot abide
    Uxoricide,[2]
Whence certain of their sex have died
    Unknowing—
Have vanished from the ones they love,
Nor stood upon the order of
    Their going;
Since dead by either word is just
    As dust—
Let me suggest, to be discussed,
    A moral:
Can't men be more *uxorious*,[3]
And wives more *maritorious*[4]?
To drive uxoricide away,
To keep mariticide at bay—
    Don't quarrel.

                —W.R.E.

A lighter note:

Some of My Best Friends Are Mules

I don't deny I'm *mulierose*,[5]
But this is also true:
Though mules and I are very close,
I'm fond of women, too.

                —W.R.E.

---

[2] Murder of a wife by her husband. [3] Fond of one's wife, even to excess. [4] Fond of one's husband, the same way. [5] Fond of all women.

11

When came th' eleventh, it was plain
The questions were inside my brain.

It was inevitable that someone would eventually produce "trichotomy" in print. It is clearly formed from "dichotomy" on the assumption that di- implies two and -chotomy something like separation. This is not the case; the roots are dicha *meaning "apart" and* tomia *meaning "cutting." What then should "trichotomy" mean? Since the Greek root* tricho- *means "hair," what has unintentionally been produced is the Greek for "haircut."*

—TIMES HIGHER EDUCATIONAL SUPPLEMENT

Etty's up to Her Tricks Again

Dear Etymology cooked up a prank while in her bath:
She'd lead some poor infatuee adown the garden path.
And knowing me for such a one—I thought she thought
    a lot o' me—
She laid a trap to fool me with a brand new word: *trichotomy.*

Dichotomy's "division into two opposing states,"
Di- meaning "two," and *-chotomy* "cuts off, or separates."
She therefore, as she soaped her back, assumed I would agree
That since *dichotomy*'s from *two, trichotomy*'s from *three.*

But though I love dear Etty, yet I trust her not a whit,
Nor swallow what she gives me without checking it a bit.
Now *di-,* or *dicho*'s not just two, but any number more;
That being so, I wondered what the *tri-* was needed for.

I found a sober magazine, and lo! 'twas printed there
That *tricho* isn't "three" at all—the word is Greek for "hair."
Trichotomy's a "haircut"! When our grandsires still were snits,
A shave and a *trichotomy* would cost a man six bits.

It follows from this reasoning (if anybody cares),
Discussion of trichotomy is really splitting hairs.
So grant, dear Etty, that your prank has turned into a flub,
And I will come and soap your back and wash you in the tub.

—W.R.E.

I am too old to be part of a drug generation and have no use for stimulants or depressants that can be smoked, sniffed, injected, or swallowed in a capsule. My indulgence has been alcohol, a far more widely used and equally addictive poison that knows no limits of age or era.
—TOM WICKER

THE *WALL STREET JOURNAL* REPORTS THAT up to two parts per billion of something called nitrosamines have been found in certain Scotch whiskeys, while levels of the substance as low as ten parts per billion have produced tumors in laboratory animals. This finding is not likely to reduce consumption of whiskey appreciably, and neither is the effort to lump alcoholic beverages with tobacco, marijuana, heroin, and the like as addictive and dangerous drugs. What will cut down drinking is the calorie count. We are less worried about dying than about getting fat.

I remember whiskey with respect and fondness and hope that someday we two may meet again. As Carlyle considered fire, so I consider whiskey—the most dreadful of masters, but what a servant! The following sixteenth-century encomium by an unknown writer has lost no force in more than three hundred years.

[Whiskey] drieth up the breaking out of hands and killeth the flesh wormes, if you wash your hands therewith.

It scowreth all the scrufe and scalds from the head, being therewith dailie washt before meals. Being moderatelie taken it sloweth age, it strengtheneth you, it helpeth digestion, it cutteth flegm, it abandoneth melancholie, it relisheth the heart, it lighteneth the mind, it quickeneth the spirits, it cureth the hydropsie, it healeth the strangurie,* it pounceth the stone, it expelleth gravell, it puffeth awaie all ventositie,† it keepeth and preserveth the head from whirling, the eies from dazzeling, the toong from lisping, the mouth from maffling, and the heart from swelling; the bellie from wrenching, the guts from numbing, the hands from shivering, and the sinewes from shrinking, the veines from srumbling,‡ the bones from aking and the marrow from soaking. Ulstadius also ascribeth thereto a singular praise and would have it to *burne, being kindled,* which he taketh to be a token to know the goodness thereof. And trulie it is a sovereign liquore if it be orderlie taken.

Speak but one rhyme, and I am satisfied:
Cry but "Ay me!" Pronounce but "love" and "dove."
—WILLIAM SHAKESPEARE

In the Beginning Was the Word.
—John 1:1

When lovely Joan Didion
Mislaid her enchiridion[1]
And could find no succedaneum[2]
To replenish her cranium,
She prayed to the Deity
To affirm her haecceity[3];
For lovely Joan Didion
Is no nullifidian,[4]
Though she thinks it absurd
That we spring from a Word.

—W.R.E.

---

* Pain in urination.
† Flatulence.
‡ Perhaps an early misprint; but neither grumbling nor crumbling seems right.
[1] handbook; manual. [2] substitute. [3] thisness; also, the character of being here and now. [4] an unbeliever.

Morality consists in suspecting other people of not being legally married.
—GEORGE BERNARD SHAW

I T IS PERHAPS TRUE THAT A THOROUGHLY balanced relationship between couples in love has not yet become the established norm; some even argue that the state of affairs is shifting faster than the flesh can follow. Still, few of us would exchange the occasionally bizarre mating rituals of our day for the manner of choosing a wife described in this seventeenth-century anecdote:

> Sir William Roper, of Eltham, in Kent, came one morning, pretty early, to my Lord, with a proposal to marry one of his daughters. My Lord's daughters were then both together abed in a truckle-bed in their father's chamber asleep. He carries Sir William into the chamber and takes the sheet by the corner and suddenly whips it off. They lay on their backs, and their smocks up as high as their armpits. This awakened them, and immediately they turned on their bellies. Quoth Roper, I have seen both sides, and so he gave a patt on the buttock he made choice of, saying, Thou art mine. Here was all the trouble of the wooing. This account I had from my honoured friend old Mrs. Tyndale, whose grandfather, Sir William Stafford, was an intimate friend of this Sir W. Roper, who told him the story.
> —AUBREY'S *BRIEF LIVES*

 Graciousness and courtesy are never old-fashioned.
—EMILY POST

T H E *WALL STREET JOURNAL* DESCRIBES a young woman, who, although obviously gracious and considerate to the core, still has a wee way to go on etiquette. She takes a class in that subject for budding society maidens in Atlanta, Georgia. Timothy K. Smith opens his article about her this way:

ATLANTA—Gentle reader, allow us to present Missy De Fiore, who is dining at the moment:

Leaning over the white table-cloth, Miss De Fiore takes a silver fork, tines down, in her left hand, a fish knife in her right. Elbows tucked against the sides of her off-the-shoulder taffeta gown, she glances down at her *saumon en croûte* and pauses.

"Hmm," Miss De Fiore says. "Looks like somebody stepped in it."

Orthoepy: correct or accepted pronunciation.

Cacoepy: bad or incorrect pronunciation.

—Webster's New International Dictionary, *Second Edition*

ORTHOEPY IS PRONOUNCED *or'*tho.ep'i. Cacoepy may be pronounced either *kak'*o.ep'i or ka.*kō'*e.pi. It follows that if you say or.*thō'*e.pi for orthoepy, that is cacoepy, while either *kak'*o.ep.i or ka.*kō'*e.pi for cacoepy is orthoepy.

It is a good general rule to pronounce words the way your peer group does, unless you have set your heart on joining a group of higher (or lower) social and financial standing, in which case it is advisable to adopt the pronunciation of the group you lust after. Consulting your dictionary is a good idea, too, but bear in mind that one dictionary frequently disagrees with another and that they all, as Peter Finley Dunne said of the Supreme Court, follow the election returns or some lexicographic equivalent; if enough people of standing begin pronouncing a word a new way, the dictionary will ultimately go along. Bear in mind also that any pronunciation accepted by a dictionary, not just the one first listed, is correct; after all, two pronunciations can't both be put first.

In the lines below Robert and Roberta disagree on the pronunciation of certain words, and in most cases they are both right. Ira Gershwin to the contrary, the fact that you say tomato and your true love says tomahto need not stand in the way of a long and happy union.

Let Us Utter Our Love in Sweet Sounds

Roberta said "he.*gem'*o.ny,"
    And Robert "*heg'*e.mo'ny";
And yet they paired as perfectly
    As cheese and macaroni.

Her past from his was *dis'*pa.rate,
    And his from hers dis.*par'*ate;
And yet their love was infinite
    As rabbit's love for carrot.

That he drank coffee and she tea
    Could not their ardor bury;
He called her taste a *vā'*ga.ry,
    She called his a va.*gā'*ry.

If he awoke with stomach sour,
    Or she in spirits poor,
She'd tell him that his face was *dour,*
    And he that hers was *dour.*

She found him bright beyond all men,
    He found her superhuman;
She magnified his *ac'*ū.men,
    He lauded her a.*cū'*men.

Though they might disagree a bit,
    Their love would overcome it;
His love for her was *con'*sum.mate,
    And hers for him con.*sum'*mate.

Their profiles psychological
    Were *oral,* hers; his, *anal;*
And he detested the ba.*nal',*
    While she abhorred the *bā'*nal.

His ring she took, he hers again;
It was a happy omen
That he adored her *ab'*do.men,
While she loved his ab.*dō'*men.

—W.R.E.

My punishment is greater than I can bear.
—*GENESIS 4:13*

IT WAS 1936, I WAS ON MY UPPERS, and I had to make my way from Chicago to Washington, D.C. For a fraction of what a bus would have cost I booked passage in a rusting Cadillac sedan, vintage 1928, along with these other members of the Depression generation:

• Two fat, disagreeable brothers in their twenties, who argued between themselves when they were not making sport of the driver;
• A roustabout from Ringling Brothers and Barnum & Bailey who was adjusting to the loss of an eye—a guy wire had snapped it out of his head as he was setting up the apparatus for a trapeze performance;
• And a sixty-year-old blind man, a pieceworker in a broom factory, whose ability to tell one funny story on the heels of another has since been matched, as far as I know, only by Ronald Reagan.

Our driver was a middle-aged, Russian-born Jew, with a thick accent and watery, red-rimmed eyes. He was short, tubby, and unshaven; he wore an open vest but no jacket; and his shirttail hung out behind. As he drove he muttered to himself, nodding or shaking his head.

He was a timorous driver, never exceeding forty. He also overcompensated in his steering, corkscrewing between the left and right limits of his lane. Fifteen miles west of Harrisburg, Pennsylvania, a police car flagged us to a stop for lack of a taillight. The driver rolled down his window, lifted his voice in a wail, and released tears that

The policeman promptly arrested the Russian. . . .

played tag down his bristly cheeks. "Oi!" he cried. "I'm poor man! I vant to die! I vant to!"

A glance inside was enough for the policeman to guess that the car was carrying passengers illegally, but there was no proof—"Ve're all friends from a child," insisted the driver between sobs. We might have escaped with a warning if one of the fat brothers had not snapped, "Why in hell are you lying? You're in a legitimate business, ain't you? We paid our money, didn't we?" The policeman promptly arrested the Russian and ordered us all to the police station, where it took him half an hour to find a judge.

This is the way the trial went:

JUDGE (*after reading the charge aloud*): How do you plead? Guilty or not guilty?

DRIVER: But, Your Honor, I don't know vot dot means.

JUDGE: Were you carrying paying passengers without a transport license?

DRIVER: I'm a leetle deaf, I don't hear vell.

(*A plea of "not guilty" is entered for him, and the officer describes the arrest. Then:*)

JUDGE: What is your story of what occurred?

DRIVER: (*weeping*): I am poor man. I verk at Brigg's Manufacturing, in Detroit. I am honest. I never been in no trouble before.

JUDGE: There is always a first time.

DRIVER: I come to Chicago. I am laid off few days. I have a friend, he say, "Here's some poor boys vant to go to New York. You take them, I pay gas and oil."

JUDGE: Come now—weren't you supposed to get $6.66 out of every $10 fare?

DRIVER: I'm a leetle deaf; I don't hear vell.

(*Judge repeats.*)

DRIVER: Oh no, Your Honor—just gas and oil.

JUDGE: Why did you lie to the officer?

DRIVER: Oi! I'm poor man! I vant to die! I vant to!

JUDGE: Why did you lie?

DRIVER: I'm a leetle deaf; I think he say, "Vhere you get this car?"

JUDGE: Guilty as charged. Ten dollars and costs or five days in jail.

DRIVER: Oi, my vife she vill fainted.

No more Cadillac for us. It looked as if we were all going to have to walk. But the arresting officer called me to one side. "Look, fella," he said, "I'm driving the prisoner into Harrisburg. If you move up the road, away from the others, I'll give you a lift."

"Could you take the blind man, too?" I asked.

He could, and did, and at Harrisburg I caught a bus, and that is the end of the story.

Book (OE boc; *Dn* beuke; *G* Buche, *a beech tree).
Possibly derived from the use of beech bark for
carving names before the days of printing.*
—BREWER'S DICTIONARY OF PHRASE AND FABLE

Book (A. S. *Bōc*, "Beech")

When England was an infant still,
   And writing was a caper
Known but to priests, their hard-won skill
Proved vain; how could they write until
   Someone invented paper?

The heaven they sailed for, jibe and tack,
   They may have got a sight on;
But could not send a message back
To chart their holy course, for lack
   Of anything to write on.

One day the Bishop chanced to see,
   While strolling through his park,
Some woodsmen fell a beech; the tree
They chopped in pieces two or three,
   And peeled away the bark.

With idle fingernail he traced
   Upon that bark a sonnet.
His senses reeled; his pulses raced;
He cried, "Our Lord this bark hath graced,
   For we can write upon it!"

And so they could, and so they did;
   That bark they made a scroll of.
The Scriptures, long in pulpit hid,
They trotted out, and oped the lid,
   And copied down the whole of.

That beech-bark scroll they called a *beech*.
   In centuries succeeding,
Beech turned to "book." And books still teach
Their lore to any and to each
   (Though many have stopped reading).

                        —W.R.E.

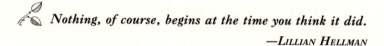 *Nothing, of course, begins at the time you think it did.*
                         —*LILLIAN HELLMAN*

THAT IS PARTICULARLY TRUE OF WORDS. Most of them originated in the long-forgotten past and occasionally mean something quite different from what they did at the start. Still, we can tie down the date of some word origins rather precisely. We know, for instance, that an Irish physicist named George Stoney coined the word *electron* in 1891; that *brunch* first saw the light in *Hunter's Weekly* in 1895; that E. Digby Baltzell put together the acronym WASP for "white Anglo-Saxon Protestant" in 1964; that in 1775 J. F. Blumenbach thought up the term *Caucasian* to apply to the chief races of Europe, North Africa, and southwest Asia.

    Other birthday words:

- 1865. *Entropy.* Coined by Rudolf Clausius from the Greek verb *entrepein,* meaning "to reverse."
- 1884. *Tabloid.* On March 14 Messrs. Burroughs, Wellcome & Co. registered "tabloid" as a trademark applied to condensed medical pills. The name was soon borrowed for racy newspapers of smaller-than-usual dimensions.

- 1895. *Golliwog.* A kind of bogeyman, named from the black doll designed by Florence Upton for the Golliwog tales written by her sister Bertha. Perhaps suggested by "pollywog."
- 1899. *Hooligan.* The Hooligans, Irish immigrants to London, were rough types. In January 1899 the *Pall Mall Gazette* observed: "The proprietor of Lord Tennyson (in wax), says it was a certain young man who Hooliganed about and threw the late Laureate's head at him." Hooligan quickly became a synonym for ruffian in many languages, including Russian.
- 1905. *Smog.* On July 3 the London *Globe* reported, "The other day at a meeting of the Public Health Congress, Dr. Des Voeux did a public service in coining a new word for the London fog, which was referred to as 'smog,' a compound of 'smoke' and 'fog'."
- 1907. *Blurb.* First used on a book jacket embellished with a drawing of a pulchritudinous young lady whom author Gelett Burgess dubbed Miss Belinda Blurb; since used for any brief commendatory notice, as on a book jacket.*
- 1923. *Robot.* Robot, cognate in Slavic languages to "orphan," entered English in the play *R.U.R.*, by Karel Capek. The initials stand for *Rossum's Universal Robots*, the name of a firm in the play that manufactures mechanical beings, enslaved by men.
- 1935. *Googol.* The mathematician Edward Kasner asked his nine-year-old nephew, Milton Sorotta, for a word to describe the number 10 followed by 100 zeros. Milton suggested "googol." A googolplex is a googol followed by 100 zeros.
- 1939. *Quark.* Used in Joyce's *Finnegans Wake* ("Three quarks for Mr. Marx") and adopted by physicists to represent any one of three subatomic particles that have been proposed as the fundamental unit of matter.
- 1940. *Ecdysiast.* A stripteaser. H. L. Mencken provided the term to stripteaser Georgia Sothern as "a new and more palatable word to describe [a practitioner of] this art." It is from "ecdysis" (Greek *ekdysis*), the scientific term for molting.
- 1943. *Genocide.* Raphael Lemkin created this miscegenation between Greek *genos* (race or tribe) and Latin *cide* (killing).

* The 1907 date is according to the *Oxford English Dictionary* Supplement. *Reader's Encyclopedia* sets the origin of the word in 1914.

- 1949. *Middlebrow*. Coined by Russell Lynes for a person of middling culture.
- 1952. *Egghead*. A sophisticate; highbrow. Said to be originally an epithet for an intellectual who supported the presidential candidacy of Adlai Stevenson, whose head was bald and allegedly reminiscent of an egg.

Acrostic. A composition, usually in verse, in which one or more sets of letters, . . . when taken in order, form a word or words.
—WEBSTER'S NEW INTERNATIONAL DICTIONARY, *SECOND EDITION*

THE NUMBER OF HIDDEN WORD ARRANGEMENTS that can be tucked into an acrostic verse is limited only by the ingenuity and patience of the versifier. In the example below, the letters that open each line, taken downward in order, make a word. So do the letters that open the fourth word of each line and those that open the final word of each line. The three words are anagrams of one another and serve to remind us that velleity can be a considerable impediment in a love affair. (It's all spelled out in Answers and Solutions.)

The Adroitly Demonstrated Idolatry
of a Dilatory Man

If dreaming a dream could achieve
Dominion of you, I'd start dozing.
Or if I learned how to receive
Love's kiss through a feint at opposing
All kisses, I'd try that.
                    (Does it
Take fervor and oomph if one's to
Redden ashes to raging fires lit?
You don't require *yearning,* do you?)

                    —W.R.E.

> *The "word problem" was to draw and letter a word so that it remained legible as a word while illustrating what the word defined.*
> —MARK SOPPELAND

WRITING SUPPOSEDLY STARTED AS PICTURES of objects. These gradually became symbols and then combinations of symbols, or signs, called hieroglyphs. From these evolved the letters of the alphabet, each letter or combination of letters representing sounds that in turn stand for ideas or things.*

Pictures remain a uniquely powerful form of communication, and as long as there has been writing, there has also been an impulse to turn the alphabet back into physical representation. The ancient Greeks amused themselves by shaping verses the way Procrustes shaped victims—chopping the desired outlines into their living flesh. They would arrange a poem on wine in the shape of a wineglass, or one on an eagle to resemble a flying bird.

A book called *Words*, created by Mark Soppeland "and his friends," shows 144 words so drawn as both to give their spelling and illustrate their meaning. The following knittelverse borrows some of these picture words.

The Old and the Young of It†

The NIGHT is dark and damp

and COLD;

The LEAVES have left the tree;

* Some examples of hieroglyphs appear on pages 39, 109, and 110.
† Drawings reprinted, with permission, from *Words* by Mark Soppeland. Copyright © 1980 by William Kaufmann, Inc., Los Altos, California 94022. All rights reserved.

He hugs the , for he is old;

She does .

He warms his  before the flame,

And piteously murm-

urs, "Adam's , and Eve's the same,

And greedy waits the ."

The  flicker, as in pain;

She hears his dreary mumble:

"Soon  are all that will remain,

And even they will .

What monuments I thought to  !

What 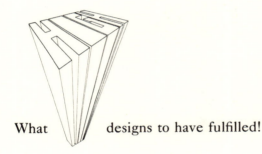 to have slain!

What  designs to have fulfilled!

Now  alone remain."

So  run his

dismal nights,

While she, too young to think

Of aught but ,

 lights,

and coats of priceless ,

With naught but  in her heart,

A  inside her head,

Expects the CLOUDS will all depart

As soon as he is dead.

—W.R.E.

Philologists who chase
A panting syllable through time and space,
Start it at home, and hunt it in the dark
To Gaul, to Greece, and into Noah's ark.
—WILLIAM COWPER

MORE WORD ORIGINS:

Ouch (Old High German Nusca, "Necklace")

You just said "Ouch." Did you refer
To the "ouch" ecclesiastic, sir?—
A brooch, or clasp, or buckle, say,
Often bejeweled in fine display,
Useful for priest or bishop or pope
To fasten his vestment, perhaps his cope?
Germanic was *nusca*, Old English *nouch;*
The *n* dropped off, and it turned to "ouch,"
In just the way the venomous nadder
Molted its *n* and became the *adder.*
(But it seems more likely your "ouch" comes from
Missing the nail, and hitting your thumb.)

—W.R.E.

Bastard (Old French Bâtarde)

The Primal Urge (or Primal Hex,
As Misanthropes refer to Sex)
Is thought by some of young estate
An impulse inappropriate
For dodderers past thirty. How
These young must grieve that for ten thou-
sand years stooped couples, long since clay,
Played all the games kids play today!

Particularly do these rhymes
Refer to medieval times,
When on secluded benches, pairs
Would nuzzle, generating heirs.
The crop of such a furtive clench
Was known as "offspring of the *bench*"—
In German, *Bänchling.*

          In those days
French muleteers used in wanton ways
Packsaddles, their accustomed bed.
And if (I pun) tail turned up head,
Folks called the infant got so fast
"The child of a *packsaddle* (*bast*).
Their word we borrowed with good reason,
Since bastards here are much in season.

               —W.R.E.

Virgins and Crooked-foot Chairs

Not only was an amulet, necklace, or brooch an *ouch* to our forebears, but a rocker was a *crooked-foot chair*, while a *virgin* was a stone bottle (of the sort that holds spruce beer), filled with boiling water and tucked into bed where the feet could rest against it for warmth.

And he shall separate them one from another,
as a shepherd divideth his sheep from the goats.
         —MATTHEW 25:22

IN SOME PLACES THERE IS ONLY ONE DOOR to the restroom, available on a first-come-first-served basis, with an inside lock. Usually these are plainly labelled, but a noteworthy exception was a Melbourne pub; its sign was HERE."

So begins Robinson Rowe's painstaking, historic report on the labels that distinguish the male from the female varieties of relief stations. *Word Ways*, which carried the article, listed several vivid met-

aphors, including ← *Visitors* *Inmates* → at a (pre–women's lib) so-
rority house, and ← *Pointers* *Setters* → at a restaurant called the Dog
House. I mention these here because there was no room for them in
the following sonnet.

ᅠᅠᅠᅠ← *Ladies*ᅠᅠᅠ*Gentlemen*→

When urgent nature whispers low, "Thou must,"
And male and female answer to the call
In public places, they repose their trust
In signs that point each gender to its stall.
Passé is ← *Ladies*ᅠᅠ*Gentlemen* → ; too coy's
The modern mood for such an honest line;
Today it's ← *Adam*ᅠᅠᅠ*Eve* →[1]; or ← *Gulls* and *Buoys* →[2]
Or ← *Harlequin* next door to *Columbine* →[3];
ᅠᅠᅠ← *Beaux*ᅠᅠ*Belles*→[4]; ← *Colts*ᅠᅠ*Fillies* →[5];
ᅠᅠᅠᅠ← *Heifers* (never *Cows*)
Across from *Bulls* →[6]; and ← *Bucks* across from *Squaws* →[7];
Here,ᅠ ← *Jane;*ᅠ there,ᅠ *Tarzan* →[8];ᅠ ← *Angels* here,ᅠ there
ᅠᅠᅠ*Devils* →[9];
← *Trunks* eye *Bikinis* →[10]; ← *Dudes* and *Dolls* →[11] hint revels.

Yet pudency still slows sign writers' pens;
Where are the restrooms labeled ← *Cocks* and *Hens* → ?

ᅠᅠᅠᅠᅠᅠᅠᅠᅠᅠᅠᅠᅠᅠᅠᅠᅠᅠᅠᅠᅠᅠᅠ—W.R.E.

Restrooms, Italian Style

Charles F. Dery's scrapbook contains the entry, "A New York City pub
named PAPARAZZI has rest rooms marked PAPARAZZI and MAM-
MARAZZI." There is still a restaurant of that name in the New York
telephone book, and I trust there has been no change in the signs on
the restrooms; but even if they no longer exist physically, they are
immortal.

[1] At the Paradise Inn, near Seattle. [2] Cove Bar, Naubimmy, Michigan. [3] A little
theater. [4] The Moulin Rouge, New Orleans. [5] At several racetracks. [6] The Cow Palace, White Sulphur Springs, Montana. [7] The Wigwam, near Long Beach, California.
[8] The Jungle Inn. [9] The Hades Club (a bar). [10] At an ocean bathhouse. [11] The Doll
House, near San Francisco.

It was a brave man who first swallowed an oyster.

—DEAN SWIFT

OYSTERMEN AROUND HERE USED TO PAY the state $10 a year for licenses, without inspection. When the state jumped the price to $140 a while back, it decided to justify the increase by sending someone to make sure everything was sanitary.

So one morning a gleaming black car with a gold seal on the side pulled up at the oyster dock, and out stepped a serious-looking young woman in a tailored suit. She had an appointment with Peter Heckes (you will recognize him if you ever come across him at the Oysterville store; he is the burly one with a full black beard that is getting silver flecks in it), and when they had shaken hands she asked which was his oyster dredge. The first one, he said; but not knowing a dredge from a dinghy she headed for a gillnetter-crabber on the wrong side of the dock, and he had to straighten her out. Then she looked at his boat and explained to him how important it was to wash off the deck between loads of oysters, but not to use the water around the dock because it might contain dangerous bacteria, and he agreed with everything she said, and they got along fine.

But the Kemmer boys were less lucky. They had a fresh load of oysters aboard their dredge, waiting to be trucked out next day, and she warned them to cover the oysters with a tarpaulin overnight, so that sea gulls would not pattern-bomb them. What is more, she said, they would have to fill in the narrow cracks between the boards of their decking, because dangerous bacteria love cracks.

So the Kemmers were not overly happy, and a few days later the other oystermen were upset as well when they received a paper from her with a title like "rat feces," only she used a more vulgar term. I won't repeat the whole message as it is too graphic for family reading, but it started this way:

Imagine for a moment, if you will, there there is a rat or gull dropping on top of the oysters on your dredge. Imagine, now, your shellstock being hoisted into a shucking plant, after the dropping has been spread down through the pile by the rain. Inside the plant, the shuckers' gloves and knives thoroughly distribute the dissolved droppings throughout the shucked product, and splash it onto the bench, walls, and floors for further transference. . . .

Well, by the end of the message it was clear that something along the lines of the bubonic plague was about to ravage the nation on account of that rat or gull dropping, and Peter thought she was going too far. She should have known that those oysters were safer inside their shells than the gold is in Fort Knox—it takes a skilled shucker to force them open, even with special equipment, and besides, before the shucking begins the shells are hosed as clean as a baby's breath.

So before her next visit he made some preparations. He and Ruby, his wife, first studied carefully the appearance of sea gull droppings. Then Ruby bought frosting and chocolate, which Peter took to his dredge. He splashed a patch of white frosting nearly the size of a saucer on the deck where it could not be overlooked and sprinkled it with yellow and brown gel and brown chocolate bits. There were similar splotches about, but that was the biggest one.

The young woman appeared the next day in her tailored suit and was so cordial that Pete almost felt ashamed of himself. She paid no attention to the smears, and he finally had to point out that apparently a good many sea gulls had been around recently. "Oh, that's no problem," she said. "Just be sure to rinse the deck before you load the oysters."

Pete said he understood that the acid in the droppings would kill off any germs, but she disagreed. "Oh no," she said. "Sea gull droppings are full of fecal coliform."

"As a matter of fact I kind of *like* the stuff, myself," said Pete. He bent over, scraped a fingerload of his vanilla mix from the deck, and popped it into his mouth. "Not bad," he said, scooping up another fingerful and extending it to her. "Here, give it a try." She gobbled, held up her hands to protect her face, and made a dash for the rail of the dredge.

When she had regained her composure Pete told her it was all a put-on, and she began to laugh, and after that they were good friends.

"But when she was getting into her car," he says, "she looked kind of thoughtful and said, 'Pete, I really think every *two* years is often enough to check oyster dredges, don't you?'"

12

*A dozen mentions. Isn't it
Past time for you and me to quit?*

Ka. In Egyptian mythology, a sort of double
which survived after a man's death if a statue were
made into which it might enter. . . .
—WILLIAM ROSE BENÉT

THE KNITTELVERSE BELOW CLARIFIES the differ-
ence between the ka of Egypt, a spirit, and the ka of Scotland, a
kind of grackle. It does not deal with the expression "Ka me, ka thee,"
meaning "You scratch my back and I'll scratch yours," or with the Ka
of Hinduism, "the unknown god."

How to Tell the Scottish from the Egyptian Ka

The ka, deemed deathless on the teeming Nile,
In Scotland lives for but a fleeting while.
Come, rain down tears for that poor Scottish ka—
He ca's his little ca', and gangs awä;
Though sometimes rather he may gang awô,
And not awä, when he has cawed his caw.

The Scottish ka's a jackdaw. Don't forget
That jackdaws are entirely formed of *khet*,
The "part corruptible," Egyptians say.
That is, the Scottish ka is mortal clay
(Or mortal clô, or maybe mortal clä;
In any case, it's bad news for the ka).

Not so the ka of Egypt; through and through
The lucky creature's essence of *sahu*.
The Flesh has fled, and Spirit is the whole.
(Egyptians say *sahu* instead of *soul*.)
Souls have no gang awäing, gang awôing;
They hang around the place, and keep on cawing.

It fuddles me to travel. When I stay
In Scotland, and espy a ka, I pray.
Were I in Egypt, and a ka I saw,
I'd try to pray, but probably I'd caw.

Another word beginning in *k* deserves its own knittelverse:

*In Zambian Currency, the
Kwacha* Is Worth 100 Ngwees
(Pronounced "Ngways")*

O you kwacha!
Once I've gotcha
I'll have a hundred ngwees!
A kwacha's smaller
Than a Yankee dollar. . . .
But it ain't hay these days.

—W.R.E.

 *Dogberry: Masters, it is proved already that you are little better
than false knaves, and it will go near to be thought so shortly.*
—WILLIAM SHAKESPEARE

DOGBERRY WAS USING A GENERALLY unintended rhetorical device—a trope called *hysteron proteron*, from the Greek
for "the latter [put as] the former." An example given by Puttenham in
1589 was "My dame that bred me up and bare me in her womb."
Muammar Qaddafi, more the strong man of Libya at the time than he
appears to be today, was indulging in hysteron proteron when he said,
"We are capable of destroying America and breaking its nose."

---

* I could not find it in today's foreign exchange listings.

In another book I described the rhetorical device this way:

Hysteron, proteron, backward inclined:
Hindermost forwardmost, foremost behind:
"Mother, you reared me, and bore me also";
"Let us die nobly, and plunge on the foe";
"Soon we shall marry, and first we'll divorce"—
Topsy is turvy, and cart precedes horse.

But how much more elegantly this comic strip makes the point!

THE BORN LOSER ˙ by Art Sansom

Reprinted by permission of NEA, Inc.

If you are not a saint, and sometimes even if you are, it is necessary to deceive one's fellow creatures on many important matters.
—JOHN COWPER POWYS

NOW THAT THE EVOLUTIONISTS HAVE retired Satan to the sidelines, Martin Gardner emerges as our Great Deceiver. Modeling himself after Old Scratch, he operates by letting us deceive ourselves. The following puzzles are from his Flimflam Files, cited by Ronnie Shushan in *The Book of Sense and Nonsense Puzzles*. The answers are always self-evident—and are also in Answers and Solutions—but that does not mean they will leap instantly to your mind.

1. Explain the meaning of this acronym: ETMOTA.
2. What is the opposite of "not in"?
3. Which would you prefer—that a lion ate you or a tiger?
4. Punctuate the following couplet to make it rhyme:
   There was an old farmer and he/Was deaf as a post.
5. You throw a die twenty times and it comes up five on seventeen out of the twenty. What's your best bet for the next roll?
6. How do you keep a moron in suspense?
7. Said a carpenter to his assistant: "Dawitcanooseeeyeoteyeo-utullaails?" What was he trying to say?

Digital Alphabet

One Mr. Essen was served a dreadful restaurant meal—lukewarm soup, wilted salad, yesterday's fish. When handed the bill, he wrote these digits on it, handed it to the waiter, and stalked out. You need only determine the message (it's also in Answers and Solutions):

1 0 2 0 0 4 1 8 0

—RONNIE SHUSHAN

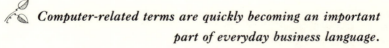

*Computer-related terms are quickly becoming an important
part of everyday business language.*

—JARED TAYLOR

THE TROUBLE IS, THEY KEEP TRESPASSING into lay language as well. Are dentists trying to improve bites or bytes? Is the baud rate the number of prostitutes per square bed? Does artificial intelligence mean cribbing on an economics exam? Everyday English is difficult enough; it is unfair to have to learn computerese, too.

In Times Before Men Turned to Twits
(A Complaint About Computerese)

In times before men turned to twits,
A shave and haircut cost six bits.
When men were men, and iron-jawed,
Six bits would also pay a bawd.

But since computers hove in sight,
It takes eight *bits* to make a *byte*.
A *baud* is eight *bits* too. Now this
Is not the kind of bawd you kiss,

But shows how fast a *modem* acts
In processing computer facts.
And *modems* are not madams, who
Kept bawds, not *bauds*, as retinue.

When men were men, a man who had
A bawd was treated as a cad.
But now a *CAD* is a machine
That works up drawings on a screen.

New words are fine—we have to use them.
My problem is that I confuse them.
I wish the days would come again
When bawds were bawds, and men were men.

—W.R.E.

Contemporary Love Song

My love is a computer with a thousand K of RAM.
It never asks for caviar nor yet prosciutto ham.
Champagne and gourmet cooking are the farthest from its thoughts;
The nourishment I give it is a meager 20 watts.
It's never watching TV when I want to have a chat,
And when I'm through conversing, I can turn it off like *that*.

It never brings me flowers or takes me to a show,
But it doesn't seek affection, or other quid pro quo.
It doesn't kiss me softly or cuddle me in bed,
But it has such lovely software! And I'll take that instead.

—R. P. BOAS

*Due to unknown motives, Jones left a letter for several
days on his desk, forgetting each time to post it. He ultimately
posted it, but it was returned to him from the Dead-Letter Office
because he forgot to address it. After addressing it and
posting it a second time, it was again returned to him,
this time without a stamp. He was then forced to recognize
the unconscious opposition to the sending of the letter.*

—SIGMUND FREUD

IT SEEMS REASONABLE THAT SOMEWHERE inside us
there should be a flip side to the emotions we consciously feel and
the decisions we consciously make—a gagged dissent that cannot
change what we think but can at least punish us by giving us a headache
or persuading us to forget to stamp a letter. We suppress dissenting
opinions, and so do the words we speak. Simply juggle the letters
around, and they become different words altogether. That is the idea
behind anagrams; ASPIRED becomes PRAISED becomes DESPAIR
becomes DIAPERS.

You can trick some words into becoming their opposites by changing them one letter at a time, leaving the other letters unaltered. That
is what I did in the pigmy-giant doublet on page 176, and I do it again
here. Just fill in the right words.

He'd Kiss the Toe That Kicks Him

"Oh, * * * *!" exclaimed the lovelorn lad;
"This * * * * is driving me quite mad;
But all the * * * *, should she enslave me,
I'd much prefer that no one * * * * me."

Better Hunt up Those Prayer Beads

Your * * * creaks, reluctant to respond;
It's * * * where the muscles used to be.
Your * * * to joys of which you've grown too * * * *
Has loosed: fine drinks, fine * * * *, especially
Fine women. Time, old * * * *, to look beyond.
You shuffle and you hack; your breath is * * * *.
Flesh has betrayed you. Time to tend your * * * *.

They Might Try Bundling

* * * * * * is the time to * * * * * *,
Time to watch the dusk grow * * * * * *;
When it's * * * * * * to firefly glow,
Time to let * * * * * * passion flow.
Kisses' fires aren't * * * * * * by sweat;
* * * * * * hugs are sweeter yet.
No. To * * * * * * love, to still
Sound of * * * * * * on the hill,
Needs a season * * * * * *, colder;
Needs a * * * * * * dourer, older.
Those who * * * * * * , close-embraced,
Will in * * * * * * days turn chaste.
Love's the * * * * * *, till it's chilly;
In the * * * * * *, love seems silly.*

—W.R.E.

I won't define the missing words this time, but the first missing word
of each doublet is given (upside down) below. The full answer is in the
back.

damn body summer.

* Not everyone agrees with this conclusion.

Democrats seldom make good polo players . . .
Republicans usually wear hats. . . .

> *I often think it's comical*
> *How Nature always does contrive*
> *That every boy and every gal,*
> *That's born into the world alive,*
> *Is either a little Liberal,*
> *Or else a little Conservative!*
> —W. S. GILBERT

THERE IS AN INACCURATE IMPRESSION getting about that all Republicans are conservatives and all Democrats liberals. That is not quite the distinction that Will Stanton drew in this 1960s *Ladies' Home Journal* article (Congressman Andy Jacobs, Jr., of Indiana, ran it in the Congressional Record twice), but it comes close. Do you suppose the congressman is a Republican or a Democrat?

HOW TO TELL A DEMOCRAT FROM A REPUBLICAN

- Democrats seldom make good polo players. They would rather listen to Béla Bartók.
- The people you see coming out of wooden churches are Republicans.
- Democrats buy most of the books that have been banned somewhere. Republicans form censorship committees and read them as a group.
- Republicans are likely to have fewer but larger debts that cause them no concern. Democrats owe a lot of small bills. They don't worry either.
- Republicans usually wear hats and almost always clean their paintbrushes.
- Democrats give their worn-out clothes to those less fortunate. Republicans wear theirs.
- Republicans employ exterminators. Democrats step on the bugs.
- Republicans have governesses for their children. Democrats have grandmothers.
- Democrats name their children after currently popular sports fig-

ures, politicians, and entertainers. Republican children are named after their parents or grandparents, according to where the most money is.

- Large cities such as New York are filled with Republicans, up until 5 P.M. At this point, there is a phenomenon much like an automatic washer starting the spin cycle. People begin pouring out of every exit of the city. These are Republicans going home.
- Republicans tend to keep their shades drawn, although there is seldom any reason they should. Democrats ought to, but don't.
- On Saturday, Republicans head for the hunting lodge or the yacht club. Democrats wash the car and get a haircut.
- Republicans raise dahlias, Dalmatians and eyebrows. Democrats raise Airedales, kids and taxes.
- Democrats eat the fish they catch. Republicans hang them on the wall.
- Republicans smoke cigars on weekdays.
- Republicans have guest rooms. Democrats have spare rooms filled with old baby furniture.
- Republican boys date Democratic girls. They plan to marry Republican girls, but feel they're entitled to a little fun first.
- Democrats suffer from chapped hands and headaches. Republicans have tennis elbow and gout.
- Republicans sleep in twin beds, some even in separate rooms. That is why there are more Democrats.*

 Together we must rise to ever higher and higher platitudes.
—RICHARD J. DALEY, LONGTIME MAYOR OF CHICAGO

CHICAGO IS AN ALGONQUIAN WORD meaning "field of wild onions," and the pungency of the city's political life makes the name appropriate. A particularly memorable Chicago mayor was Richard J. Daley, who took office in 1955 and ruled the city for nearly

* For a similar problem besetting what remains of Europe's aristocracy, see page 106.

twenty years. Mayor Daley was the last of the old-time bosses, but he may well be remembered longest for his malapropisms, rivaled only by those of motion picture producer Samuel Goldwyn. The examples below are from Peter Yessne's book *Quotations from Mayor Daley*.

Chicago, said the mayor, was going to become "the aviation cross-words of the world." About that world he was an optimist; "It is amazing," he predicted, "what they will do when they get the atom harassed." Sometimes he even sounded thin-skinned: "They have vilified me," he said of his opponents, "they have crucified me, yea they have even criticized me."* He started a speech: "Ladies and gentlemen of the League of Women Voters . . ."

"This administration has always taken the position," he declared, "that an ounce of protection is worth a pound of cure." And, again: "Gentlemen, get the thing straight, once and for all—the policeman is not there to create disorder, the policeman is there to preserve disorder."

> *And the man said, The woman whom thou gavest to be with me, she gave me of the tree, and I did eat.*
> —GENESIS 3:12

ROGER ANGELL TELLS A STORY along this line: An ancient dame, widowed and alone in the cavernous house where her husband and children had once bustled, was at length called away by her Maker. Her heirs had to decide what part of the litter of her lifetime they should throw out and how they should divide the remainder. They were particularly interested in the attic, rumored to hold among its steamer trunks and bird cages and string-tied bundles of newspapers, its bedsprings and bottomless chairs and curvilinear dress models, a letter to a forebear written in Abraham Lincoln's own hand. Unfortunately, an exhaustive search revealed no such trophy. They did find, however, a yellowed envelope that bore in a spidery hand the

---

* This is one of those hysteron proterons I was talking about on page 274.

legend "Great-Uncle Ezra's foreskin." They opened the envelope and reverently shook out a powdery residue—all that remained above-ground of their grandmother's great-uncle.

I thought of that attic yesterday during a visit to Sir John Soane's Museum in Lincoln's Inn Fields, London. If a great-grandparent of yours had never thrown anything away; if that great-grandparent had been wealthy and of informed and eclectic taste; if the time had been the eighteenth century; if the leavings had been masterpieces and oddities of art assembled from most parts of the earth—then you might have had the luck of working your way through litter like that left by Sir John Soane (1753–1837), a brilliant fellow from a humble family, who rose to become architect of the Bank of England, having already had the good sense to fall in love with and marry a wealthy woman.

The museum was Sir John's home, and the entire mansion, not just the attic, is crammed with his acquisitions, some heartbreaking in their loveliness, others simply unexpected and intriguing. The place is so packed that some exhibits are tucked away inside the walls on pivoting trays. You can bring out the paintings in Hogarth's *A Rake's Progress* one by one, tip each upright, and study it at leisure before returning it to its hiding place. The sensation is a bit like watching an extremely slow motion film.

Some windows look out on, or into, a tiny enclosed garden containing, with much else, a monument perhaps ten feet high, almost as elaborately carved as the monstrosity in Edinburgh that memorializes Sir Walter Scott. The legend on the base is a tribute to Sir John's deceased Welsh terrier: "Alas, poor Fanny!"

Each visit to Sir John's reveals something previously missed, and yesterday, in a sort of bow window without the windows, I came across a set of drawings by the eighteenth-century artist James Barry, showing scenes from Milton's *Paradise Lost* and *Paradise Regained*. One, called *Adam's Detection*, made me laugh so heartily that I had a copy struck off to keep me in good spirits at home.

The scene is the Garden of Eden. Above, in the sky, sits Jehovah, lifting an admonitory finger at fallen Adam and Eve. But he is not a glowering God; there is tenderness in his face, perhaps even a repressed smile.

Eve, on her knees, cowers, regarding Him in terror over her shoulder. Adam, however, stands erect, returning God's gaze in outraged

Adam's Detection

innocence. He is shrugging; his arms are thrust forward, palms up. You can almost hear him saying, "What do you expect? You gave us the tools, and aren't we supposed to do the job?"

Look at the reproduction on the previous page. There may be something perverted about my sense of humor, but I think it is one of the funniest paintings I have ever seen.

Nyx (Greek), Nox (Latin). The lively imagination of the ancients associated with this mysterious goddess of night a control over illness, sufferings, dreams, misfortunes, quarrels, war, murder, sleep, and death. She was supposed to inhabit a palace in the lower world jointly with Day. When the latter entered the palace, Night rode out in a chariot drawn by two black steeds, and accompanied by many stars, traversed the heavens till daybreak, when she returned to the palace.
—ALEXANDER S. MURRAY

NYX (OR NOX) ENCOURAGED ME TO WRITE a knittelverse that features words starting with the letter *n*, and I did; but fewer *n* words rallied round than I had expected.

Summer Insomnia
I wonder—is it Nyx or Nox
    That's goddess of the night?
I'll worship either, if she blocks
    This vespertinal plight:

There is a nikin,* far too sweet
    And young for lustful plot—
So young that in the summer heat
    She walks out nelipot†;

* A dear, unformed young thing.
† Barefoot.

And every eve as I lie here
    And count her charms again,
She and another, her compeer,
    Play outside in the lane.

Great Nyx-Nox, if my love you'd win,
    Pray warn her she must not
Play nievie-nievie-nick-nack* in
    The lane outside my cot!

Not that indecent images
    Disturb my early sleep
Of amatory scrimmages,
    And vows I would not keep . . .

But stop Time's wheel, and Death defy!—
    To make the matter plain,
Let *her* lie old in bed, while *I*
    Play nick-nack in the lane!

                      —W.R.E.

Mathers is much troubled by ladies who seek spiritual advice, but one has called to ask his help against phantoms who have the appearance of decayed corpses, and try to get in bed with her at night. He has driven her away with one furious sentence, "Very bad taste on both sides."

                      —W. B. YEATS

IT IS A FINE THING TO RESIST TEMPTATION, but to turn the enticement itself into something repulsive seems to me to be going too far. If I were to store up credits in heaven by keeping phantoms out of my bed, the phantoms would look like Helen of Troy or Marilyn Monroe.

* A children's choosing game.

An Unclean Mind Is a Perpetual Feast.
—VOLTAIRE

An unclean mind's a perpetual feast?
So *that's* why the fat has all gone to my head!
An unclean mind's a perpetual feast?
My body is pure, but my mind is a beast
That gorges on images better unsaid.
An unclean mind's a perpetual feast?
So *that's* why the fat has all gone to my head!

—W.R.E.

I protest that I do not consider the verse that follows to be tasteless. In fact, I do not even consider it to be off color.

. . . Triste Est

Somniferous the sweet surcease;
We lie entwined, in separate peace.
Then, in the way of sated lovers,
She sighs, "Dear, you've got all the covers."

—W.R.E.

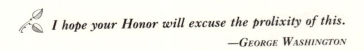 *I hope your Honor will excuse the prolixity of this.*
—GEORGE WASHINGTON

I LEFT YOU ON PAGE 237 HALFWAY through the longest sentence of my acquaintance, feeling you had taken as much as could be expected without a respite. Now you have rested and are ready for the remainder of Laurie Winer's 854 words. Try to read them aloud without taking a breath.

. . . New York City librarian told me, that the longest sentence in literature is the last 40,000 words of James Joyce's *Ulysses*, which does contain two periods but which is really a poem, a chant, or free association that disintegrates at times to a point where it is unrecognizable as formal grammar or even as English (". . . I can see   his   face   clean shaven Frseeeeeeeeeeeeeeeeeeeeeefrong that train . . .") and clings only, as the critic Roy K. Gottfried points out, to a morphemic structure, and which, it should be said, is quite beautiful and evocative, but although while Joyce broke ground and freed his prose from the tyranny of syntax, he did not write a 40,000-word sentence) unless you give it to someone who actually wrote an extremely long sentence, as Marcel Proust did in his seven-volume masterpiece (first published as eight volumes, though *Bookmen's Bedlam* calls it eleven and another reference book, *Felton & Fowler's Best, Worst, and Most Unusual*, remembers it as sixteen—these record books seem to get none of the numbers right) *Remembrance of Things Past*, which contains in it a famous, perfect 958-word (in the C. K. Scott Moncrieff translation) sentence (it begins "Their honour precarious, their liberty provisional . . .") that appears near the start of the fourth book, *Sodome et Gomorrhe* or, as it is known in English, *Cities of the Plain*, just after the narrator has witnessed a homosexual encounter between Jupien the tailor and the Baron de Charlus, an encounter that initiates a rumination on the part of our young hero, whose creator was himself a half-Jewish homosexual, on the tenuous situation of the homosexual in society and on how he is like the Jew in respect to the duplicity of his life, seeking to assimilate and yet compelled to remain different, permeated with the pain of the ever-present knowledge that, because of what he is, he gives cause to others to snub him, alienate him, or hate him, and of how this difference, shared by members on the highest and lowest rungs of society, bonds the ambassador to the felon, or the prince to the ruffian, for here is a sentence that does not suffocate the reader with its verbiage (as might the work of certain Teutonic runners-up for the longest sentence, such as Thomas Bernhard or Hermann Broch); here is a sentence whose length befits its subject matter and its context in the whole; here is a sentence that can be parsed; here is a sentence that should be called the longest in literature (taking into account the possibility that there exist longer grammatical sentences— maybe some crank somewhere wrote a one-sentence book—but we are biased in favor of our titleholder's also being a genius) by the Guinness people; so we suggest they change their Faulkner entry.

Now.

·······

> *I prefer rather than to smell well*
> *not to smell of anything at all.*
> —MARTIAL

THE SEAMAN BROTHERS, THOUGH their accomplishments were many, were not familiar with the epigrams of the Latin author Martial, who flourished close to 2,000 years ago and besides wrote in a foreign language. If Liney Seaman had read the works of Martial, he never would have made his mistake.

Peter Heckes tells me that in the early 1920s, perhaps even a few years earlier, Liney and his older brother, Mort, were young bachelors living across the bay, more or less, from Oysterville. They decided to attend a dance at Smith Island, up the Naselle River.

Liney, to make himself fragrant for the occasion, rolled, in his only suit, in a bed of wild peppermint that grew behind the house. It was a cool day, and he did not notice that some animal had relieved itself there not long before.

The brothers then got in their launch and took off. They were soon dancing their hearts out. As the room and Liney grew warmer, a young woman with whom he was swooping about the floor said, "Liney—do you smell anything?"

"Unh-uh," said Liney.

After they had swooped on awhile, she said again, "Liney—are you *sure* you don't smell anything?"

"Oh, *that!*" said Liney modestly. "Don't mention it, ma'am. That's just my own natural aroma."

Which may or may not have been the reason Liney remained a bachelor all his life. Mort did, too; out of fraternal loyalty, I suppose.

The following knittelverse features two words beginning with *o*: *olent* and *olid*. As you scarcely need telling, *olent* means fragrant. *Olid* means the opposite.

Olent's Not in Love with Olid

Beth debouched from bath of bubble,
Sweet of scent and tempting trouble.

From the pigpen Hank, her neighbor,
Rushed still reeking from his labor.
Beth would not be kissed by Hank;
She informed him that he stank.
Hank to sty retreated dolent:
He was *olid*, she was *olent*.

—W.R.E.

*My father, now in his ninety-second year, hails originally
from Providence, Rhode Island. He had the experience from time to time
of being exposed via the local newspaper to the poetic efforts of one
Edward Leland Strong, known as "the Pawtucket Poet"—Pawtucket
being a small town abutting Providence. The first two stanzas
of the enclosed "poem" remained locked in my father's memory,
and I recall hearing them from early childhood. Recently
the full work was located and typed out—a gem of purest ray serene.*

—Daniel G. Donovan

THE PAWTUCKET POET'S INTOLERABLE poem, reprinted here, was first published February 15, 1911.

Sunrise Over the Banigan Building

When sere and yellow leaf is doomed
And Nature's winter nights are done,
I love to wander all around
The Building called the Banigan.
Oh stately pile of whitish gray,
Like sentinel at the city's gate,
One morning I stood by thy pave
At twenty minutes to 8.

The sun was up, and his rosy tints
Was reflexed from each pane,
Then thoughts of Mammon crossed my mind
And how men work for gain.
Behold, in this stately pile
Lawyers are waiting for their prey;
And brokers too, with hypnotic smile,
Butchering to make a holiday!

Why should a scene of Nature's joy
Be spoiled by sordid gold?
I suppose it will be just the same
Till the judgment day unfold.
What is the use of this stately pile
Devoted to such use?
For such a travesty on progress
There can be no excuse.

And so when the sun gilded my thoughts
With Nature all around,
I thought how pathetic is man,
And my eyes fell to the ground.
Oh build your mounds of bricks and stones,
But the false is not the real,
And sadly then did I turn away
To eat my morning meal.

*The acrostic was probably invented about the same time
with the anagram, tho' it is impossible to decide whether the
inventor of the one or the other were the greater blockhead.*
—JOSEPH ADDISON

MR. ADDISON'S REMARK IS AS UNFAIR to the acrostic
as it would be, say, to the sonnet, or indeed to language itself.
A sonnet may indeed be inane; also, an acrostic may lie at the heart of

a noble poem. The octet below is only a knittelverse, but that is because I can't write anything better, not because the initial letters of the lines, taken in order, make a word.

Acrostic

Aesthetes think puns are called *paronomasia*.[1]
Chronograms once had for name *eteostic*.[2]
Riddles, the scholars say, started in Asia.
Ormonyms fool you—they're *bidiagnostic*.[3]
Scrabble's no game for a man with *aphasia*.[4]
Tongue-twisting preachers are called *pentecostic*.[5]
If you have even a touch of *ergasia*,[6]
Certainly you have unlocked this acrostic.

—W.R.E.

The acrostic in the following sonnet is not simply a device; the poem flows from it. The author, Peter Dickinson, composed the lines to celebrate a marriage; the octet spells out the given name of the bride, and the sestet that of the groom.

. . . x 2*
(*For Arabella and Jeremy*)

Astounding to think of the binary ancestors
Receding back into time, yet mustering here,
As individuals meaningless, bones under moors,
But alive in this place by having been one of a pair,
Each pair doubling the unsummable sum,
Lover with lover, power beyond power of two . . .
Look! To your wedding the generations have come,
All those powers, here, in this hour, in you.

[1] Greek: "with a slightly altered meaning." [2] Greek: "years in a row." [3] Greek: "can be taken in two ways." [4] I don't need to tell you what that means. [5] Or that. [6] Greek: "work"; "disposition toward work."
* Copyright © 1989 Peter Dickinson

Justly then we rejoice, for at such places, such hours,
Exact at the point where line intersects with line
Remaking the timeless mathematical sign,
Energies funnel to a focus, chance becomes willed,
Moments are filled with lifelines, themselves fulfilled . . .
You stand at the fortunate crossroads. Yours are the powers.

Once a homophone, on whim,
Told a passing homonym,
"Homonym? Don't make me laugh—
You're a cheesy homograph!"
Cried the other, "That's baloney!
Shut your mouth, you homophoney!"
—W.R.E.

MAYBE WE SHOULD GO OVER the difference between homophones and homonyms (see page 177) once more.

- *Homophones* differ from one another in origin, meaning, and sometimes in spelling—but never in sound.
- *Homonyms* differ from one another in origin, meaning, and spelling, but never in sound.

So homophones that do not differ from one another in spelling are also homonyms. It will go hard with you in later life if you forget this.

Next comes *homograph*.

The dictionary next to my desk says that a *homograph* (Greek for "with the same letters") is one of two or more words identical in orthography but different in derivation and meaning—as *fair*, meaning *market*, and *fair*, meaning *beautiful; lead*, meaning *to conduct*, and *lead*, meaning *metal*. It fails to say what it shows in the second example: that homographs, unlike homophones and homonyms, *may* differ from one another in pronunciation. And what are homographs that differ from one another in pronunciation?

You are right. They are now *heteronyms*.

For what does the same dictionary say a heteronym is? It is "a word spelled like another, but differing in sound and sense, as *sow*, a pig; *sow*, to strew seed."

To the best of my intent and knowledge, there are various homophone-homonym-homograph combinations in the truncated drama that follows—but no heteronyms.

A Lass, a Lass, Aisle Dye a Made

(*Ella enters stage right, Stella stage left*)

ELLA: High.

STELLA: Low.

ELLA: Ewe seam feint and warn, deer. Ewe grown and mown. Aye here yew side awl weak.

STELLA: Yew grown and mown two. Aye herd ewe.

ELLA: Owe, how yore ayes stair! Yew are sew tents! Yew real!

STELLA: Ella, ewe mussed have guest my pane.

ELLA: Neigh—*hour* pane, deer suite. Aye am blew to. Weir awl, awl a loan, yew and eye.

STELLA: Hour tiers floe. Weir retches.

ELLA: Ewe are sew write, suite hart! But wee no the colonel of hour pane. It is hour knead of a hansom mail.

STELLA: A lass, threw sum grate miss chants weave mist hymn.

ELLA: Ewe no, deer, weave bin chased for daze.

STELLA: Owe, can that bee sew? Hoo chaste us? Sum buoy?

ELLA: Know, know, ewe no know won chaste us, oar wee wood knot bee chased.

STELLA: A lass, a lass, aisle dye a made.

ELLA: Aye two mussed dye a made, a lass, a made unmaid, a lass.

STELLA: Buy, suite.

ELLA: Buy, buy, deer.

(*Exeunt, weeping*)

—W.R.E.

Wilt thou have this Man to be thy wedded husband, to live together after God's ordinance in the holy estate of Matrimony? Wilt thou love him, comfort him, honor, and keep him in sickness and in health; and, forsaking all others, keep thee only unto him, so long as ye both shall live?
The Woman shall answer *I will.*

—*The Form of the Solemnization of Matrimony,*
The Book of Common Prayer

Bridal Morn

The maidens came
    When I was in my mother's bower;
I had all that I would.
    The bailey beareth the bell away;
    The lily, the rose, the rose I lay.
The silver is white, red is the gold;
The robes they lay in fold.
    The bailey beareth the bell away;
    The lily, the rose, the rose I lay.
And through the glass window shines the sun.
How should I love, and I so young?
    The bailey beareth the bell away;
    The lily, the rose, the rose I lay.

—Medieval verse

13

A dozen and one times we chat;
All is silence after that.

> *Starting words in the middle and spelling them in both directions lifts the pallid pastime of Ghosts* out of the realm of children's parties and ladies' sewing circles and makes it a game to test the mettle of the mature adult mind.*
>
> —JAMES THURBER

IN OTHER WORDS, GHOSTS BECOMES Superghosts—one of those games I read about but don't play. Thurber hunted through his mind for two hours for a word besides "phlox" that has "hlo" in it. "I finally found seven," he writes: " 'matchlock,' 'decathlon,' 'pentathlon,' 'hydrochloric,' 'chlorine,' 'chloroform,' and 'month-long.' " The Superghost aficionado, according to Thurber, spends moody hours wondering "why he didn't detect, in yesterday's game, that 'cklu' is the guts of 'lackluster' and priding himself on having stumped everybody with 'nehe,' the middle of 'swineherd.' "

I find in the mail a typewritten postcard from J. Bryan III, reading

Dear Mr. Espy:
    I L I L
    I L I W
I've never played the game with anyone who could solve either of these combinations.

Fortunately, Mr. Bryan inked in on either side the letters that are required. If you find yourself at a loss, look at Answers and Solutions.

---

* Tony Augarde in *The Oxford Guide to Word Games* explains Ghosts as follows: "The first player thinks of a word of three or more letters, and calls out its first letter. The second player adds another letter, which continues but does not complete a word, and so on, until one player is forced to finish a word. Any player who adds a letter can be challenged by the next player to say what the word will be. Any player who loses such a challenge or completes a word becomes 'a third of a ghost.' When he loses again, he becomes 'two-thirds of a ghost' and the third time he is 'a whole ghost' and is out of the game."

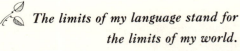
Gloucester: O! let me kiss that hand!
Lear: Let me wipe it first; it smells of mortality.
—WILLIAM SHAKESPEARE

It Often Comes into My Mind

When sun leaps up and sun dips down,
When leaves spring green and leaves fall brown,
It often comes into my mind
That this is leaving me behind.

When tides wash out and tides wash in,
When what will be is what has been,
It often comes into my mind
That this is leaving me behind.

When morrows sink in yesterdays,
And peaks grow dim with valleys' haze,
It often comes into my mind
That this is leaving me behind.

When you, with but a door between,
Are gone as if you had not been,
It often comes into my mind
That this is leaving me behind.

—W.R.E.

The limits of my language stand for
the limits of my world.
—EMIL LUDWIG

CAN ONE LANGUAGE ACTUALLY EXPRESS anything of importance that another language cannot? Can French reveal more about women, or Inuit about snow, or Chinese about dragons?

Few, except perhaps for the French, would argue that English is not the richest of tongues. Can it really say more than the rest, then—more plainly—and in subtler detail?

And what about the *sounds* of a language? Is there really something to the old saying, "English for horses, French for business, German for command, Italian for lovemaking, Spanish for addressing one's God"? And is there a difference between the soul of the man who says "Gawd" and the one who says "Gahd"?

What (wrote George Lyttleton, who was English, to his friend Rupert Hart-Davis, English also)

> are you to do about America, where the *sound* of words is differently interpreted? I remember a rather good Galsworthian play about the iniquity of cutting down the copse in front of some country house. It pleased in London, but on Broadway they thought cutting down the copse meant a reduction in the size of the police force, and were baffled.

I raise these questions; I do not answer them. That will have to wait until I have decided whether to say *a.cū'men* or *ac'ū.men*.

A man's real possession is his memory.
In nothing else is he rich,
in nothing else is he poor.
—ALEXANDER SMITH

IF MEMORIES, RICH OR POOR, prove too troublesome, we bury them away in our subconscious, pile earth on them, jump up and down on it, and leave the spot unmarked. Thereafter they return only in disguise, as ghosts or nightmares. But why do so many innocuous, even pleasant events disappear as totally? Perhaps memory is limited in capacity, like a bathtub; once the water has risen to the overflow level, an equal amount must be lost for everything gained.

In 1938 I made a two-month trip to Mexico for a magazine, to write an article about President Cárdenas's "each one teach one" program for cutting down illiteracy. The magazine was *The Nation;* they were to pay me $75, not a bad price, and I was to cover my own expenses. My letters home made it clear that I was having the time of my life; yet I have very little independent memory of what happened, and none whatever of anything reported here:

Mexico City, 6 September 1938

Dear folks:

My companions coming south included a passenger agent for the Mc-Cormick lines and an English-born postal employee who wears size fourteen shoes that curve towards each other like parentheses. At Mazatlan we all walked the beach; the passenger agent stripped to his shorts and plunged into the surf, while the rest of us strolled on. When the agent returned to shore, all his clothes were waiting for him except the shoes. The postal employee offered a spare pair of his size fourteens, but the passenger agent preferred to walk barefoot for half an hour until we found a shoe store.

We spent Friday and Saturday at Guadalajara. You hear the city before you see it. The *calendrias*—four-wheeled carriages—have constantly jangling bells; the bicycles boast horns that would shame an American fire engine; the trolley cars clang; and the cathedral bells ring endlessly. Besides the regular strokes, there are combinations that warn of approaching church services, others that plead with you to hurry, and still others that say sorry, we had to start without you.

The city is ablaze right now with *llamaredas*. They are a climbing plant with flowers of a flame-color so vivid that I almost averted my eyes, as if to avoid the direct sun. We watched the painter Orozco working on a mural, and were impressed. Moments later we were no less impressed by an ancient Indian in a dirty serape cutting drawings into new clay pots.

Oh—we also visited a cathedral that featured in its nave a coffin containing the body of a bishop, a very holy man dead these three hundred years. Worshipers in need of heavenly intercession rap three times on the coffin, and then make their requests. Notes of gratitude for wishes fulfilled, generally written in pencil, are pasted to the top and sides. One thanked the dead bishop for restoring the fidelity of a husband, and another for easing the pain in a woman's legs.

I am told that when the bishop died, a mule train started across the mountains with his body, but bandits abducted it, perhaps hoping for a ransom. Three days later, a mule with the holy remains still draped across its back appeared at the cathedral door, struck the cobblestones three times with its hoof, and dropped dead.

JACKSON, Miss., Dec. 8.—The American Civil Liberties Union today asked a Federal court to overturn Mississippi's decision to light a cross on a 20-story state office building for the Christmas season. "There has never been a Federal court that has upheld a cross display on a public building," Hilary Chiz, executive director of the Mississippi chapter of the civil liberties group, said at a news conference.

—AP

Mz. Chiz

Who iz
Mz.
Chiz?
Why iz
Mz.
Chiz
Afizz?

      For this:
      An edifice
      In Old Miss
      Where a mys-
      tic sign of bliss
      But no Kriss

Kringle iz.
To Mz.
Chiz

      This

Iz
Monkey biz.

      This

Cross iz
Why Mz.
Chiz
Cross iz.

Merry Christ-
mas, edifice
in Old Miss!
Merry Christ-
mas, Kriss!
Merry Kriz-
mas, Mz.
Chiz!

—W.R.E.

 Inflation is like sin; every government denounces it
and every government practices it.
—SIR FREDERICK LEITH-ROSS

ON THE LONG-GONE FIRST DAY of Christmas when My True Love began sending his cumulative gifts, no one had heard of inflation. My True Love found his trees and his fowl in the forest, his maids and milch cows on the farm. For a meal that included an abundance of ale and venison, any number of lords, ladies, and pipers would start dancing, leaping, and piping. George Johnson reminded me that this blissful state of affairs can never return. He sent me a Chicago newspaper story pointing out that if My True Love had acquired those same gifts in modern times, they would have cost him $587,878.78 (slightly higher west of the Rockies). Here are the calculations:

- *First day*. "The first day of Christmas, my true love sent to me/A partridge in a pear tree." Six-foot potted pear: $15.99. Crested wood partridge: $100. Since this, like the later gifts, is repeated each of the twelve days, the total comes to $1,391.88.
- *Second day*. Two turtle doves, $50 a pair. For eleven days, $550.
- *Third day*. Three French hens, $5 each. $150 for ten days.
- *Fourth day*. Four calling birds. The researchers (based at the University of Illinois's Chicago Circle Campus) decided on canaries

with a good color and a quality chirp; $49.50 apiece, $198.00 per day for nine days: $1,782.

- *Fifth day.* Five gold rings. Fourteen karat or twenty-one karat? The song does not say. But at the time the dispatch was written, Tiffany's was offering a 15 percent discount on rings in quantities of five. Five rings a day for eight days, fourteen karat, $3,162. Twenty-one karat, $12,750.
- *Sixth day.* Six geese a-laying, at $50 per goose. Here the pricing becomes complicated. To lay eggs, says the dispatch, requires the help of a companion, and geese mate for life. So not six but twelve geese are required each day. I question the premise. I know little about geese, but when I was a boy on the farm our hens required no prompting from the other sex to lay eggs. They needed help only to lay *fertile* eggs. Taking the researchers at their word, twelve geese a day for the seven remaining days of Christmas means forty-two pair, or eighty-four individual geese. The cost: $4,200.
- *Seventh day.* Seven swans a-swimming, times six. If My True Love is willing to settle for mute swans, he can have forty-two birds for $10,500. If he insists on trumpeters, he will be hit for $52,500.
- *Eighth day.* Eight maids a-milking. The cost here is based on the cows—eight of them for five days. If they are high-class Holsteins, producing 15,000 pounds of milk a year each—enough to sour anyone on milk for life—the agricultural school will rent them out for $132,979.20. The milkmaids are thrown in free, which is understandable. No explanation is given for the last twenty cents.
- *Ninth day.* Nine ladies dancing. There is room for maneuver here; it depends on how one defines the word *lady*. The price given for chorus girls in the dispatch is $9,690, including a van to transport them. But ballerinas would come to $90,000. They would need a musical accompaniment, and what the newspaper account calls a "chest of viols" would raise the ante by another $23,000, including air fare from the East Coast and lodging.
- *Tenth day.* Ten lords a-leaping, then twenty, then thirty. First-class on British Airways, first-class accommodations in Chicago for three days—$143,760.
- *Eleventh day.* Eleven pipers piping. If they are from the Pipe-fitters Union, the total charge will be $4,158. For nonunion bag-

pipers the price is only $2,022, and they come in their own cars.
• *Twelfth day.* Twelve drummers drumming. Just $300.

The dispatch lists a few extra expenses: rental of Chicago's Navy
Pier for twelve days, including adjoining space for the animals: $38,400;
fifty pounds of seed for partridges, doves, and canaries, cracked corn
for the hens, hay and mixed grain for the cows: $137.50.

Whether the total is exactly $587,878.78 depends on which of the
variables you pick and also on whether you are renting those dancers
and leapers or buying them. The charge for the rings is too high,
though. The line is about ringdoves, not finger rings. Ringdoves are
much like pigeons, and pigeons are not scarce in Chicago. In fact, I
imagine the city fathers would pay My True Love to take them away.

Hickey. Of unknown origin. From original application to
devices used in electrical trades, it was quickly embellished to
doohickey, meaning a gadget or tool used to manage some simple
operation. Of still further interest is the variety of picturesque
expressions for the same concept and idea, like* do(o)dad,
rigmajig, thing(a)bob *and* what-do-you-call-it. *1. Of dermatalogic
interest is application of the word to a pimple* (papulo-pustule) *and to
the erythematous and later ecchymotic mark* (passion purpura) *of a
playful bite or pinch, usually on the cheeks (of the face or buttocks),
the neck or breasts, incurred in hanky-panky.*
—A DICTIONARY OF DERMATOLOGICAL WORDS, TERMS, AND PHRASES,
MORRIS LEIDER AND MORRIS ROSENBLUM

THE FOREGOING EXTRACT ARRIVED from Dr. S. A.
Rosenthal, of the Department of Dermatology at the New York
University Medical Center. My emotions were aroused:

* See pages 90 and 211.

The Hickey

Deep in a dictionary medical,
'Mid other items tricky,
Behold an epidermal pedicle
Identified as *hickey!*

"Of root unknown, but full of riches,"
The definition reads—
"As, gadgets for electric switches;
From this same word proceeds

"*Doohickey,* for a tool that can
Abet some trifling aim—
So unpretentious that a man
Cannot recall the name;

"Sometimes called *doodad, thingumbob,*
And other terms as simple;
Upon the skin, a vexing knob—
In laymen's terms, a *pimple;*

"But oft an ecchymotic* mark
On buttock formed, or cheek,
Or throat, or breasts, from after-dark
Pinch, nibble, bite, or tweak

"By lovers (to such whims addicted)
On loved parts, plump or lanky.
This hickey's oftenest inflicted
In course of hanky-panky."
—W.R.E.

* Discolored by an effusion of blood beneath the skin.

*The Homunculus, Sir, in however low and ludicrous a light
he may appear, in this age of levity, to the eye of folly or prejudice
. . . consists as we do, of skin, hair, fat, flesh, veins, arteries,
ligaments, nerves, cartilages, bones, marrow, brains, glands,
genitals, humours, and articulations;—is a being of as much
activity—and, in all senses of the word, as much and as truly our
fellow-creature as my Lord Chancellor of England.*

—LAURENCE STERNE

MY DICTIONARY LISTS THREE STRAINS of homunculus. Number one is "a diminutive man; pygmy; manikin." Number two is the human fetus, evoked by Tristram Shandy, with a little help from Laurence Sterne, in *The Life and Opinions of Tristram Shandy, Gentlemen.*

The homunculus that was Tristram-to-be came within a spasm's space of never existing at all, when at a critical instant his mother-to-be asked his father-to-be whether he had not forgotten to wind the clock. Now, the rules for creation of a homunculus require that at the starting gun thousands of importunate suitors burst from the gate and race toward the object of their affections, who waits passively at the finish line. The winner melts into her bosom, and the losers perish of exhaustion and despair. The winner and his darling are merged into one—a homunculus. In Tristram's case, by reason of the query about the clock, the starting gun all but missed fire.

We come now to homunculus number three, generally confined to medical dictionaries. It is a drawing—a simulacrum for physicians in which each part of the human body is proportional in size to the amount of attention it requires of the brain. Dr. Goodwin M. Breinin informed me about number three and was kind enough to draw me the accompanying illustration. The eyes, about the relative size of millwheels, apparently require as much attention from the nervous system as all our other parts combined. The thumbs are second in size only to the eyes. From the viewpoint of the brain, we consist essentially of eyes and thumbs; the rest is little more than material for holding these two

together. Who would have dreamed that such elaborate neural guid-
ance is required for the thumb to counterpoint the other fingers? To
me, thumbs have always stood for bumbledom. The thumb is the thing
you hit with your hammer when you miss the nail.

There are times when Dr. Breinin, were he present, might note a
distinct resemblance between me and homunculus number three:

Homunculus to His Mistress

In me, my dear, as in Homunculus,
The bits and pieces correspond in size
To their demands upon the abacus
Men call the Brain. Homunculus has eyes
Thrice larger than his head, and thumbs, though less,
Thrice larger than his hands.
                                    This rule applies
To me at midnight; for, as you undress,
    I am all eyes;
But when the longed-for, sweet encounter comes,
    I am all thumbs.
                                    —W.R.E.

GMB '80

Heap on more wood!—the wind is chill;
But let it whistle as it will,
We'll keep our Christmas merry still.
—Sir WALTER SCOTT

DYLAN THOMAS'S CONVERSATIONS ABOUT XMAS
(*Continued from page 224.*)

SELF: The Uncles sat in front of the fire, took off their collars, loosened all buttons, put their large moist hands over their watch-chains, groaned a little, and slept. Mothers, aunts, and sisters scuttled to and fro, bearing tureens. The dog was sick. Auntie Bessie had to have three aspirins, but Auntie Hannah, who liked port, stood in the middle of the snowbound backyard, singing like a big-bosomed thrush. I would blow up balloons to see how big they would blow up to; and, when they burst, which they all did, the Uncles jumped and rumbled. In the rich and heavy afternoon, the Uncles breathing like dolphins and the snow descending, I would sit in the front room, among festoons and Chinese lanterns, and nibble at dates, and try to make a model man-o'-war, following the Instructions for Little Engineers, and produce what might be mistaken for a sea-going tram. And then, at Xmas tea, the recovered Uncles would be jolly over their mince-pies; and the great iced cake loomed in the centre of the table like a marble grave. Auntie Hannah laced her tea with rum, because it was only once a year. And in the evening there was Music. An uncle played the fiddle, a cousin sang Cherry Ripe, and another uncle sang Drake's Drum. It was very warm in the little house. Auntie Hannah, who had got on to the parsnip wine, sang a song about Rejected Love, and Bleeding Hearts, and Death, and then another in which she said that her Heart was like a Bird's nest; and then everybody laughed again, and then I went to bed. Looking through my bedroom window, out into the moonlight and the flying, unending, smoke-coloured snow, I could see the lights in the windows of all the other houses on our hill, and hear the music rising from them up the long, steadily falling night. I turned the gas down, I got into bed. I said some words to the close and holy darkness, and then I slept.

SMALL BOY: But it all sounds like an ordinary Xmas.

SELF: It was.

SMALL BOY: But Xmas when you were a boy wasn't any different to Xmas now.

SELF: It was, it was.

SMALL BOY: Why was Xmas different then?

SELF: I mustn't tell you.

SMALL BOY: Why can't Xmas be the same for me as it was for you when you were a boy?

SELF: I mustn't tell you. I mustn't tell you because it is Christmas now.

Modernity here were a fig leaf; wax candles were burnt instead of gas or electric light; and even the telephone was enshrined in a Florentine casket.

—COMPTON MACKENZIE

THE PRESIDENT OF OBERLIN COLLEGE sent the faculty a memorandum reading as follows:

Camus, I believe, defined modern man as one who drinks coffee, reads newspapers, and engages in sex. By this measure, it is virtually impossible to be a modern man or woman in the Rice Faculty Lounge as it now exists. To rectify this unfortunate situation, I am arranging for coffee to be served (at a modest cost to the drinker) during weekday mornings and early afternoons, and for newspapers to be available there. These earth-shaking innovations will bring the Faculty Lounge two-thirds of the way into the modern world—probably as far as it should go.

And, of course, there is nothing to stop the faculty members, between sips of coffee and glances at newspaper headlines, from building hopes, laying plans, engaging in schemes, and even passing notes, all aimed at going the last third of the way into the modern world. Somewhere outside the Faculty Lounge, of course.

. . . .

More than five hundred years after the heyday of the English archer, his terminology may still be heard in everyday speech, in proverbial wisdom, and in the imagery of literature.
—PETER A. DOUGLAS, VERBATIM

MR. DOUGLAS IS NOT DRAWING the long bow. Here are some of the terms he describes as descending from either the bow and arrow or the crossbow, that dread weapon which many once feared might destroy civilization, if not mankind:

Bull's-Eye!

Should bruited atom bomb
Make mush of manly marrow,
Perspective may lend calm:
Start talking bow-and-arrow.

You say, "Brace up!" One point you may have missed—
That "brace up" first conveyed "to brace a bow"—
"To draw the bowstring tighter." Let me list
More terms passed on by archers long ago:

The arrow's target was a *butt,* or bank
Of earth. That's why the target of a joke
Is now the *butt.* The butt contained a *blank*—
A white spot that a well-aimed shaft would poke—

Whence our *point-blank*—"directly aimed; just so."
"I still have arrows in my quiver" means
"I have alternatives," as does "My bow
Has more than just one string." More origins:

The final shot, which settled tourney prizes,
Was called the *up*shot; it resolved all doubt.
So "upshot of the matter" *summarizes:*
"With all facts in, here's how the case turns out."

In crossbow days, the missile was a *bolt*.
We shoot our *bolt* still; *bolts* come from the blue.
When we say *bolt* of lightning, *bolting* colt,
To *bolt* off—these are crossbows' residue.

> *Though bow-and-arrow battle*
> *No more feeds men to worms,*
> *We still embroider prattle*
> *With bow-and-arrow terms.*

—W.R.E.

> *Just a wee doch-an'-dorris*
> *Before we gang awa'* . . .
> —SIR HARRY LAUDER

DID YOU ASK WHAT SOCIAL CUSTOMS were like when I was young? Well, though our urges may have been identical with those of today, we manifested them differently. And it does seem to me that we had more fun than our children and grandchildren do. But there!—maybe it is quite the other way around—maybe they are enjoying every minute of every twenty-four hours and are just hiding it from us. A story that Tony Kischner tells probably bears on the subject, but I am not sure which way it points.

Tony presides over the Shoalwater Restaurant fifteen miles or so south of Oysterville. He worked his way up in the business in Seattle and was once a waiter. One evening he waited on a young man and woman who were clearly in a festive mood. They had two drinks before dinner and looked deeply into each other's eyes as they raised their glasses. They held hands between courses, ordered caviar and the costliest steak, chose the most expensive, if not the best, Burgundy on the wine list, clinked their goblets together, and looked into each other's eyes again. As he brought their after-dinner cordials, Tony worked up courage to say, "You two must be celebrating something. Are you getting married?"

"No," they replied in happy chorus; "we are getting divorced."

His wife, his children, his garden fill up his day,
as snip-snap-snorum does his evening.
—MELESINA TRENCH

So WHAT, I ASKED FIRST MYSELF and then the dictionary, is snip-snap-snorum? I could not answer, but the dictionary
came through, saying it is a "round game of matching sequences; see
Earl of Coventry." I saw Earl of Coventry—"a card game in which the
eldest hand lays a card on the table, and the other players in turn try to
match it." I also saw another dictionary, which called snip-snap-snorum
"a round game of cards, played (esp. by the young) in various ways, in
which the players on turning up the requisite cards respectively call
'snip,' 'snap,' and 'snorum.' " A quotation followed from Robert
Southey: "It had been found convenient to set down the children to
Pope Joan, or snip-snap-snorum, which was to them a more amusing
because a noisier game." I looked up Pope Joan. It is a game "played
with an ordinary pack of cards minus the eight of diamonds (called the
'Pope Joan')." The game is named after a fabulous female, who was
supposedly elected to the papacy in 855 as John VIII and "died in
childbirth during a solemn procession." Besides being a card game,
Pope Joan is "a circular revolving tray with eight compartments."

So snip-snap-snorum either is, or is similar to, Earl of Coventry,
Pope Joan, and a circular revolving tray. It is also a key element of this
knittelverse, featuring certain words that begin with the letter *s* and a
few that do not:

S. On Sploring[1] and Snip-snap-snorum[2]

A picnic is a pasture feast;
A pyknic[3] is a fat-stuff.
But nothing care we two, at least,
That *this* stuff leads to *that* stuff.

---

[1] Carousing. [2] A card game. [3] A fatty.

So we shall splore[4] among the cows,
And on the grass sit stodging[5];
If lambs come bounding as we smouse,[6]
Let others do the dodging.

Let others jog, their waists to shear—
Slipe[7] lipids[8] off by diet;
We'll lean against some Jersey's rear,
And sloam[9] in God's own quiet.

Let others scuddle[10]; let them strain,
And fitness pamphlets study;—
Though we grow squaddy,[11] we'll remain
As seely[12] as a scuddy.[13]

While they do push-ups on the lea,
And play the cockalorum,[14]
Our briskest exercise will be
A hand of snip-snap-snorum.

                              —W.R.E.

*Neurosis does not deny the existence of reality;
it merely tries to ignore it; psychosis denies it and
tries to substitute something else for it.*
                              —SIGMUND FREUD

WHERE DOES *HYSTERIA* COME IN? It is a psychoneu-
rosis common to both sexes; but the word comes from the Greek
for "womb," and many a man has the impression that it is primarily a
female problem. Technically, a man, lacking a womb, cannot suffer

---

[4] Frolic. [5] Stuffing ourselves. [6] Eat with gusto. [7] Peel, pare, strip. [8] Fats. [9] Slumber,
doze. [10] Hurry about. [11] Stout, heavy. [12] Blissful. [13] A naked child. [14] A bantam cock;
a self-important person.

from hysteria. "Woman's reason," said George Meredith, "is in the milk of her breasts"; a man has no breasts. It is an undeniable fact, though, that the symptoms of hysteria are quite as prevalent among men as among women.

You will be glad to know, then, that there is a sex-neutral word for hysteria. It is *tarassis* (from Greek *tarassein*, "to disturb"). Yet maybe it is not sex-neutral; my dictionary defines it specifically as "hysteria in males."

> *One Tarassis = One Hysteria.*
>   *Or Does It?*
>
> L. P. Beria*
> Could not have hysteria.
> Jackie Onassis
> Cannot have tarassis.
> The words disagree
> Genderally.
>
>
> That's been the idea
> Since the tritavia†
> Of my tritavia;
> Been drilled in us
> Since the tritavus‡
> Of my tritavus.
>
>
> *Different name—*
> *Symptoms the same*
>   —W.R.E.

---

* He ran the OGPU for Stalin.

† A great-grandmother's great-grandmother.

‡ A great-grandfather's great-grandfather.

*Affectation is an awkward and forced
imitation of what should be genuine and easy, wanting
the beauty that accompanies what is natural.*

—JOHN LOCKE

THE HEROES OF THIS LAST KNITTELVERSE are three highly dignified words, two Greek and one Latin, that begin with *u*.

U. Mr. Ultrafidian,[1] Meet Mr. Ucalegon[2]

There's something fine in Latin. Something—oh,
How should I say it? Something like . . . you know . . .
Well, *fine!* Like, I could call a man
(A sucker, natch) an *ultrafidian!*

And Greek's great too. They've even got a noun
For "neighbor with a house that's burning down"!
I kid you not. They turn the firehose on,
And shout across, "Hi there, *ucalegon!*"

I'm for the classics. Like . . . you'll think I'm loony . . .
But honey, just you listen. You're my *uni-
cumissimus*[3]—my very most unique!
Hey, Latin's good for grammar. So is Greek.

—W.R.E.

---

[1] One who is ultracredulous. [2] Defined in the verse. [3] *Unicum* is a thing unique in its kind. So *unicumissimus* is very unique, uniquer than unique—egregious in grammar, but delightful in lovers.

> *With the single exception of Homer, there is*
> *no eminent writer, not even Sir Walter Scott, whom*
> *I can despise so entirely as I despise Shakespeare*
> *when I measure my mind against his. . . . It would positively*
> *be a relief to me to dig him up and throw stones at him.*
> *—G. B. SHAW**

At Last, the Real Shakespeare (II)†

GEORGE BERNARD SHAW DID NOT DOUBT that Shakespeare really wrote the plays and poems that bear his name; Shaw's point was that they were lousy. Generally, the contention that the name Shakespeare was a pseudonym for someone else is turned the other way around—the man, say his critics, simply lacked the background, the breeding, the culture, and the connections required to create the masterpieces attributed to him. According to this argument, Ben Jonson was thinking of someone else when he wrote after the Bard's death:

> This figure that thou here seest put,
> It was for gentle Shakespeare cut,
> Wherein the graver had a strife
> With Nature, to out-do the life.
> O could he but have drawn his wit
> As well in brass, as he has hit
> His face, the print would then surpass
> All that was ever writ in brass:
> But since he cannot, reader, look
> Not on his face, but on his book.

If Shakespeare was not Shakespeare, who was? Perhaps, goes one theory, he did play a small part in a sub-rosa committee set up by Queen Elizabeth, with Raleigh or de Vere in charge, such writers as

---

* Tolstoy took a similar position.

† See page 132 for (I).

Bacon, Marlowe, Fletcher, and Beaumont participating, and Shakespeare running the errands. Under the guise of entertainment, the group would have been carrying out propaganda for the queen.

In any event, goes the claim, some person or persons of culture and connections must have crafted certain masterpieces and forged Shakespeare's name to them. Among the suspects have been Edward de Vere (earl of Oxford); William Stanley (earl of Derby); Kit Marlowe; and Francis Bacon. The Baconian thesis is built around tortured anagrams; one Dr. Isaac Platt, for instance, anagrammed the word "honorificabilitudinitatibus" in *Love's Labour's Lost* into *"Hi ludi, F. Baconis nati tuiti orbi"*—tortured Latin, he claimed, for "These plays, the offspring of F. Bacon, are preserved for the world."*

That none of the ciphers proves its point means only that the decipherers were attempting to identify the wrong man. By good luck, I have been able to correct this error. One day, as I reread Jonson's *To the Memory of Shakespeare*, my eye paused on the line that described him as one of "small Latin and less Greek." Why, thought I in some astonishment, that is an exact description of *me!* The resemblance was too strong to be mere coincidence. Moreover, I had—have—in all other respects the background, the breeding, the great connections, that Shakespeare was alleged to lack. I felt an instant moral certainty that I had composed the Shakespeare canon; all that was needed for proof was to locate my name anagrammed in one of the texts. This I set out to do.

It was not easy; but I am persistent. In Sonnet 56, I found five letters on succeeding lines that—taken in order, though not in succession—spelled "To Wil." Scarcely conclusive, since the Wil referred to could have been William S. himself; but a promising beginning. In Sonnet 54, he got as far as "To Willar." In 60 he managed "Willard Esp." At last, in 114, he worked in the whole name—"Willard Espy"—and threw in the Spanish-language huzzah "olé" for good measure. The letters, moreover, are arranged with elegant symmetry, one to a line. The proof is conclusive. You doubt me? See for yourself.

* But the word was used in writing at least five hundred years before Shakespeare's time.

At last, the real Shakespeare!

Sonnet 114

Or *w*hether doth my mind being crown'd with you,	W
Dr*i*nk up the monarch's plague, this flattery?	I
Or whether sha*l*l I say mine eye saith true,	L
And that your *l*ove taught it this alchemy.	L
To m*a*ke of monsters and things indigest	A
Such che*r*ubims as your sweet self resemble,	R
Creating every ba*d* a perfect best,	D
As fast as obj*e*cts to his beams assemble?	E
O, 'ti*s* the first, 'tis flattery in my seeing,	S
And my great mind most kingly drinks it u*p;*	P
Mine e*y*e well knows with what his gust is 'greeing,	Y
And to his palate d*o*th prepare the cup;	O
If it be poison'd, 'tis the *l*esser sin	L
That min*e* eye loves it and doth first begin.	E

—WILLIAM SHAKESPEARE (PEN NAME OF W.R.E.)

There you are. The word's gotten out.

ANSWERS AND SOLUTIONS

· ·

PAGE 29
ESPYramids Up

Faith Rewarded

The missing words: A, AS, SEA, APES, SPARE, SPREAD, PRAISED, PAR-
ADISE

The complete verse: A sailor, as he set to sea
                                  To bring back apes from Barbary,
                                  Prayed, "Father, spare me and I swear
                                  I'll spread Thy glory everywhere!"
                                  He praised the Lord, nor felt surprise
                                  To wake next morn in paradise.

And They're Smooth Going Down

The missing words: A, AT, EAT, LATE, ALTER, RELATE, TREACLE,
LACERATE

The complete verse: A man at dinner would not eat.
                                    He said, "Of late I like food sweet.
                                  Please alter what you serve to me;
                                  I best relate to sugared tea
                                  And treacle. They are cloying, but
                                  They do not lacerate the gut."

At Least He Knows What He Wants

The missing words: A, AT, ART, TEAR, TRADE, ARDENT, TRAINED,
STRAINED, RESTAINED, DISHEARTEN

The complete verse: A critic at an art display
                                    Could scarcely tear himself away;
                                  He said, "I'll trade my Paul Gauguin
                                  With ardent joy for your Derain.
                                  To excellence my eye is trained;
                                  I know what's fine, and what is strained.
                                  Your canvas is restained, I see,
                                  But that does not dishearten me."

PAGE 32
Shakespeare Didn't Always Say It First

1. If ye should lead her into a fool's paradise (as they say), it were a very gross kind of behaviour (as they say).
   —*Romeo and Juliet*, ACT II, SC. 3, l. 169

2. I'll not budge an inch, boy.
   —*The Taming of the Shrew*, ACT II, SC. 1, l. 14

3. He receives comfort like cold porridge.
   —*The Tempest*, ACT II, SC. 1, l. 10

4. And art made tongue-tied by authority.
   —SONNET 66
   (The word *tongue-tied* also appears in *A Midsummer Night's Dream*, *The Winter's Tale*, *1 Henry VI*, *Richard III*, and *Julius Caesar*.)

5. But be it as it may, I here entail/The crown to thee.
   —*3 Henry VI*, ACT I, SC. 1, l. 194

6. But, for my own part, it was Greek to me.
   —*Julius Caesar*, ACT I, SC. 2, l. 59

7. For a score of kingdoms you should wrangle,/And I would call it fair play.
   —*The Tempest*, ACT V, SC. 1, l. 175

8. I am a man more sinn'd against than sinning.
   —*King Lear*, ACT III, SC. 2, l. 288

9. In despite of the teeth of all rhyme and reason.
   —*The Merry Wives of Windsor*, ACT V, SC. 5, l. 95
   (Also "Neither rhyme nor reason," *The Comedy of Errors*.)

10. I have been in such a pickle since I saw you last that I fear me will never out of my bones.
    —*The Tempest*, ACT V, SC. 1, l. 281

11. Therefore, 'tis high time that I were hence.
    —*The Comedy of Errors*, ACT III, SC. 2, l. 162

12. An eye-sore to our solemn festival.
    —*The Taming of the Shrew*, ACT III, SC. 2, l. 103

13. Make a short shrift, he longs to see your head.
    —*Richard III*, ACT III, SC. 4, l. 97

14. The more fool you for laying on my duty.
> —*The Taming of the Shrew*, ACT V, SC. 2, l. 129

15. The game is up.
> —*Cymbeline*, ACT II, SC. 3, l. 107

16. He will give the devil his due.
> —*1 Henry IV*, ACT I, SC. 2, l. 122

17. And if I do not leave you all as dead as a door-nail, I pray God I may never eat grass more.
> —*2 Henry VI*, ACT IV, SC. 10, l. 43

18. If the good truth were known.
> —*The Winter's Tale*, ACT II, SC. 1, l. 199

The truth being known,/We'll all present ourselves.
> —*The Merry Wives of Windsor*, ACT IV, SC. 4, l. 64

19. Pray, let us not be laughing-stocks/To other men's humours.
> —*The Merry Wives of Windsor*, ACT III, SC. 1, l. 88

20. What! will the line stretch out to the crack of doom?
> —*Macbeth*, ACT IV, SC. 1, l. 117

21. Eight yards of uneven ground is threescore and ten miles afoot with me, and the stony-hearted villains know it well enough.
> —*1 Henry IV*, ACT II, SC. 2, l. 25

22. But 'tis all one to me.
> —*The Winter's Tale*, ACT V, SC. 2, l. 131

23. To make a virtue of necessity,/And live, as we do, in the wilderness.
> —*The Two Gentlemen of Verona*, ACT IV, SC. 1, l. 62

24. I have not slept one wink.
> —*Cymbeline*, ACT III, SC. 4, l. 103

25. To dance attendance on their lordships' pleasures.
> —*Henry VIII*, ACT V, SC. 2, l. 37

26. My own flesh and blood to rebel!
> —*The Merchant of Venice*, ACT III, SC. 1, l. 37

27. To be or not to be.
> —*Hamlet*, ACT III, SC. 1, l. 56

28. A countenance more in sorrow than in anger.
> —*Hamlet*, ACT I, SC. 2, l. 231

29. But this denoted a foregone conclusion.
    —Othello, Act III, sc. 3, l. 429

30. True it is that we have seen better days.
    —As You Like It, Act II, sc. 7, l. 120

31. Caesar, I never stood on ceremonies.
    —Julius Caesar, Act II, sc. 2, l. 13

32. All is not well; I doubt some foul play.
    —Hamlet, Act I, sc. 2, l. 254

33. But in the end, the truth will out.
    —The Merchant of Venice, Act II, sc. 2, l. 88

34. Some of us would lie low.
    —Much Ado About Nothing, Act V, sc. 1, l. 51

35. Thy wish was father, Harry, to that thought.
    —2 King Henry IV, Act IV, sc. 5, l. 91

36. I cannot tell what the dickens his name is.
    —The Merry Wives of Windsor, Act II, sc. 2, l. 20

37. Our revels are now ended. These our actors,/As I foretold you, were all spirits, and/Are melted into air, into thin air. (Not "vanished," as in my list.—W.R.E.)
    —The Tempest, Act IV, sc. 1, l. 148
    (*Othello* has "Go, vanish into air, away!")

38. *Clown*: Let me not be pent up, sir: I will fast, being loose. *Boy*: No, sir; that were fast and loose; thou shalt to prison.
    —The Merchant of Venice, Act III, sc. 2, l. 100

39. *Boy*: Yes, that a' did, and said they were devils incarnate.
    —Henry V, Act II, sc. 3, l. 31

40. How all the other passions fleet to air,/As doubtful thoughts, and rash-embraced despair,/And shuddering fear, and green-ey'd jealousy.
    —The Merchant of Venice, Act III, sc. 2, l. 100
    (See also *Othello*.)

41. This is the short and the long of it.
    —The Merry Wives of Windsor, Act II, sc. 2, l. 62

42. But while thou livest, keep a good tongue in thy head.
    —The Tempest, Act II, sc. 2, l. 117
    (I find no example of *civil* tongue.)

PAGE 56
It Was John Buchan

E is a vowel, like A, I, and O;
YE, though now rare, is the plural of "you."
YES has the opposite meaning of "no."
These further facts may be useful to you:
ESPY did not write *The Thirty-nine Steps*—
Though, come to think of it, neither did *PEPYS*.

PAGE 67
Rebuses

1. All in all. 2. Paradise lost. 3. Off again, on again. 4. Mixed nuts. 5. Forever Amber. 6. Split level. 7. Horseback. 8. Reading between the lines. 9. Tricycle. 10. Backward glance. 11. Neon lights. 12. Touchdown. 13. Life after death. 14. Just between you and me. 15. Man overboard.
The Italian-American rebus: You comma church. Rosie missed her period.

PAGE 68
Words Under Sail

Bill Beavis describes the origins of the nautical terms as follows:

1. *Tar.* Abbreviation of *tarpaulin* (canvas covered with tar or other waterproof material and used for covering hatches and the like).
2. *Cut of his jib.* The triangular *jib* was the first sail one would see as a ship approached. The jib sails in French and Spanish ships were generally higher than the English, giving an early indication of whether friend or foe was approaching.
3. *Took her aback.* When the helmsman was negligent and allowed the wind to get in front of the sails, practically every sail would suddenly blow out in reverse, sometimes bringing the masts down. The ship was *taken aback*.
4. *Brought her up short.* Stopping a ship with her anchors—only done in an emergency or by accident. The masts whip, everything shudders, doors slam, sleeping men are thrown from their bunks.

5. *Took the wind from her sails.* An engaging ship would attempt to get between the opponent and the wind so that the latter's sails would be blanketed; she would stop and present herself as a helpless target.

6. *Three sheets to the wind.* The sheets are the ropes that control the triangular-shaped jib sails, of which there were usually three. These would be let go as the ship was headed into the wind previous to paying off on a different tack, and during this period the ship would stagger and falter like a drunk.

7. *Listless.* A still, calm day when there was not enough wind to fill the sails. On such a day, the ship did not *list*.

8. *In the doldrums.* The doldrums were the windless patch in the Atlantic where sailing ships might sit for days like dead things. The word has overtones of unhappiness.

9. *Under the weather.* This originally referred to seasickness, often caused by bad weather.

10. *Shake it up.* The expression refers to the speed with which the sail would begin to shake should the helmsman allow his concentration to lapse.

11. *Get cracking.* The crack was the sound a straining sheet rope made when eased, signifying that the wind had freed and the speed would increase.

12. *Bear up.* A ship bore up when she could bring her head into the wind and make good progress.

13. *Scant.* From a situation in which a ship could just hold her own going to windward and was in continual danger of being blown off course. It thus means "scarcely sufficient."

14. *Bore down.* Steered toward an object (usually an enemy ship) without considering the wind.

15. *Sailing too close to the wind.* Pointing so high into the wind that forward pressure was lost, as indicated by the flapping of the sails.

16. *Touch and go.* Barges, unable to spare a crew member to sound the depth of the water, would move toward the side of the river until the bottom touched, and then go about on the other tack. Sometimes the ship would sink—hence the risk associated with "touch and go."

17. *Slant.* From an old Norse word for "breeze," the slant was the angle at which the ship was headed into the wind. Hence an attitude, point of view.

18. *All square.* The yards of a properly kept ship were kept all square—at right angles to the mast—when she was in port. Crews applied the expression to the payment of their debts at the end of a voyage.

19. *Footloose.* The foot is the bottom edge of the sail. The large barges that traded on the Thames did not lace the foot to the boom but simply tied the sheet rope in the corner, leaving the sails "loose-footed." Hence *footloose* for "free; untrammeled."

PAGE 80
ESPYramids Down

Those Were the Good Old Imperialist Days

The missing words: FLINDERS, FRIENDS, FINDER, INFER, FINE, FIE, IF, I

The complete verse: When Captain Flinders sailed the sea
His friends were filled with jealousy;
For "Finder keeper!" he would cry
As each new isle he scudded by;
And I infer from what I read
The isles he kept were fine indeed.
(Do I hear "Fie!"? If you could do
The same, you would; and I would too.)

The Chronic Crisis Down on the Farm

The missing words: HARVESTS, TRASHES, SHEARS, HARES, RASE, SEA, AS, A

The complete verse: The farmer can't his harvests stem;
He trashes more than half of them.
He shears his sheep, the wool's forgot;
The hares he traps he leaves to rot;
He raises corn to rase it; he
Throws corn and barley in the sea,
And as a rule leaves none for me.

The 7:21 Is Late Again

The missing words: TRANSMIT, TRANSIT, STRAIN, TRAIN, RAIN, RAN, AN, A

The complete verse: Transmit this message, little verse:
The transit system's getting worse.
Commuters still endure the strain
Of rushing off to catch the train;
Still run in rain and hail and snow
As ran their fathers long ago;
Still find an empty railroad track:
The train is stalled a few miles back.

PAGE 83
Pell's Pastiche

- Hafiz, real name Shams-ud-din Mohammed; fourteenth-century Persian lyric poet.
- Jack London, American journalist and novelist, 1876–1916.
- Emily Post, American authority on etiquette, 1873–1960.
- Orpheus, legendary Greek poet and musician, son of Apollo and Calliope.
- Norman Mailer, American novelist and journalist, 1923–   .
- Denis Levertov, American poet, 1923–   .
- W. Somerset Maugham, British novelist, short-story writer, and playwright, 1874–1965.
- Octavio Paz, Mexican poet, 1914–   .
- Dorothy Parker, American poet, short-story writer, and wit, 1893–1967.
- Johann Sebastian Bach, German composer, 1685–1750.
- Conrad Aiken, American poet and critic, 1889–1973.
- Erik Satie, French composer, 1866–1925.
- Robert Benchley, American humorist, 1889–1945.
- H. L. Mencken, American author, critic, and editor, 1880–1956.
- Mark Schorer, American critic and novelist, 1908–   .
- Theodore Dreiser, American novelist, 1871–1945.
- William Inge, American playwright, 1913–1973.
- C. P. Snow, British novelist and critic, 1905–1980.
- Haile Selassie, emperor of Ethiopia, 1891–1975.
- Erich Maria Remarque, German novelist, 1898–1970.
- Heinrich Böll, German novelist, 1917–   .
- Thomas Middleton, British playwright, 1570?–1627; Drew Middleton, American writer on military affairs, 1913–   .
- Juno, wife of Jupiter, principal god of the Romans.
- Charles Alfred Cripps, English lawyer and statesman, 1852–1941.
- Calvin Trillin, American journalist, 1935–   .
- Peter DeVries, American novelist and humorist, 1910–   .
- Edith Sitwell, English poet and writer, 1887–1964; also her brothers Osbert (1892–1969) and Sacheverell (1897–19–?).
- Ford Madox Hueffer, better known as Ford Madox Ford, British novelist, critic, and editor, 1873–1939.
- Arnold Auerbach, American author and humorist, 1912–   .
- Jean Anouilh, French dramatist, 1910–1987.

- John Dryden, English poet, critic, and dramatist, 1631–1700.
- Friedrich Wilhelm Nietzsche, German philosopher and poet, 1844–1900.
- Lytton Strachey, English writer, 1880–1932.
- Marjorie Kinnan Rawlings, American novelist, 1896–1953.
- Heinrich Heine, German poet, 1797–1856.
- Truman Capote, American novelist and short-story writer, 1924–1984.
- M. Marsden Glass, American playwright and fiction writer, 1877–1934; also Philip Glass, American composer, 1937–   .
- Rainer Maria Rilke, German poet, 1875–1926.
- Rosamond Lehmann, British novelist, 1904?–   ; also Lotte Lehmann, German operatic and concert singer, 1888–1976.
- George Ade, American humorist, 1866–1944.
- Samuel Pepys, English diarist, 1633–1703.
- Émile Zola, French novelist, 1840–1902.
- Amy Lowell, American poet and critic, 1874–1925; James Russell Lowell, American critic, poet, and humorist, 1819–1891; Robert Lowell, American poet, 1917–1977.
- Sir Max Beerbohm, British critic, author, and caricaturist, 1872–1956.
- Günter Grass, German novelist, 1927–   .
- Louis Untermeyer, American poet and anthologist, 1885–1977.
- Michel de Montaigne, French essayist, 1533–1592.
- George Bernard Shaw, British playwright of Irish origin, 1856–1950.
- Sarah M. Fuller, American writer and literary critic, 1810–1850.
- Thomas Hardy, English novelist and poet, 1840–1928.
- Stefan Zweig, Austrian playwright, author, and biographer, 1881–1942.
- Mickey Spillane, American detective story writer, 1918–   .
- Edward N. Westcott, American novelist and banker, 1846–1898.
- John Fowles, English writer, 1926–   .
- Jean Genet, French playwright and poet, 1910–   .
- Saki. Real name H. H. Munro, English short-story writer and novelist, 1870–1916.
- Geoffrey Hellman, American author and editor, 1907–1977; also Lillian Hellman, American dramatist and screenwriter, 1905–1979.
- Lewis Mumford, American social and literary critic, 1895–19–?.
- George P. Baker, American teacher of playwrighting, 1866–1935; Russell Baker, American journalist, 1935–   ; Josephine Baker, American night-club star, 1906–1975.
- Immanuel Kant, German philosopher, 1724–1804.
- Geoffrey Chaucer, English poet, 1340?–1400.
- See previous reference.

- Algonquin, an American Indian tribe; also, a New York hotel frequented by literary figures.
- René Descartes, French philosopher and mathematician, 1596–1650.
- Mary Halleck Foote, American writer, 1847–1938.
- Baruch (or Benedict) Spinoza, Dutch philosopher, 1632–1677.
- Sir Edward Creasy, English historian, 1812–1878.
- Kingsley Amis, English novelist, 1922–   .
- Parra. Unknown to me.
- Alfred Noyes, English poet and essayist, 1880–1958.
- V. I. Ivanov, Russian poet, 1866–1949; also V. V. Ivanov, Russian novelist, 1895–1963.
- F. García Lorca, Spanish playwright and poet, 1899–1936.
- May Sarton, American poet and novelist, 1912–   .
- Mateo Alonso, Argentine sculptor, 1878–1955.
- Lord Edward Dunsany, Irish dramatist and short-story writer, 1878–1957.
- Damon Runyon, American short-story writer and journalist, 1880–1946.
- François Villon, French poet, 1431–1463?.
- Edwin Muir, Scottish poet and literary critic, 1887–1959; also John Muir, American naturalist, 1838–1914.
- Marguerite Duras, French novelist, 1914–   .
- Anonymous, one of our most prolific writers, background uncertain.
- Sigmund Freud, Austrian psychoanalyst, founder of psychoanalysis, 1856–1939.
- Elinor Wylie, American poet, 1885–1928; Philip Wylie, American fiction writer, 1902–1971.
- Safa, in Muslim myth, the Arabian hill where Adam and Eve came together.
- See previous reference.
- Natalie Sarraute, French novelist, 1901–   .
- Giuseppe Verdi, Italian operatic composer, 1813–1901.
- Edgar Allan Poe, American poet and story writer, 1809–1849.
- Nelson Algren, American novelist and story writer, 1909–1981.
- George Sand, French novelist, 1804–1876.

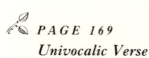

PAGE 169
Univocalic Verse

Persevere, ye perfect men;
Ever keep these precepts ten.

Pell's Pastiche *(continued)*

- Edgar A. Guest, English-born versifier and humorist popular in the United States, 1881–1959.
- Euclid, Greek mathematician, 450?–374 B.C.
- Dorothy L. Sayers, English detective-story writer, 1893–1957.
- Jesse Martin Unruh, Democratic politician, 1922–   .
- John Cheever, American novelist and story writer, 1912–1982.
- David Broder, American journalist, 1929–   .
- Wilfred Owen, English poet of World War I, 1893–1918.
- Sir Arthur Conan Doyle, British novelist, detective-story writer, 1859–1930.
- H. G. Wells, British novelist and historian, 1866–1946.
- Marcus Tullius Cicero, Roman statesman and philosopher, 106–43 B.C.
- Egerton Castle, English novelist, 1858–1920; Irene Castle, American dancer, 1893?–1969.
- Pliny. Gaius Plinius Secundus, Roman scholar, 23–79 A.D.
- Miguel de Cervantes, Spanish novelist (born Alcalá de Henares), 1547–1616.
- Samuel Butler, English satirical poet, 1612–1680; Samuel Butler, English satirist, 1835–1902.
- Alfred Alistair Cooke, British-born American journalist and broadcaster, 1908–   .
- Paul Valéry, French poet and man of letters, 1871–1945.
- Bennett Cerf, American publisher and anthologist, 1898–1971.
- Isak Dinesen, Danish short-story writer and novelist, 1885–1962.
- Gregory Nunzio Corso, American poet, 1930–   .
- Peter Ustinov, English actor, 1921–   .
- Leo Tolstoy, Russian novelist, 1828–1910.
- John Bigelow, American writer and diplomat, 1817–1911.
- John Barth, American novelist, 1930–   .
- Edna Ferber, American novelist and playwright, 1887–1968.
- Marianne Moore, American poet, 1887–1972.
- Richard Steele, English essayist and playwright, 1672–1729.
- Vachel Lindsay, American poet, 1879–1931.
- Claude Monet, French impressionist painter, 1840–1926.
- St.-John Perse, French poet, 1887–1975.
- Henry David Thoreau, American poet and writer, 1817–1862.
- Thomas Fairfax, English general under Cromwell, 1612–1671.
- Rumer Godden, English novelist, 1909–   .
- Friedrich Dürrenmatt, Swiss dramatist and novelist, 1921–   .
- Edith Wharton, American novelist, 1862–1937.
- Ronald Firbank, English writer, 1886–1926.

- Publius Vergilius Maro, Roman poet, 70–19 B.C.
- John Philip Sousa, American composer and bandmaster, 1854–1932.
- John Hersey, American novelist and war correspondent, 1914–   .
- Robert Graves, English poet and novelist, 1895–1985.
- John B. Priestley, English novelist and journalist, 1894–1984; Joseph Priestley, English clergyman and chemist, 1733–1804.
- E. E. Cummings, American poet, 1894–1962.
- Joan Didion, American novelist, 1934–   .
- Maxfield Parrish, American artist and illustrator, 1870–1966.
- Saul, first king of Israel, anointed by Samuel, c. 1025 B.C.
- David Merrick, American theatrical producer, 1912–   .
- Old King Cole, a merry old soul, dates unknown; William Cole, American anthologist and light-verse writer, 1919–   .
- Ernest Thompson Seton, British-born Canadian writer and naturalist, 1860–1946.
- Robert Penn Warren, American poet and novelist, 1905–1989.
- See previous entry.
- Frederick Pohl, American science fiction writer, 1919–   .
- William Pitt (the Elder), English statesman, 1708–1778; William Pitt (the Younger), "probably England's greatest prime minister," 1759–1806.
- Eugene O'Neill, American dramatist, 1888–1953.
- Frederic Peret, American science fiction writer, 1919–   .
- John Dos Passos, American novelist and short-story writer, 1896–1970.
- John Hay, American statesman and author, 1838–1905.
- Venus, Roman goddess of love, beauty, and the hunt.
- Walter Thomas Layton (first Baron Layton), English economist and publicist, 1884–1966.
- Jack Kerouac, American "beat" poet and novelist, 1922–1969.
- James Thurber, American writer, humorist, and cartoonist, 1894–1961.
- Maurice Maeterlinck, Belgian poet and dramatist, 1862–1949.
- Hans Otto Storm, American novelist, 1895–1941; also Theodor Storm, German writer, 1817–1888.
- John Cowper Powys, English critic and novelist, 1872–1963.
- Alfred Kazin, American literary critic, 1915–   .
- Charles Lutwidge Dodgson (Lewis Carroll), English author and mathematician, 1832–1898.
- Edward Everett Hale, American clergyman and author, 1822–1909; Nathan Hale, American Revolutionary hero, 1755–1776.
- Thomas Stoppard, Czechoslovakian-born English dramatist, 1932–   .
- Erich Fromm, American psychoanalyst, 1900–1980.
- Gustave Flaubert, French novelist, 1821–1880.

- Arthur Rimbaud, French poet, 1854–1891.
- Guillaume Apollinaire, French poet, 1880–1918.
- Molière, pseudonym of Jean Baptiste Poquelin, French actor and playwright, 1622–1673.
- Huey Long, American lawyer and politician, 1893–1935.
- See previous reference.
- Thomas Pynchon, American novelist, 1937–   .
- Stéphane Mallarmé, French poet, 1842–1898.
- Austin Clarke, Irish poet, 1896–1974.
- Herman Wouk, American novelist, 1915–   .
- Jean-Paul Sartre, French novelist and critic, 1905–1980.
- Jean Jacques Rousseau, French philosopher, 1712–1778.
- Hans Fallada, German novelist, 1893–1947.
- Louisa May Alcott, American author and reformer, 1832–1888.
- Eudora Welty, American novelist and story writer, 1909–   .
- Daniel Defoe, English novelist and journalist, 1659?–1731.
- Sidonie Gabrielle Claudine Colette, French semiautobiographical novelist, 1873–1954.
- John Updike, American novelist, critic, and poet, 1932–   .
- Henry Hazlitt, American editor and author, 1894–   ; William Hazlitt, English essayist, 1778–1830.
- Simone de Beauvoir, French writer, 1908–   .
- Oppeln, a town in Upper Silesia, Prussia.
- Max Frisch, Swiss novelist, 1911–   .
- Jane Eyre, heroine of an 1847 novel by Charlotte Brontë (1816–1855).
- Franz Kafka, Czech novelist and story writer, 1883–1924.
- Saul Bellow, American novelist, 1915–   .
- Hans (Jean) Arp, French artist and poet, 1887–1966.
- Charles Baudelaire, French poet, 1821–1867.
- Lafcadio Hearn, American journalist and author, 1850–1904.
- Boris Pasternak, Russian novelist, 1890–1960.
- Guy de Maupassant, French novelist and story writer, 1850–1893.
- Margaret Hungerford, Irish novelist, 1855?–1897.
- Gore Vidal, American novelist, 1925–   .
- Bret Harte, American story writer, poet, and journalist, 1836–1902.
- Jonathan Swift, Anglo-Irish poet and satirist, 1667–1745.
- Leon Trotsky, Russian Communist Party leader, 1879–1940.
- Quintus Horatius Flaccus, Roman lyricist and satirist, 65–8 B.C.
- Donald Hall, American poet, 1928–   ; James Norman Hall, American novelist, 1887–1951.
- Paul Gustave Doré, French illustrator and painter, 1833–1883.

- Alfred Jarry, French dramatist and novelist, 1873–1907.
- Hyperion, a Titan of Greek mythology, sometimes personified as the sun.
- Laurence Sterne, English novelist, 1713–1768.
- Sir Henry Rider Haggard, English novelist, 1856–1925.
- Hermann Hesse, German novelist and poet, 1877–1962.
- Allen Tate, American poet and critic, 1899–1979.
- Rex Stout, American detective story writer, 1886–1975.
- Novalis, pseudonym of Friedrich Leopold von Hardenberg, German romantic poet, 1772–1801.
- James Purdy, American novelist, 1923– .
- Chester Bowles, American advertising man and politician, 1901–19–?.
- Philippe Soupault, French poet, novelist, and biographer, 1897–19–?.
- Jane Austen, English novelist, 1775–1817.
- Bertolt Brecht, German playwright and poet, 1898–1956.
- Dr. Johannes Faustus, magician, astrologer, soothsayer, and hero of Marlowe's *Tragical History of Dr. Faustus* and Goethe's *Faust*; 1480?–1540.
- Donald Barthelme, American novelist and story writer, 1931–1989.
- Aesop, reputed Greek author of *Aesop's Fables*, c. 620–560 B.C.
- Jan Vermeer, Dutch painter, 1632–1675.
- Unknown to me.
- Thornton Wilder, American dramatist, 1897–1975.
- Icarus, in Greek mythology, son of the artificer Daedalus; killed by flying too close to the sun.
- Charles Lamb, English essayist, 1775–1834.
- Frédéric Chopin, Polish composer for the piano, 1810–1849.
- Leon Uris, American novelist, 1924– .

PAGE 175

Doublet

The missing words: PIGGY, BIGGY, DIGGY, DINGY, RINGY, BINGY, BINGE, TINGE, SINGE, SINCE, WINCE, WINCH, WENCH, WELCH, BELCH, BEECH, BEACH, BRACH, BRACT, BRANT, GRANT.

The verse in the clear:

The Little Fellow Who Tried to Grow Big

A PIGMY to grow to great stature resolved.
To handle the first of the problems involved,
He changed to a Piggy. And next, to grow biggy,
He rooted potatoes out, diggety diggy.
The church bells dinged "Dingy," the church bells ringed "Ringy,"

To count off the hours as that beast stuffed its bingy.
(Although you may find that last word a bit alien,
It simply means *stomach* to any Australian.)
He swelled and he swelled, and went on with his binge,
Till his snout was all bruised, with a mottleish tinge.
Each gulp gave his gullet a singe as it passed,
Since his throat had grown raw from engorging so fast.
The pain made him wince; yet he ceased not to sup
Till only a winch could have lifted him up.

A wench was out walking her dog (she was Welch),
And she happened to hear that poor animal belch.
Beneath a tall beech tree she came on him lying,
As huge as a whale on a beach, and as dying.
'Twas love at first sight. But her dog was a brach,
Whose reason for living was porkers to catch.
As a bract in a blink from a leaf will burst out,
As a brant in a wink will dive after a trout,
With no grant of mercy the hound seized the hog.
One swallow—no pigmy. Just one GIANT dog.

PAGE 177

Oh, Be Not Mean

Oh, be not mean to your dear horse,
For it's not fair, you see.
A horse is great in size of course,
While we of course are wee;
But he (at least so I am told)
Was not allowed a soul,
And so must die out in the cold,
And wind up in a hole;
While we have souls to waste, I trust,
And when we find the way

To heaven's gate (for so we must)
Who, who would say us nay?

PAGE 197

Pell's Pastiche (continued)

- St. Francis Xavier, "the apostle of the Indies," 1506–1552.
- Publius Ovidius Naso, Latin poet, c. 43 B.C.–?17 A.D.
- John Dickson Carr, English-born American detective story writer, 1905–1977.
- Rafael Sabatini, Italian novelist, 1875–1950.
- John Steinbeck, American novelist, 1902–1968.
- Gay Talese, American journalist and author, 1932–   .
- Vance Bourjaily, American novelist, 1922–   .
- Georges Braque, French painter, 1882–1963.
- William Wordsworth, English poet, 1770–1850.
- Ezra Pound, American poet, 1885–1972.
- George Orwell, English novelist, essayist, and critic, 1903–1950.
- Pearl S. Buck, American novelist, 1892–1973.
- Marc Chagall, Russian painter, 1887–1985.
- Amado Nervo, Mexican poet, 1897–1919.
- Johann Wolfgang von Goethe, German poet, dramatist, and novelist, 1749–1832.
- Henrik Ibsen, Norwegian dramatist, 1828–1906.
- Jorge Luis Borges, Argentine poet and writer, 1899–1986.
- Nikolai Gogol, Russian novelist and playwright, 1809–1852.
- Hilaire Belloc, English writer of light verse, fiction, biography, 1870–1953.
- See previous reference.
- Paul Grabbe, Russian-born American writer, 1912–   .
- Alain Robbe-Grillet, French novelist, 1922–   .
- Euripides, Greek playwright of the fifth century B.C., ranked with Aeschylus and Sophocles as the greatest of Greek dramatists.
- Carl Sagan, American astronomer and writer, 1934–   ; Françoise Sagan, French novelist, 1935–   .
- Pindar, Greek lyric poet, 522?–443 B.C.
- Horace Walpole, English politician and man of letters, 1717–1797; also Sir Hugh Walpole, English novelist, 1884–1941.
- Marcel Proust, French novelist, 1871–1922.
- Alexander Sergeyvich Pushkin, Russian poet, dramatist, and novelist, 1799–1837.
- Vladimir Nabokov, Russian-born American author and critic, 1899–1977.

- Stendhal, pseudonym of Henri Beyle, French novelist, 1783–1842.
- Howard P. Lovecraft, American novelist of the supernatural, 1890–1937.
- Hieronymus Bosch, Dutch painter, 1450?–1516.
- Kenneth Patchen, American poet, 1911–1972.
- Christopher Isherwood, English novelist and short-story writer, 1904– .
- Apollo, Greek god identified with the sun and masculine beauty.
- James Joyce, Irish novelist, 1882–1941.
- Lord Acton (John Dalberg), English historian, 1834–1902.
- Oscar Wilde, Irish-born English playwright and poet, 1854–1900.
- Edward Albee, American playwright, 1928– .
- Prometheus, a Greek Titan punished by Zeus for giving fire to mankind.
- Noah, Old Testament ark builder who, with his family and representative animals, survived the Flood.
- Albert Camus, French novelist and philosopher, 1913–1960.
- Jules Verne, early French science fiction novelist, 1828–1905.
- Alphonse Daudet, French novelist, 1840–1897.
- Robert Emmet, Irish nationalist, 1778–1803.
- Robinson Jeffers, American poet, 1887–1962.
- Anaïs Nin, American poet, 1903–1977.
- Pablo Picasso, Spanish-born French painter, 1881–1973.
- Étienne Marcel, fourteenth-century French politician, d. 1358.
- Thomas Mann, German-born American novelist and playwright, 1875–1955; Horace Mann, American educator, 1796–1859.
- Anatole France, French novelist, 1844–1924.
- Shalom Aleichem, Yiddish writer, 1859–1916.
- S. J. Liebling, American satirist and critic, 1904–19–?.
- José de Goya, Spanish painter, etcher, and lithographer, 1746–1828.
- Marquis Donatien de Sade, French novelist, playwright, and pervert, 1740–1814.
- Prosper Mérimée, French novelist, 1803–1870.
- Ernest Hemingway, American novelist and story writer, 1899–1961.
- Clifford Odets, American dramatist, 1906–1963.
- Carl Jung, Swiss psychiatrist and founder of analytical psychology, 1875–1961.
- Evelyn Waugh, English novelist, satirist, and critic, 1903–1966; also Alec, his brother, novelist, 1898– .
- Terry Southern, American writer, 1924– .
- Honoré de Balzac, French novelist, 1799–1850.
- Charles Sackville, English poet and courtier, 1638–1706; also Thomas Sackville, English poet and diplomat, 1536–1608; and V. M. Sackville, English novelist and poet, 1892–1962.

- Victor Hugo, French novelist, dramatist, and poet, 1802–1885.
- Joan Miró, Spanish painter, 1893–1974.
- Marcel Duchamp, French painter and sculptor, 1887–1968.
- Dada, a literary and artistic movement that flourished during World War I.
- Anita Loos, American humorous writer, 1893–1981.
- Eugene Ionesco, Rumanian-born French playwright, 1912–   ; also Take Ionescu, Rumanian statesman, 1858–1922.
- Homer, name given the unknown Greek poet or poets who wrote *The Odyssey* and *The Iliad,* between 1200 B.C. and 850 B.C.

PAGE 218
Essaying Montaigne

Wiser men can create for themselves a repose altogether spiritual, their souls being strong and vigorous; but mine being of the ordinary sort, I need the comforts of the flesh to help me sustain myself; and age having recently stolen away those I enjoyed most, I train and sharpen my appetite for what remains most suitable to this different season. We have to hang on to life's pleasures tooth and claw as the years wrench them one after another from our fists. "Let us enjoy ourselves; only the days we give to pleasure are ours. Soon you will be no more than a cinder, a shade, a fable."

PAGE 230
More Rebuses

1. Mixed doubles. 2. To shrink back. 3. Inverted commas. 4. Wings outspread. 5. Condescending. 6. *J'ai assez obéi à elle.* (I have obeyed her enough.) 7. Humpback. 8. Mix-up. 9. Sliced bread. 10. Up in arms over nothing at all. 11. Turncoat. 12. World without end Amen. 13. Mixed-up kid.

PAGE 240
Dery's Double Trouble

1. shilly-shally	6. flipflop
2. powwow	7. palsy-walsy
3. lovey-dovey	8. hurly-burly
4. hobnob	9. tip-top
5. hoity-toity	10. rickrack

11. fuddy-duddy
12. riprap
13. tittle-tattle
14. hurdy-gurdy
15. singsong
16. zigzag
17. bigwig
18. pellmell
19. namby-pamby
20. higgledy-piggledy
21. mishmash
22. dilly-dally
23. crisscross
24. superduper
25. hodgepodge
26. boogie-woogie
27. walkie-talkie
28. riffraff
29. pitter-patter
30. roly-poly
31. hocus-pocus
32. knickknack
33. chitchat
34. humpty-dumpty
35. dingdong
36. randan
37. flimflam
38. hanky-panky
39. teeny-weeny
40. wishy-washy
41. wingding
42. willy-nilly

 PAGE 261

The initial letters of each line, in sequence, spell *idolatry*; of the fourth word in each line, *dilatory*; and of the last word in each line, *adroitly*. The three words are anagrams of one another.

 PAGE 262

The Old and the Young of It

The night is dark and damp and cold;
The leaves have left the tree;
He hugs the fire, for he is old;
She does embroidery.

He warms his hands before the flame,
And pitifully murm-
urs, "Adam's dust, and Eve's the same,
And greedy waits the worm."

The candles flicker, as in pain;
She hears his dreary mumble:
"Soon bones are all that will remain,
And even they will crumble.

"What monuments I thought to build!
What dragons to have slain!
What high designs to have fulfilled!
Now books alone remain."

So backward run his dismal nights,
While she, too young to think
Of aught but dancing, neon lights,
And coats of priceless mink,

With naught but bubbles in her heart,
A rock inside her head,
Expects the clouds will all depart
As soon as he is dead.

PAGE 275
Martin Gardner's Flimflam Files

1. Explain the meaning of this acronym.
2. In.
3. You would prefer that the lion ate the tiger.
4. Change post to p - o - s - t.
5. Bet on 5. The die is probably loaded.
6. This question will be answered in a future book.
7. "Damn it, can't you see I've got my mouth full of nails?"

PAGE 276
Digits as Words

1 0 2 0 0 4 1 8 0 = I ought to owe nothing for I ate nothing.

PAGE 278
Doublets

He'd Kiss the Toe That Kicks Him

"Oh, damn!" exclaimed the lovelorn lad;
"This dame is driving me quite mad!
But all the same, should she enslave me,
I'd much prefer that no one save me."

(Proceeds from *damn* to *save*: damn, dame, same, save.)

Better Hunt up Those Prayer Beads

Your body creaks, reluctant to respond.
It's bony where the muscles used to be.
Your bond to joys of which you've grown too fond
Has loosed: fine drinks, fine food, especially
Fine women. Time, old fool, to look beyond.
You shuffle and you hack; your breath is foul.
Flesh has betrayed you. Time to tend your soul.

(Proceeds from *body* to *soul*: body, bony, bond, fond, food, fool, foul, soul.)

They Might Try Bundling

Summer is the time to simmer,
Time to watch the dusk grow dimmer;
When it's dimmed to firefly glow,
Time to let dammed passion flow.
Kisses' fires aren't damped by sweat;
Damper hugs are sweeter yet.
No. To hamper love, to still
Sound of harper on the hill,
Needs a season harder, colder;
Needs a warder dourer, older.
Those who wander, close-embraced,
Will in wanner days turn chaste.
Love's the winner, till it's chilly;
In the winter, love seems silly.

(Proceeds from *summer* to *winter*: summer, simmer, dimmer, dimmed,
    dammed, damped, damper, hamper, harper, harder, warder, wander,
    wanner, winner, winter.)

 PAGE 293

Alas, Alas, I'll Die a Maid

(Ella enters stage right, Stella stage left)

ELLA: Hi.
STELLA: 'Lo.
ELLA: You seem faint and worn, dear. You groan and moan. I hear you sighed
    all week.

STELLA: You groan and moan too. I heard you.

ELLA: Oh, how your eyes stare! You are so tense! You reel!

STELLA: Ella, you must have guessed my pain.

ELLA: Nay—*our* pain, dear sweet. I am blue too. We're all, all alone, you and I.

STELLA: Our tears flow. We're wretches.

ELLA: You are so right, sweetheart! But we know the kernel of our pain. It is our need of a handsome male.

STELLA: Alas, through some great mischance we've missed him.

ELLA: You know, dear, we've been chaste for days.

STELLA: Oh, can that be so? Who chased us? Some boy?

ELLA: No, no, you know no one chased us, or we would not be chaste.

STELLA: Alas, alas, I'll die a maid.

ELLA: I too must die a maid, alas, a maid unmade, alas.

STELLA: 'Bye, sweet.

ELLA: 'Bye, 'bye, dear.

(Exeunt, weeping.)

PAGE 299

Superghosts

o I L I L y
b a I L I W i c k

INDEX

Names (*Except for Those of Fictitious or Mythical Characters*) Mentioned in This Book

A Abraham, 145 • Adam (the first man), 18, 68, 90–91, 211, 284 • Adams, J. D., 173 • Adams, John, 40 • Adams, John Quincy, 41 • Addison, Joseph, 76, 122, 292 • Ade, George, 4 • Akenhead, Edmund, 233 • Alexander, Dr., 92 • Alexandra, Tsarina, 106 • Alfred, Lord Tennyson, 7, 260 • Allen, Dale S., 139 • Allen, Mary Wood, 210–211 • Alfonso XIII, 106, 227 • Anderson, Jimmy, vi, 53–55 • Andreas, Dwayne, 128 • Angell, Roger, 283 • Aquinas, Thomas, 226 • Aristotle, 52 • Armstrong, Neil, 127 • Arthur, Chester Alan, 124 • Auden, W. H., 32 • Augarde, Tony, 18, 299

B Bacon, Sir Francis, 137, 320 • Baker, Russell, 163 • Balluff, Rose E., 142 • Baltzell, E. Digby, 259 • Balzac, Honoré de, 137 • Barham, R. H., 251 • Barnes, Julian, 11, 117 • Barry, James, 284 • Barth, John, 173 • Basch, Buddy, 154 • Basselin, Olivier de, 117 • Bawer, Bruce, 146 • Beatrice (Dante's beloved), 188 • Beaudoin, John T., 127 • Beaumont, Francis, 320 • Beavis, Bill, 68 • Belloc, Hilaire, 88 • Benchley, Robert, 118 • Benenson, James, Jr., 149 • Benet, William Rose, 273 • Bennett, Arnold, 52, 217 • Beria, L. P., 316 • Berne, Stanley, 189 • Bernhard, Thomas, 289 • Bernstein, Ted (Theodore), 4 • Berta (mother of Charlemagne), 180 • Beukel (Beukelz), William (Wilhelm), 234 • Bierce, Ambrose, 197, 245 • Billebaw, Laird of, 117 • Birkets, Sven, 63 • Bismarck (Bismarck-Schönhausen, Prince Otto Edward Leopold von), 238 • Blake, Bud, 114 • Blake, William, 98, 202 • Blumenbach, J. F., 259 • Blumenthal, Walter Hart, 236 • Boas, R. P., 278 • Bock, Ian, 139 • Boleyn, Anne, 181 • Bombaugh, C. C., 169, 183–184 • Bonaparte, Napoleon, 131, 140, 213 •

Bonner, Paul, 35 • Borgmann, Dmitri, 71 • Bragonier, Reginald, Jr., 211 • Braybrooks, Lord, 56 • Breinin, Goodwin M., 27, 188, 308–309 • Brennan, Francis (Hank), 93 • Breton, André, 10 • Brooks, Maxey, 67, 154 • Brooks-Baker, Harold, 105–106 • Brown, David, 141 • Brummel, Beau (George Bryan), 127 • Bryan, J. III, 299 • Buchan, John, 56 • Buchanan, James, 124 • Bull, John, 174 • Burgess, Gelett, 260 • Burns, Robert, 121 • Bush, George H. W., 126 • Butler, Samuel, 69, 153 • Byron, Lord George Gordon, 137

C Cade, Jack, 167 • Calepino, Ambrosio, 117 • Calvin, John, 137 • Camus, Albert, 311 • Cantab, a, 230 • Capek, Carol, 260 • Cardenas, Lazaro, 301 • Carlyle, Thomas, 137, 250 • Carroll, Lewis (Charles Lutwidge Dodgson), 167, 175, 224 • Carter, James Earl, 126 • Carter, Ms. P., 151 • Cassidy, Edward, 75–76 • Castro, Fidel, 40 • Cavendish, Lady Frederick, 163 • Céline, Louis Ferdinand, 173 • Centlivre, Susanna, 33 • Cervantes, Miguel de, 33 • Chagall, Marc, 159 • Chao, Lillian, 38 • Charlemagne, 180 • Charles II, 117, 182 • Charlie, Bonny Prince, 160 • Charlus, Baron de, 289 • Chase, Stuart, 138 • Chesterfield, Lord, 243 • Chisholms of Nova Scotia, 160 • Chiz, Hilary, 303–304 • Church, Dudley F., 28, 142 • Clausius, Rudolf, 259 • Cleopatra, 181 • Cleveland, Grover, 124 • Clinton, Lady, 163 • Clough, Arthur Hugh, 188 • Cohen, Philip M., 48, 230 • Cole, Charles Woolsey, 112 • Cole, William R., 235 • Coleridge, Samuel Taylor, 16, • Condax, Kate Delano, 149 • Confucius, 145 • Coogler, J. Gordon, 65 • Coolidge, John Calvin, 125 • Coombs, Pat, 30 • Coué, Emile, 58 • Cousins, Norman, 152 • Cowley, Malcolm, 236 •

First Lines of Verses (not by W. R. E.)

First Lines of W. R. E. Knittelverses

A Sampling of Verbal Phenomena Mentioned in This Book

PERMISSIONS

Grateful acknowledgment is given to the following for permission to reprint copyrighted material:

Page 4, excerpt from *The Owl in the Attic*, by James Thurber. Published by Harper & Row. Copyright © 1931, 1959 by James Thurber.

Page 5, "The Tree That Did Not Fall on a Sixpence," from *The Letters of Evelyn Waugh*, edited by Mark Amory. Copyright © The Estate of Laura Waugh 1980. Copyright © in the introduction and compilation Mark Amory 1980. Reprinted by permission of Ticknor & Fields, a Houghton Mifflin Company, and Sterling Lord Literistic, Inc.

Page 12, excerpt from "You, Too, Can Strengthen English, and Write Good," by Maggie Sullivan. Copyright © 1985 by The New York Times Company. Used by permission.

Page 30, excerpts from *The Book of Heroic Failures*, by Stephen Pile. Copyright © Stephen Pile. Reprinted by kind permission of Rogers, Coleridge & White, Ltd.

Pages 37 and 38, "A Language That Has Ausgeflippt" and "Don't Kiss Me," by Otto Friedrich. Copyright © 1986 by Time, Inc. Reprinted by permission.

Pages 122, 222, and 310, excerpt from *Conversations About Xmas*, by Dylan Thomas. Copyright © 1954 by New Directions Publishing Corporation. Reprinted by permission of New Directions Publishing Corporation and the Trustees for the Copyrights of Dylan Thomas.

Page 127, excerpt from *The Phrase-Dropper's Handbook*, by John T. Beaudoin & Everett Martin. Copyright © 1976 by Richard Dempewolff and Benjamin R. Hofter, trustees for Lisa K. Beaudoin, Stephanie B. Piper, John C. Beaudoin, and Mark T. Beaudoin. Reprinted by permission of Doubleday, a division of Bantam, Doubleday, Dell Publishing Group, Inc.

Pages 137 and 239, excerpts from "On Language" columns, by William Safire, published in the *New York Times Magazine*. Used by permission of the author.

Pages 139 and 213, excerpt from "Games" columns, *Omni* Magazine. Copyright © 1982, 1985, 1986 by *Omni* Magazine. Reprinted by permission of Omni Publications International, Ltd.

Page 142, excerpt from *The Grasshopper Trap*, by Patrick F. McManus. Copyright © 1985 by Patrick F. McManus. Reprinted by permission of Henry Holt and Company, Inc.

Page 151, "Lady," from *The Spectator*. Reprinted by permission.

Pages 173–174, excerpts from *Rotten Reviews*, ed. Bill Henderson (Wainscott, New York: Pushcart Press, 1986). Reprinted by permission of Pushcart Press.

Pages 204 and 205, "At Sixty, Juliette's Mass of Hair" and "I'd Rather Have Your Wrinkles, Jane," from *Two Hundred Poems from the Greek Anthology*, by Robin Skelton. Published by McClelland and Stewart, Toronto, and the University of Washington Press, Seattle. Copyright © 1971 by Robin Skelton. Reprinted by the kind permission of Robin Skelton.

Pages 208–209, excerpt from the Peterborough column, the *Daily Telegraph*, London. Used by permission.

Page 212, excerpt from *Newsweek*, May 12, 1986. Copyright © 1986 Newsweek, Inc. All rights reserved. Reprinted by permission.

Page 224, "If Big Nose Louie Turns You Off, Try Buying a Piece of Mad Dog," by Beatrice Garcia. Copyright © Dow Jones & Company, Inc., 1985. Reprinted by permission of the *Wall Street Journal*. All rights reserved worldwide.

Page 225, memo reprinted from the December 2, 1988, issue of *Publishers Weekly*, published by the Bowker Magazine Group of Cahners Publishing Company,